National
Service
in Singapore

Other Related Titles from World Scientific

Perspectives on the Security of Singapore: The First 50 Years
edited by Barry Desker and Cheng Guan Ang
ISBN: 978-981-4689-32-8
ISBN: 978-981-4689-33-5 (pbk)

Critical Issues in Asset Building in Singapore's Development
edited by S Vasoo and Bilveer Singh
ISBN: 978-981-3239-75-3

Managing Diversity in Singapore: Policies and Prospects
edited by Mathew Mathews and Wai Fong Chiang
ISBN: 978-1-78326-953-2

National Service
in Singapore

Editors

Ho Shu Huang
Graham Ong-Webb

S. Rajaratnam School of International Studies, NTU, Singapore

We World Scientific

NEW JERSEY · LONDON · SINGAPORE · BEIJING · SHANGHAI · HONG KONG · TAIPEI · CHENNAI · TOKYO

Published by

World Scientific Publishing Co. Pte. Ltd.

5 Toh Tuck Link, Singapore 596224

USA office: 27 Warren Street, Suite 401-402, Hackensack, NJ 07601

UK office: 57 Shelton Street, Covent Garden, London WC2H 9HE

Library of Congress Cataloging-in-Publication Data
Names: Ho, Shu Huang, editor. | Ong, Graham Gerard, 1975–   editor. | Lau, Albert, 1956–
    National service and citizen soldiers.
Title: National service in Singapore / [edited by] Shu Huang Ho, Graham Ong-Webb.
Description: Hackensack, New Jersey : World Scientific, [2018] |
    Includes bibliographical references and index.
Identifiers: LCCN 2018021941| ISBN 9789813149212 (hardcover) |
    ISBN 9789813203037 (softcover)
Subjects: LCSH: Draft--Singapore. | National service--Singapore. | Singapore.
    Armed Forces--Recruiting, enlistment, etc.
Classification: LCC UB345.S54 N37 2018 | DDC 355.2/2363095957--dc23
LC record available at https://lccn.loc.gov/2018021941

British Library Cataloguing-in-Publication Data
A catalogue record for this book is available from the British Library.

For any available supplementary material, please visit
https://www.worldscientific.com/worldscibooks/10.1142/10264#t=suppl

Desk Editor: Jiang Yulin

Typeset by Stallion Press
Email: enquiries@stallionpress.com

About the Contributors

Nur Diyanah Binte Anwar is a Senior Analyst with the Centre of Excellence for National Security at the S. Rajaratnam School of International Studies (RSIS), Nanyang Technological University, Singapore. She attained her Master of Science in Asian Studies from RSIS, and her Bachelor of Social Science (Honours) in Political Science with a minor in Sociology from the National University of Singapore. Her focus in the Social Resilience Programme revolves around identity issues, social policies, inequality, and the relations between state and society.

Priscilla Cabuyao is a former Senior Analyst at the Centre of Excellence for National Security, S. Rajaratnam School of International Studies (RSIS), Nanyang Technological University, Singapore. Her analyses on comparative politics, social integration policies, and national narratives have taken various forms such as policy reports, newspaper and magazine commentaries, and journal articles. She received her MSc in International Relations from RSIS in 2014.

Samuel L. W. Chan is an Adjunct Lecturer at the University of New South Wales (UNSW) in Canberra, Australia. His education background includes a BSc with Honours Class 1 in Statistics (UNSW), an MSc in Russian and East European Studies (University of Oxford), and a PhD in International and Political Studies (UNSW). He is the co-author of *Defence* (Straits Times Press & Institute of Policy Studies, 2015), and *Ready, Decisive, Respected: Chronicling Our Army's Overseas Operations (1970–2015)* (Straits Times Press & Ministry of Defence, 2015).

Chang Jun Yan is Associate Research Fellow at the S. Rajaratnam School of International Studies (RSIS), Nanyang Technological University, Singapore. He has published in various academic journals. He is currently pursuing a PhD at the University of Queensland, School of Political Science and International Studies. His thesis topic deals with the macro-securitisation of what he calls the "Blue Dread" China Threat Thesis. Prior to joining RSIS, he served as a combat officer in the Republic of Singapore Navy. In 2012, he was deployed for Operation *Blue Sapphire* (Maritime) [OBS (M)], Singapore's contribution to counter-piracy operations in the Gulf of Aden and the Somali Basin.

Ho Shu Huang is an Associate Research Fellow at the S. Rajaratnam School of International Studies (RSIS), Nanyang Technological University, Singapore. He is concurrently pursuing a PhD with the Department of Defence Studies, King's College London. Shu Huang has a B.A (Honours) degree in History from the National University of Singapore, as well as an MSc in Strategic Studies from RSIS. Prior to joining RSIS, Shu Huang worked for the Singapore Army to set up the Army Museum of Singapore. His affiliation with the military continues to this day, though now in the realm of professional military education and research on Singapore defence issues. Shu Huang is the co-author of *Singapore Chronicles: Defence* (Straits Times Press & Institute of Policy Studies, 2015).

Albert Lau is Associate Professor at the Department of History, National University of Singapore, where he had served as Head of Department and also Vice-Dean of the Faculty of Arts and Social Sciences. He obtained his doctorate in history from the School of Oriental and African Studies in London. He is the author of *The Malayan Union Controversy, 1942–1948* (Oxford University Press, 1990) and *A Moment of Anguish: Singapore in Malaysia and the Politics of Disengagement* (Times Academic Press, 1998). He is also one of the authors of *A New History of Southeast Asia* (Palgrave Macmillan, 2010) and the editor of *Southeast Asia and the Cold War* (Routledge, 2012). His areas of research include Malaysian and Singapore political and constitutional history and the international history of Southeast Asia.

Leong Chan-Hoong is Head of Social Lab at the Institute of Policy Studies, National University of Singapore (NUS). He received his PhD in psychology from Victoria University of Wellington, New Zealand, and MSc in statistics from NUS. His research centres on immigration, social resilience, and the management of cultural diversity. He is Principal Investigator for various national surveys including the Geo-spatial Analysis on How the Social and Built Environment Influence Attitudes to Immigrants (Ministry of Culture, Community and Youth, 2018), the State of the Overseas Singaporeans Survey (Overseas Singaporeans Unit, 2017), and Youth Study on Transitions and Evolving Pathways in Singapore (National Youth Council, 2017). Chan-Hoong is currently a board member of the National Integration Workgroup on Communities. He is a Fellow of the International Academy for Intercultural Research, and he sits on the Editorial Board for the *Asian Journal of Social Psychology*. He reviews manuscripts and research grant proposals submitted to various journals and international research agencies, including *Applied Psychology: An International Review*, *Journal of Cross-Cultural Psychology*, the Israel Science Foundation, and Israel Ministry of Science, Technology and Space. He was Consulting Editor for the *International Journal of Intercultural Relations* (2013–2014), and Editor for the 2013 and 2018 Special Issues, *"Multiculturalism: Beyond Ethnocultural Diversity and Contestations"*, and *"Viewing Intercultural Adaptation and Social Inclusion through Constructs of National Identity"*, respectively.

Bernard Fook Weng Loo is an Associate Professor with the Military Studies Programme and coordinator of the Master of Science (Strategic Studies) degree programme at the S. Rajaratnam School of International Studies, Nanyang Technological University, Singapore. He completed his doctoral studies at the Department of International Politics at the University of Wales, Aberystwyth in 2002. His research interests encompass war studies, strategic theory, conventional military strategies, strategic challenges of small and medium powers, and the problems and prospects of military transformation.

Graham Ong-Webb is a Research Fellow at the S. Rajaratnam School of International Studies, Nanyang Technological University, Singapore. He currently resides with the Executive Deputy Chairman's Office where he conducts research for the Future Issues and Technology portfolio. He was formerly attached to the Military Studies Programme at the School. Graham is the editor of *IHS Jane's Chemical, Biological, Radiological, and Nuclear (CBRN) Response Handbook*, 4th Edition (IHS Jane's, 2011) and *Piracy, Maritime Terrorism and Securing the Malacca Straits* (Institute of Southeast Asian Studies, and the International Institute of Asian Studies, Leiden University, 2006). A Commonwealth Scholar, Graham completed his PhD at the Department of War Studies, King's College London. As an Operationally-Ready National Serviceman, Graham is a commissioned army officer serving as a Commanding Officer of a National Service armoured infantry battalion. He is also an Honorary Aide-de-Camp to the President of Singapore. He graduated from the 14th National Service Command & Staff Course at the Goh Keng Swee Command and Staff College as Distinguished Graduate.

Kai Ostwald is an Assistant Professor in the School of Public Policy & Global Affairs and the Department of Political Science at the University of British Columbia (UBC), Canada. He is also Director of UBC's Centre for Southeast Asia Research and Associate Editor (Southeast Asia) of *Pacific Affairs*. He received a PhD in Political Science from the University of California, San Diego, and an MA from the National University of Singapore. He was also a Visiting Associate at ISEAS-Yusof Ishak Institute. His work focuses broadly on issues of political development, nation building, and ethnic politics in Southeast Asia, particularly Singapore, Malaysia, Indonesia, and Myanmar.

Terri-Anne Teo is a Research Fellow at the Centre of Excellence for National Security, S. Rajaratnam School of International Studies, Nanyang Technological University, Singapore. She holds an MSc in International Relations and PhD in Politics from the University of Bristol. Terri-Anne has taught courses on international relations, political theory and multicul-turalism. She has written about Singapore's identity politics, youth and meritocracy, and perceptions of citizenship. Building on this research, she is currently working on a monograph that examines multiculturalism in Singapore, and an edited volume on postcolonial governmentalities.

Norman Vasu is Senior Fellow and Deputy Head of the Centre of Excellence for National Security at the S. Rajaratnam School of International Studies, Singapore. He is the author of *How Diasporic Peoples Maintain Their Identity in Multicultural Societies: Chinese, Africans, and Jews* (Edwin Mellen Press, 2008), editor of *Social Resilience in Singapore: Reflections from the London Bombings* (Select Publishing, 2007), co-editor of *Nations, National Narratives and Communities in the Asia-Pacific* (Routledge, 2014), as well as *Immigration in Singapore* (Amsterdam University Press, 2015). His research on multiculturalism, ethnic relations, narratives of governance, citizenship, immigration, and national security have been published in journals such as *Asian Survey*, *Asian Ethnicity*, *Journal of Comparative Asian Development* and *The Copenhagen Journal of Asian Studies*, and in a number of edited volumes. He was a Fulbright Fellow with the Center for Strategic Communication, Hugh Downs School of Human Communication, Arizona State University in 2012, a Visiting Senior Fellow at the Takshashila Institution, Bangalore, India in 2016 and a Visiting Scholar at the Daniel K. Inouye Asia-Pacific Center for Security Studies in Honolulu, Hawaii in 2018.

Wu Shang-Su is a Research Fellow at the S. Rajaratnam School of International Studies, Nanyang Technological University, Singapore. He is attached to the Military Studies Programme at the school's constituent unit, the Institute of Defence and Strategic Studies. His research interests include military modernisation, Taiwan issues, railway and international relations. Shang-Su's articles, commentaries and op-eds have been published in the *Pacific Review*, *Defence Studies*, *Naval War College Review*, *East Asia Forum*, and the *National Interest* amongst others. He is also the author of *The Defence Capabilities of Small States: Singapore and Taiwan's Responses to Strategic Desperation* (Palgrave, 2016).

Contents

Introduction

National Service (NS) is one of Singapore's foundational public policies and an enduring pillar of its national defence. It was first implemented by the British in 1954, amended by the Singapore government in 1967 to provide the manpower to defend a fledgling independent nation and finally codified into its present form in 1970. Today, NS comprises a period of full-time uniformed service, presently between 22 to 24 months, in the Singapore Armed Forces (SAF), Singapore Police Force (SPF) or Singapore Civil Defence Force (SCDF). Enlistment for full-time service typically occurs at age 18. This is followed by a period of operationally-ready duties comprising 10 annual in-camp trainings (ICT). Officers are liable for duty until the age of 50, and other ranks, till age 40. Most, however, finish their NS obligations before those ages by meeting the requisite number of ICTs. Some opt to continue their NS under the Reservist on Voluntary Extended Reserve Service (ROVERS) scheme until their respective statutory age requirements. Still others continue serving past that age under the NS Volunteer Scheme. National Servicemen (NSmen) serve in most vocations and ranks.

Singapore commemorated the 50th anniversary of NS in 2017. The year-long "NS50" commemoration acknowledged the service of over 1 million NSmen, as well as others who had supported and contributed to the development of NS over the years. To the Singapore government, NS has "fulfilled a critical need for defence and security" and also "provided the peace and stability" facilitating Singapore's development. No other government policy has been commemorated at such a scale. Arguably, none affects the Singaporean way of life to the extent that NS does. In addition to its role in Singapore's defence, NS is also deeply woven into Singapore's political and social fabric. In one way or another, Singaporeans and long-term residents have had a stake in NS. NSmen, past and present, have naturally shouldered the biggest responsibilities. But others — family members, friends, employers, and colleagues of NSmen — too have played significant roles in supporting the policy and institution. Consequently, many, having experienced NS directly or indirectly, have an opinion of it. Online and off-line commentary on NS matters in recent years has demonstrated a clear interest in discussing it. Recognising the importance of these perspectives, the government has also encouraged these conversations. In 2013, the Committee to Strengthen National Service (CSNS) was established to "examine how the NS system can be strengthened for the future, to better serve Singapore and Singaporeans." The CSNS reportedly engaged more than 40,000 Singapore residents to determine how NS could be improved. The Committee also commissioned a study involving 1,200 face-to-face interviews conducted by the Institute of Policy Studies (IPS) to understand public perceptions and attitudes towards NS, with its findings subsequently publicly released.

Such studies, however, have been exceptional. While opinions on NS abound, what has been noticeably lacking in conversation about NS is academic research on the topic. Despite the policy's reach and age, NS has only been marginally explored in scholarship on Singapore. With a few exceptions, it has typically been examined as an aspect of Singapore's defence policy or a location to study other phenomena, rarely a subject of study in its own right. This edited volume foregrounds NS and places it squarely on centre stage. It proffers a small collection of research by scholars and analysts from varied backgrounds contemplating the past, present and future of what has become a central Singaporean national policy and institution.

The chapters in this edited volume are organised into four parts. Its first part explores the history of NS and comprises three chapters. The first chapter is a welcomed update to Albert Lau's history of NS, *National Service*, published as a brief monograph by *Pointer*, the Journal of the SAF, in 1992. Lau necessarily revisits some of the same ground he covered earlier. He traces the decisions and developments that have given NS its key characteristics. NS has become the "backbone of Singapore's defence" and "a deeply embedded aspect of the nation's psyche and a non-negotiable requirement of citizenship". The key principles of universality and equity were adopted at its start to ensure no liable male citizen, including "sons of ... politicians, top civil servants, senior military, police and civil defence officials and high-income earners" were exempted from NS. A status-blind approach to conscription was extended to a consistent approach to punishing NS defaulters. Lau also outlines how the Singapore government mounted an extensive publicity campaign to explain the necessity of NS. This effort focused on gaining the support of community and grassroots leaders to help galvanise the public. Lau highlights past and present measures to explain how the Singapore government won what he describes as "the battle to gain broad public acceptance of military conscription as an essential part of life for Singapore's male citizens", and how it still invests considerable resources to secure continued support for NS.

Bernard Fook Weng Loo's chapter adopts a narrower historical lens by focusing on the role that Singapore's first Minister for Defence, Dr Goh Keng Swee, played in implementing NS as he raised the SAF. Dr Goh not only solved the considerable practical challenges in implementing NS, but was able to do so in a manner which overcame the initial societal and economic objections raised by Singaporeans. NS was initially not a popular policy owing to its mandatory nature and disruptiveness. The policy, however, came to be accepted as "part of the Singaporean way of life" because of its eventual "routinisation". In a decade after its implementation, NS made possible the SAF's personnel expansion by about 433%, the policy having quickly overcome initial public criticism and concern. In examining Dr Goh's role in implementing NS, Loo explains how it became the cornerstone of the SAF from its very beginning.

Ho Shu Huang's chapter highlights how NS does not merely entail military service in the SAF. Many NSmen have also served in the SPF and SCDF. To be sure, the close association of NS with the SAF is unsurprising given that the majority of every NS cohort is indeed enlisted for military service. No historical account of NS, however, is complete without examining the non-military roles NS can be served in. In his chapter, Ho charts the policy logic of non-military NS in Singapore through an exploration of its early history outside the SAF. He establishes that its inclusion was initially based on both legislative legacy and administrative necessity despite the need to quickly expand the SAF. Ho notes there had always been legislative provision for NS to be served outside the military. Defence, however, was thought to be mainly the responsibility of the SAF in the years following Singapore's independence. The preservation of Singapore's sovereignty from external aggression was the dominant concern then. Yet channelling each annual cohort of new NS enlistees entirely into the SAF was not feasible as it simply did not have the capacity to accommodate and train them all. Consequently, many served NS part-time in the Special Constabulary (SC) and Vigilante Corps (VC) under the SPF in an internal security role until the early 1980s. The 1980s saw Total Defence incorporating non-military pillars of defence formally introduced. The SCDF was formed in 1986. The decade saw a broader understanding of security functions beyond the military seeded and has developed since. Ho traces how NSmen in the SPF and SCDF became integral to Singapore's national security, with them now playing roles as important as their SAF counterparts.

The edited volume's second part comprises four chapters which explore different aspects of NS in practice. Chang Jun Yan sets the stage for this section by addressing a paradox — how does a policy which imposes a lengthy period of mandatory service in uniform still enjoy popular support? While specific aspects of NS have faced criticism, Singaporeans still broadly support NS. Chang frames his explanation using the field of International Relations Copenhagen School's concept of "securitisation". At independence in 1965, Singapore's policy elites noted objective and subjective perceptions of vulnerability in the economic, geographical, political and social realms. In order to mitigate these vulnerabilities, the Singapore government securitised them and constantly foregrounded them in public discourse and policies. The exceptional security practice of NS was a product of the securitisation of vulnerability. Using NS, Chang charts the securitisation of vulnerability in three areas across Singapore society: first in the successfully implementing NS for national defence and nation-building; second in the co-option and subsequent mobilisation of its audience, the Singapore public; and third in the entrenchment of vulnerability in the fabric of society itself and the rise of what some have observed to be a "national habit of fear" in its citizens.

Samuel L. W. Chan's chapter focuses on what is arguably the most visible aspect of NS in practice — the comparatively large SAF considering Singapore's small geographical size. This is only possible because of NS. Chan, however, notes that at independence, NS was not the only option considered to raise a credible military for Singapore's defence. If the SAF were to be a credible deterrent force, numbers, however, would matter. NS was the only feasible policy to raise, train and sustain an adequately large military force for that purpose. NS allowed the quick expansion of a small professional SAF into an integrated force capable of a multitude of missions. Today, the SAF can field about 350,000 trained personnel if fully mobilised. Using considerable empirical evidence, Chan shows in his chapter how NS makes this possible.

Kai Ostwald's chapter moves away from NS' operational role in the SAF and instead examines its nation-building one. Beyond its security function, NS also brings together the country's diverse population by inculcating in it a sense of identity and loyalty through a common experience working towards a shared purpose. Ostwald argues that Singapore's utilisation of the military as a vehicle of social transformation has global historical antecedents. Ostwald examines the effectiveness of NS in Singapore's nation-building process. He first describes how NS facilitated the creation of a new collective identity after Singapore was separated from Malaysia in 1965 when there were few collective experiences or institutions which meaningfully differentiated being "Singaporean" and "Malaysian". Together with other social vehicles such as Singlish (a colloquial local variant of English) and its public housing policies, NS has become a quintessential social "rite of passage for its male citizens" to forge a Singaporean identity and be socialised as "ideal citizens". Through surveys of two contrasting groups of NSmen who either live in barracks on weekdays (those who "stay-in") or are allowed to return home daily (those who "stay-out"), Ostwald offers a preliminary assessment of nation-building by framing the process through a theory of *socialisation* and *contact*. Both shape the attitudes and behaviours of NSmen vis-à-vis nation-building traits acquired. He posits where these mechanisms are more pronounced, "the transformative potential of NS is greater", and vice-versa.

Continuing with the theme of nation-building, Leong Chan-Hoong's chapter explores how Singapore's international outlook could impact NS. As Singapore becomes more globalised and cosmopolitan, the possibility of it becoming a "hyperculture" state, one with a fluid mix of multiple cultures that transcends traditional boundaries, increases. A growing number of immigrants and transient labour will call the city-state home. Additionally, transnational marriages are increasing. More children born from such marriages will have complicated citizenship status. These trends will affect the ethno-cultural texture of Singapore, and the subject of NS liability could become a potential fault-line between citizens and non-citizens in the years to come. Furthermore, the number of Singaporeans working and living abroad has increased, possibly impacting the operational readiness of its NS-based security forces. Leong's chapter delves deep into the changing social fabric of the Singapore nation and how this may shape the future of NS. To set up his main argument, Leong first offers a brief historical overview on the imperatives for universal conscription in Singapore, followed by a description on the guiding principles of NS, and how the role of the institution has evolved over the years. He then explores this evolving demographic landscape by examining the findings from a recent survey on attitudes to NS commissioned by the CSNS. Leong discusses how the cosmopolitan contour and having a non-distinctive Singaporean identity in an era of "hyperculturalism" can affect perceptions of NS.

The third part features contributions on two debates on NS. Terri-Anne Teo and Priscilla Cabuyao's chapter discusses the idea of dual citizenship and NS. Singapore does not allow dual citizenship. The position adopted by the Singapore government is one should be loyal to a single state and therefore possess only single citizenship. Following on, NS is often trumpeted as a marker of Singapore citizenship and a symbol of loyalty to Singapore. Dual citizenship would therefore be antithetical to NS's nation-building role. In a globalised world, could a policy of dual citizenship, however, enhance NS instead of undermining it? Teo and Cabuyao suggest that it could be possible. They argue possessing dual citizenship could be compatible with NS despite claims that it dilutes loyalty to a nation and compromises national security in times of crisis. They begin their chapter with a contextualisation of the main contentions surrounding dual citizenship and national security as far as NS is concerned. They then contest the view that NS and dual citizenship are fundamentally incompatible in Singapore. Teo and Cabuyo establish that loyalties are actually situational and multiple, finding commonality across dual nationalities and multiple identities. Be that as it may, Teo and Cabuyao acknowledge the need for prudence. With safeguards in place, the inclusion of dual citizens, however, could actually increase the NS manpower needed in times of crisis.

The contentious issue of race and NS is the second debate addressed. In their chapter, Norman Vasu and Nur Diyanah Binte Anwar explore Malays and NS in the context of a long-standing perspective that they face discrimination in where they serve it. Some view Malays as over-represented in the SPF and SCDF while under-represented in the SAF. An additional concern is whether Malays are unrepresented in military units deemed to be security "sensitive". Vasu and Nur Diyanah note MINDEF maintains that in every NS cohort, the SAF enlists more Malays than the SPF and SCDF altogether. It also reiterates Malays have been progressively integrated into "all elements of the SAF". Vasu and Nur Diyanah, however, show a complex relationship between Malays, the military and NS. They begin by outlining the significant role the Malays played in the military in pre-independence Singapore. Malays would subsequently dominate the military forces posted to Singapore when it was part of Malaysia. The fledgling SAF, however, was hollowed out of Malays post-independence because of security concerns given the difficult relations Singapore had with its neighbours, Malaysia and Indonesia, then. Without a distinctive Singaporean national identity formed yet, there was concern in some quarters then the loyalty of Malays in Singapore would lie with these states they ostensibly shared an ethno-cultural affinity with if there was conflict. Reflecting this, Malays were only selectively enlisted in the early years of NS. If they were enlisted into the SAF, Malays were deployed in only selected military vocations. Some argue this still continues. This experience of Malays in the SAF and NS remains controversial and has been variously interpreted. It is therefore crucial to understand these historical observations in context and detail, both of which Vasu and Nur Diyanah systematically provide. While acknowledging the SAF has over the years become more inclusive, Vasu and Nur Diyanah conclude still more can be done for NS' nation-building role, suggesting the setting of racial targets in the SAF where NS can be served which are more closely representative of the overall racial make-up of Singapore.

The concluding part of this edited volume offers an international perspective of mandatory service. Wu Shang-Su and Ho Shu Huang explore the evolution of conscription in Taiwan. Wu and Ho demonstrate that much like Singapore, conscription in Taiwan was traditionally justified as a key pillar of national defence against an attack by the People's Republic of China (PRC) seeking to reunify the "renegade province" with the mainland. This remained the dominant narrative for almost half a century. With the end of martial law and the "democratisation"' of Taiwan in the 1990s, the justification for continuing military conscription in Taiwan was increasingly challenged. Its importance to national defence had seemingly diminished given the apparent maturing of diplomatic relations with the PRC, notwithstanding occasional bouts of antagonism. Conscription was also poorly implemented in areas. Questions were raised over poor equipment, inadequate care of conscripts and their inappropriate deployment for non-military tasks. Responding to popular sentiment, different Taiwanese administrations have slowly but surely moved to abolish conscription and optimistically transform the Taiwanese military into an all-volunteer force (AVF) comprising regulars. In this final chapter, Wu and Ho examine how conscription has evolved from being a cornerstone of Taiwan's defence policy to its present problematic position of being a policy that Taiwan no longer wants politically but cannot yet abolish fully because of difficulties in raising an AVF.

Across its 10 chapters, *National Service in Singapore* addresses a mere handful of topics. Many other aspects of NS remain to be explored. It is hoped this edited volume inspires further academic study of NS. While NS is a policy and institution so many may already claim familiarity with given how it has involved them in one way or another, much more about it still remains to be understood. Its familiar omnipresence in multiple aspects of Singaporean life precisely makes the policy ripe for further study.

Part 1

The History of NS

Chapter 1

National Service and Citizen Soldiers: The Singapore Experience of Military Conscription

Albert Lau

When Singapore was suddenly thrust out of Malaysia in 1965, the betting odds were heavily stacked against its survival as a newly sovereign state. The island-state's diminutive size, small population, lack of natural resources, its location in a tough neighbourhood — a "region of revolt"[1] — and inability to defend itself did not augur well for a future on its own. Fifty years on, in 2015, Singapore celebrated its Golden Jubilee — in style. The once fledging state had not only defied the odds against its survival but had prospered economically in the process. Underpinning the Singapore Economic Miracle is the physical security of its sovereignty and territorial integrity provided by the Singapore Armed Forces (SAF), created from scratch after independence and built upon the bedrock of military conscription that was first introduced — albeit amid much controversy and opposition — when Singapore was still a British colony in 1954. Foisted once again in 1967, this time on a grander scale and on a post-independent citizenry unaccustomed to soldiering, National Service (NS) has come a long way since then. Today, NS is not only the backbone of Singapore's defence; it has become a deeply embedded aspect of the

---

[1] Milton Osborne, *Region of Revolt: Focus on Southeast Asia* (New South Wales: Pergamon Press, 1970).

nation's psyche and a non-negotiable requirement of citizenship — a "way of life" and a "rite of passage" for its male citizens on whose shoulders the burden and responsibility of national defence disproportionately rested. This chapter surveys the historical evolution and administration of NS in Singapore between 1954 and 2017. It focuses on not only the rationale for NS and its undergirding principles but also shows how the post-independent city-state grappled with the burdens and the challenges of foisting common defence responsibilities on its male citizenry. In particular, the story of conscription in Singapore reveals how the continual engagement of its citizenry is necessary to win the hearts and minds of each generation of Singaporeans and get them to embrace the concept of life-long NS.

The Colonial Legacy

Though military service was not unknown to Singapore,[2] the island state's first experience of NS began only in the 1950s as part of the British response to the outbreak in June 1948 of the armed communist insurgency, dubbed the "Emergency", in both Malaya and Singapore. Forced to deal with the deteriorating security situation, the British in 1952 introduced the National Service Bill requiring the part-time conscription of all eligible male British subjects and Federal citizens. The bill was passed by the Legislative Council in December 1953, which also approved the bill to set up the Singapore Military Forces (SMF). But NS was not strenuously enforced beyond the middle of 1954 as it incited violent riots by Chinese Middle School students who equated it

---

[2] As early as 1854, a Singapore Volunteer Rifle Corps had been formed to assist the police in dealing with riots. During World War I, volunteers participated in maintaining internal security and, in 1922, following the introduction of compulsory military service for all British European males between the ages of 18 and 55, the Singapore Volunteer Corps (SVC) was established. It fought along the regular British and Commonwealth troops during the Japanese invasion of Singapore during World War II. Although it was disbanded after Singapore's liberation in June 1946, it was revived in 1949 as internal security demands increased following the outbreak of the "Emergency". See T. M. Winsley, *A History of the Singapore Volunteer Corps 1854–1937* (Singapore: Government Printing Office, 1938); Gabriel Chan Eng Han, "The Volunteer Corps", *Pointer Supplement* (November 1990).

as devise to defend a colonial system benefiting only the British and the English-educated elite.[3]

While the NS ordinance remained very much in force, conscription soon gave way to a preference for regular forces as Singapore marched towards self-government under the Labour Front government from 1955. After the People's Action Party (PAP) won the 1959 Singapore elections and formed the government, it continued the policy of building Singapore's regular forces, which by 1963 saw the raising of two full-strength regular battalions of the Singapore Infantry Regiment (SIR). Arguing that an independent Singapore on its own was not economically, politically, or militarily viable, the PAP government pushed for independence through merger with the Federation of Malaya. With the formation of Malaysia, comprising the former British territories of Malaya, Singapore and the North Borneo and Sarawak, on 16 September 1963, defence and internal security became a Federal responsibility and the need to boost the recruitment of local forces was no longer considered a priority.[4]

The creation of Malaysia, however, precipitated the onset of *Konfrontasi* (Confrontation), as Indonesia sought to assert its influence over the former British territories.[5] In April 1964, the Federal government invoked the NS ordinance once more, and some 30,000 men registered for NS by May. Of the 100 who were called up, only 82 reported for service. They were sent for two months' training at Port Dickson. By mid-1965, some five batches were trained.[6] By then, however, Singapore's relationship with Kuala Lumpur had deteriorated to the point where separation seemed the only viable option. On 9 August 1965, after 23 months in Malaysia, Singapore found itself suddenly out of the Federation. When the last batch of NS conscripts returned from Port Dickson on 6 October, Singapore was already an independent state.[7] The need to build up its own military forces took on an added urgency as the

---

[3] See: Albert Lau, "National Service", *Pointer Supplement* (November 1992), 6–10.
[4] Ibid., 12–13.
[5] See: J. A. C. Mackie, *Konfrontasi: The Indonesian-Malaysia Dispute 1963–1966* (Kuala Lumpur: Oxford University Press, 1974).
[6] Mickey Chiang, *SAF and 30 Years of National Service* (Singapore: MINDEF Public Affairs Department, 1997), 25.
[7] Lau, "National Service", 14.

young republic struggled to find its own footing during a time of great uncertainty for Singapore and the region.

National Service: Reloaded

Singapore's departure from Malaysia made its physical survival a pressing concern. Surrounded by the territorial waters of Indonesia and Malaysia, the small, trading island's confined location at the southern tip of the Malay Peninsula meant that its access to the high seas was possible only through its neighbours' waters. Any serious disruption of its physical links to the outside world would seriously threaten its economic well-being and physical survival as a young state. With Indonesia just a few kilometres away, and the fires of *Konfrontasi* still smouldering, Singapore's threat environment did not improve. Its dependence on Malaysia for its water supply afforded yet another source of vulnerability.[8] At the time of independence, Singapore was in no position to defend itself. Its total defence capability consisted of the following: two understrength battalions (nearly all the officers in command were British and two-thirds of the soldiers were non-citizens hailing mainly from Malaysia); a 5,000-men police force; an ageing gunboat (called the *RSS Panglima*) to guard its territorial waters; and not a single aircraft to safeguard its national airspace. While the presence of British troops during *Konfrontasi* helped to cushion Singapore's vulnerability, the island's leaders knew that they could not expect the United Kingdom to continue to extend its security umbrella over the island once Britain's security interests no longer coincided with Singapore's. Now a sovereign state, there was no escaping the hard reality that Singapore would have to be responsible for its own defence.[9]

A small team led by newly appointed defence minister, Dr Goh Keng Swee, was hastily assembled to form the nucleus of the new Ministry of

---

[8] In his memoirs, Singapore's premier Lee Kuan Yew recalled, for instance, how his Malaysian counterpart, Tunku Abdul Rahman, had informed Lord Head, the British High Commissioner, that "If Singapore's foreign policy is prejudicial to Malaysia's interests, we could always bring pressure to bear on them by threatening to turn off the water in Johor." Lee Kuan Yew, *The Singapore Story: Memoirs of Lee Kuan Yew* (Singapore: Times Edition, 1998), 663.

[9] Lau, "National Service", 15.

Interior and Defence (MID), which was set up in October 1965. An economist by training, Dr Goh sought help from other countries to build Singapore's own defence force from scratch. He ruled out the British as he felt that, going by their record of training the Indian army, the British would want to "continue to provide the officers for a long time."[10] Several non-aligned Asian and African countries, including India and Egypt, were discreetly approached, but many of these states had reservations about assisting a then unknown state in a sensitive subject like defence. Only Israel responded positively and an agreement was reached for Israel to help train and build up the SAF.[11]

Several options were considered — and just as readily dropped. Raising a small, highly trained, regular military force was financially feasible but it was also, by reason of its size, militarily impotent. Singapore also could not depend on volunteers to supplement its small regular force as there was no assurance of getting an adequate supply of volunteers: Singapore had no tradition of soldiering and the majority race, Chinese, despised soldiering as a profession.[12] Building a large regular force, on the other hand, would be the most effective means of ensuring Singapore's security — but it came with high cost. With only a small population of less than 2 million, creating such a sufficiently large standing military force to meet Singapore's defence needs would also invariably divert scarce manpower resources to military use. On the recommendation of the Israeli advisors, the decision was taken to create a citizen's army of conscripts built around the nucleus of regulars serving in the two SIRs as the most cost- and manpower-effective solution to build a credible SAF. A detailed and systematic programme of build-up was worked out with the Israeli advisors.[13] The Singapore Armed Forces Training Institute (SAFTI) was quickly set up in February 1966 to train officers and non-commissioned officers (NCOs) and, from June 1966, the first batch of 140 officer cadets was selected from more than 2,000 applicants to undergo training and form the nucleus of the regular officer corps needed to train national servicemen. In July 1967, 117 of the 140 received

---

[10] *The Straits Times* (henceforth ST), 30 June 1992.
[11] Goh Keng Swee, "National Service and Defence Policy", in *Towards Tomorrow: Essays on Development and Social Transformation in Singapore* (Singapore: NTUC, 1973), 56.
[12] Chiang, "SAF and 30 Years of National Service", 23.
[13] Lau, "National Service", 18.

their commissions.[14] A Central Manpower Base (CPMB) was also established to register conscripts.[15]

With the military infrastructure in place, the government moved the National Service (Amendment) Bill in parliament on 27 February 1967. Under the bill, all 18-year-old Singapore citizens and permanent residents were required to be enlisted for part-time service in the volunteers-reliant People's Defence Force (PDF), Vigilante Corps, and the Special Constabulary for 12 years. As facilities and trainers were limited, only about 10%, mainly from the better educated, would be conscripted for full-time NS, spending two to three years with the army and thereafter 10 years in the reserves until reaching 40 years of age. In moving the second reading of the NS bill in parliament on 13 March 1967, Dr Goh justified its necessity on wider security and nation-building grounds. The "logical" effect of a strategically important but poorly defended Singapore, he argued, must mean that it would "revert to a colony or satellite of whoever wishes to afford it protection" — an outcome that would not only spell trouble for the region but also pose a threat to the security and peace of the world. A well defended Singapore, on the other hand, could become a valuable partner in any future regional defence scheme and a stabilising force in the region. For a recently independent and heterogeneous state like Singapore, where a strong national identity was still lacking among its multi-ethnic communities, Dr Goh maintained that participation in the military forces — and particularly when this participation was spread over all strata of society as in the case of NS — had an important nation-building aspect as well by helping to forge a sense of "loyalty and national consciousness" among its citizenry.[16] In the absence of the main opposition party, Barisan Sosialis, which had boycotted parliament since October 1966, the bill had a relatively smooth passage through the PAP-dominated House, which passed it on 14 March 1967 after considerable debate.[17] In July, the first full-time batch of 900 men was enlisted to serve in two newly-formed NS battalions, 2 and 4 SIR. Outside parliament, a

---

[14] Chiang, "SAF and 30 Years of National Service", 35.

[15] The CPMB moved from Dempsey Hill location to Depot Road venue in 1989.

[16] Singapore Parliamentary Debates (henceforth SPD), 13 March 1967, Cols. 1158–1164.

[17] Ibid., 14 March 1967, Cols. 1197–1257.

few small anti-NS demonstrations occurred but these did not detract the government from pressing ahead with NS.[18]

As the training capacity then was unable to absorb all available manpower, the government initially freely exempted or deferred young men from full-time NS who were either working (particularly as sole bread winners), or students awaiting enrolment to the university.[19] But by exempting or deferring the educated, the SAF soon found itself enlisting lower educated conscripts which resulted in a shortage of "high mental calibre" young men who could undergo officer training. Reversing course in December 1967, the government started what the *Straits Times* termed a "brain power" call-up, drafting graduating students in tertiary institutions on a selective basis. The need to speed up the build-up of its officer corps assumed even greater urgency after the shock announcement in January 1968 of Britain's intention to accelerate its military withdrawal by the end of 1971.[20]

The move to draft at short notice graduates into full-time military service, however, provoked an immediate backlash not just from graduates worried about their competitiveness but also employers nervous about the effects of such a brain drain of scarce professional and technical manpower on the growing economy. The government defended its policy by pointing out that a credible defence was necessary to ensure a safe climate for Singapore's economic growth.[21] In June 1969, the government dropped another bombshell of its own. Arguing that SAF officers had to be effectively trained, it raised the draft liability of NS officers from two to three years, evidently based on the experience of the Israeli army.[22] Not surprisingly, the unpopular move, which was

---

[18] The police had to fire tear gas and deploy its riot squads to disperse them. But the resistance was unlike the scale of the anti-NS riots of 1954. Then, Singapore was still a British colony and NS was perceived as a British scheme to protect their interests and prolong colonial rule. In 1967, however, public support had improved. Singapore had been independent for two years and, after the upheavals of *Konfrontasi* and separation, there was the gradual realisation among Singaporeans that the new-found independence thrust upon them was theirs to shoulder and defend. Chiang, "SAF and 30 Years of National Service", 31.

[19] SPD, 4 November 1970, Col. 296.

[20] Lau, "National Service", 21.

[21] ST, 17 December 1967.

[22] SPD, 11 June 1969, Col. 31.

selective and not comprehensive, prompted another row. Graduate officers complained bitterly in the press while employers expressed concern that three years of full-time NS would cause graduate conscripts to lose touch of their professional skills and the latest developments in their fields. The Chinese Chamber of Commerce's proposal of a shortened period of liability — six-month full-time training followed by part-time service thereafter[23] — was, however, unacceptable to MID which felt that it was "impossible to train an efficient defence force part-time"; nor was it prepared to "turn our best brains into poor quality privates."[24] The government assured the chamber that the shortage of professionals in commerce and industry was only temporary and would be lessened once the first batch of graduates completed their NS cycle in 1970.

By 1970, the government was ready to recalibrate its NS policy. MID was split into two ministries, the Ministry of Home Affairs and the Ministry of Defence (MINDEF), allowing the latter to focus exclusively on military matters. Britain's new Conservative government's decision to delay its military withdrawal from Singapore, at least until 1975, mitigated the immediacy of a rapid build-up — for now. The need to speedily enlist university graduates to assume leadership roles in NS also lessened as progressively larger proportions of pre-university students were drafted. To assuage public resentment over the perceived arbitrariness of its previous policy, the government in November 1970 changed NS from part-time to full-time service for all,[25] so that the intention to pursue tertiary studies was no longer a ground for exemption, and standardised NS liability across the board to two and a half years for both officers and NCOs, while the service period of other ranks remained at two years. This change was necessary to address the problem of eligible recruits deliberately failing their NCO or officer cadet's courses to avoid a third year of full-time service and at the same time to incentivise the canny Singaporean male to work all that much

---

[23] ST, 1 October 1969, 4 February 1970.

[24] ST, 12 October 1969.

[25] To avoid depleting the universities of male students, the intake into NS was staggered for two years, starting with half of the total male pre-university cohorts in 1970, to three-quarters in 1971 and 1972, and almost all in 1973 when the 1970 intake would have completed its NS cycle in time for the university session in 1973, which was adjusted to start in July to suit them, and subsequent batches.

harder to become officers for the higher status and pay.[26] The change was also recognition that an unpopular policy could not build commitment to military service and would have an adverse effect on graduate officer morale.[27] On the other hand, the new policy afforded an opportunity for the SAF to develop a quality officer corps within the service from younger full-time National Servicemen (NSF) yet to enter the universities in the belief that many of them, just starting out with their future careers unde-cided, could be persuaded to consider a career with the SAF and be attracted by SAF scholarship schemes, including the prestigious SAF Overseas Scholarship introduced in 1971,[28] for regular officers to pursue their university education. As with any change in policy, some unfairness persisted: officers commissioned before 1971 served three years; those after 1971 served six months less.[29]

While the management of conscription did not remain stagnant, and adapted to shifts in the social milieu, no fundamental change in Singapore's NS policy occurred over the next three decades. By the 1990s, however, important changes in Singapore's evolving socio-economic and demographic landscapes brought new challenges that had ramifications for its NS policy. First, one upshot of the overhaul-ing of Singapore's education system during the late 1970s and again from the mid-1990s to keep in step with the state's economic transition from an export-led industrialisation strategy to a knowledge-economy phase, and the attendant increased emphasis on lifelong learning and

---

[26] ST, 1 February 1971.

[27] Shortening the service liability, however, had one drawback: it meant that potential cadets had to be selected at the outset for the new Standard Military Course, introduced in 1974, that offered a continuous basic to officer training over nine months without the benefits of unit experience provided by the previous system based on a three-year cycle requiring training at recruit, section leader, and officer cadet levels, with unit experience in between. See: Lau, "National Service", 26–27.

[28] This scholarship is open to young NS and regular officers with outstanding academic results and who show potential to become good combat officers in the SAF. After six months in Officer Cadet School (OCS), they pursue their studies in premier overseas uni-versities. ST, 19 August 1992.

[29] See: Lau, "National Service", 27. For these affected officers, preferential treatment was offered by the government for admission to the civil service and their military service was included as pensionable service.

upgrading of professional skills amongst the country's workforce,[30] was the changing profile of better educated and more critically thinking enlistees and reservists who were less satisfied with the status quo and had "higher expectations of their NS experience."[31] Second, declining birth rates, which first appeared in the 1980s, and plummeted to an all-time low in 2010 despite the government's pro-natal policies, had not only affected Singapore's ability to sustain its economic development but also impacted the manpower base the SAF drew upon for its conscription. A pro-immigration policy, which was put in place to attract global talent, helped to alleviate the labour crunch but it had also fuelled resentment among Singaporeans who were not only worried about the increased competition and strains on infrastructure from the influx of foreign workers but were also riled that Permanent Residents (PR) and New Citizens (NC) were enjoying the benefits of citizenship without NS liabilities.[32] Third, the effects of greater regionalisation and globalisation, which Singapore embraced for its economic growth, had "brought about greater competition and increased demands in the workplace," requiring employees to relocate or travel at short notice, and made it much more challenging for reservists to juggle their careers with their family and NS obligations.[33] Fourth, changing worldwide trends moving away from

---

[30] Report of the Third Committee to Recognise the Contribution of Operationally Ready National Servicemen to Total Defence (Record III), Executive Summary.

[31] Report of the Fifth Committee to Recognise the Contribution of Operationally Ready National Servicemen to Total Defence (Record V), 1.

[32] Since the 1990s there had been a steady rise in the number of foreigners taking up citizenship in Singapore, with the average annual growth of PR and non-residents being greater than that of Singapore citizens before falling in 2010. Although first generation PRs and NCs were exempt from NS, their male children who gained PR status under their parents' sponsorship were liable for NS upon reaching enlistment age unless they decided to renounce their Singapore citizenship. See: Wilson Low, "Wither Conscription in Singapore" (Masters Dissertation submitted to the Faculty of the US Army Command and General Staff College, 2011), 41.

[33] Report of the Fourth Committee to Recognise the Contribution of Operationally Ready National Servicemen to Total Defence (Record IV), 1; Report of the Fifth Committee to Recognise the Contribution of Operationally Ready National Servicemen to Total Defence (Record V), 1.

conscripted citizen soldiers in favour of more streamlined professional "high tech" armies[34] had also put pressure on the Singapore government to justify the continuance of its conscription policy per se — especially when concerns about the influx of immigrants and the lukewarm reception to NS by liable PRs[35] had cast doubts about the fairness and relevance of military conscription among citizens and prompted calls to refine the enlistment policy.[36]

Despite such challenges, the Singapore government remained unwavering in its defence of the primacy of NS. But In 2004, in the first major change to the Enlistment Act since 1970, the government reduced the conscription period from two and a half years to two years across the board, ostensibly because technological enhancements, which reduced the time needed to train soldiers, and the 15–20% surge in the number of conscripts from 2006 would enable the SAF to maintain its operational readiness even with the shortened NS duration.[37] Notwithstanding the curtailed training period, the duration of 24 months was still relatively long compared to many other countries with a conscription-based military force.[38]

Universality and Equity

Central to the government's administration of its conscription policy since 1967 were the underpinning principles of universality and equity that

---

[34] A plethora of reasons had been suggested, focusing principally on the argument that the higher demands of operating sophisticated weaponry in today's modern and more complex battlefields required more streamlined "high tech" professional armed forces that could not be effectively substituted by a less rigorously trained conscript force. Low, "Wither Conscription in Singapore", 11–15.

[35] The Minister of Defence, Dr Ng Eng Hen, revealed on 21 November 2011 that between 2005 and 2010, about one-third of NS-liable PRs renounced their residency prior to conscription. See: SPD, 21 November 2011, Col. 618.

[36] Leong Chan-Hoong, Yang Wai Wai and Jerrold Hong, "National Service: The Holy Grail in the Management of Social Diversity", in *Managing Diversity in Singapore: Policies and Prospects*, eds. Matthew Matthews and Chiang Wai Fong (London: Imperial College Press, 2016), 321–322.

[37] Low, "Wither Conscription in Singapore", 5.

[38] Ibid., 60.

ensured that no liable male citizen, not even those hailing from rich and influential Singaporean families, was exempted. "If we have a system in which some are conscripted but others are not, there will be strong feelings of unfairness which will undermine the commitment of our NSmen," explained defence minister Teo Chee Hean in 2006. "MINDEF has always been very clear that National Service must be universal — all who are fit to serve National Service must serve."[39] No ground for exemption was therefore accepted for the category of "conscientious objectors". After the Singapore congregation of the Jehovah Witnesses, which was registered in 1962, objected to NS as their beliefs forbade them to bear arms, perform military duties, salute the state flag or swear oaths of allegiance to the state, the government duly deregistered the congregation in January 1972 on the grounds that its continued existence would not only be "prejudicial to public welfare and good order" but would also have detracted from and undermined the principle of universality on which NS was founded.[40] To prevent the rich from sending their sons overseas for studies to dodge the draft, exit controls were tightened in January 1970 for male citizens who reached the call-up age of 18.[41] When it was realised that parents were evading even this ruling by sending their sons at a young age for secondary schooling overseas, with the intention of extending their studies to university level thereafter, that exit route was sealed in July 1970 when passports were refused to male citizens below the registration age of sixteen and a half. After parents protested at the draconian measure, the ruling was modified in December 1970 to permit them to provide security by cash bond or bank guarantee instead, which would be forfeited if their sons failed to return to serve when they reached 18. Placed at Singapore dollars (SGD) $20,000 in 1970, the bond quantum was increased to half

---

[39] SPD, 16 January 2006, Col. 2004.

[40] ST, 15 January 1972. Isolated instances of conscientious objections by Jehovah Witnesses nevertheless persisted, requiring the government to court martial and sentence defaulters to detention. After two years, they were released whereupon the enlistment order was served upon them again. When they refused, they served a second two-year period of detentions, after which the government "call it quits and deem it equivalent" to they having served NS. See: SPD, 23 February 1990, Col. 1182.

[41] ST, 25 January 1970. Only government scholars and those already either in tertiary institutions abroad or selected for post-graduate studies were exempted.

the combined annual income of the parents, or SGD $75,000, whichever was higher, in 1992.[42]

From the late 1970s, NS-liable sons of influential Singaporeans — including politicians, top civil servants, senior military, police and civil defence officials, and high earners — were also specially identified and monitored under a "white horse" category, ostensibly to ensure that they would not be given any preferential treatment because of their parentage and family connections — at a time when most NSFs favoured non-combat clerical and other "soft" positions — and that their deployment based on their medical classification and vocation assignments were "scrupulously fair".[43] Since 2000, however, the "white horse" classification was discontinued as Singaporeans "have come to accept that the SAF treats its servicemen fairly" and NSFs on their part "aim higher because they know employers value those who have been officers or section commanders."[44]

In December 2005, a further rationalisation of MINDEF's deferment policy ensued to permit deferment only for pre-enlistees to gain their "basic" educational qualifications, i.e., 'A' levels, polytechnic diploma or below, and not for "higher" university degrees. Deferment was no longer allowed for pre-university students who had won places in overseas universities: they would have to serve NS first, just like everyone else, to ensure that members within the same cohort would receive roughly the same treatment in allowing them to attain their educational qualifications.

In line with its principles of universality and equality, MINDEF consistently took a tough stand against NS defaulters. In 1979, the government amended the constitution so that no one could escape his NS obligation by simply renouncing his citizenship. Only those who emigrated at a young age and had not enjoyed substantial socio-economic

---

[42] SPD, 16 January 2006, Col. 2004. In 1979, a further revision of the measure occurred. Young sons who accompanied parents or fathers transferred abroad to work and wished to pursue their secondary education overseas were exempted from the mandatory bond ruling. See: ST, 27 August 1979. They were also allowed to postpone their NS if they secured a place at the university before reaching 18 years of age but this time round the bond ruling would apply. ST, 17 September 1989.

[43] SPD, 11 November 2003, Col. 3443.

[44] ST, 19 November 2003.

benefits were allowed to renounce their citizenship without serving NS.[45] Defaulters were charged under the Enlistment Act and dealt with by the courts which would impose an appropriate sentence — imprisonment of up to three years, a fine of up to SGD $5,000 or both — based on the circumstances of each case. As most defaulters returned at a relatively young age and were still able to fulfil their NS obligations, MINDEF did not press for custodial sentences or heavier sentences until after the public backlash over the Melvyn Tan case in 2006 prompted a review. Tan, an internationally-acclaimed pianist and prodigy, who left Singapore in 1969 when he was 12 to study music in the United Kingdom, was granted a three-year deferment in 1974 (after his parents posted a SGD $30,000 bond) to further his music studies on a scholarship. When his request in 1977 for a further deferment to pursue his master's degree was disallowed, as MINDEF did not permit deferment for postgraduate studies, he defaulted, became a British citizen the following year, and duly renounced his Singapore citizenship, which he was allowed to do based on the then prevailing policy.[46] In 2005, however, after staying away for 37 years and informing the Singapore authorities, Tan returned to Singapore, ostensibly to visit his aged parents and to perform at a concert. Though Tan was duly charged for his NS offense, the composition fine of SGD $3,000 he received struck all the wrong notes and fuelled the perception that he was let off too lightly. As an indignant *Straits Times* reader put it, a fine for "thumbing your nose at a national institution just does not cut it."[47] In 2006, the government upped the maximum fine for NS defaulters from SGD $5,000 to SGD $10,000 and, for serious cases, it would also press for a jail sentence if they failed to enlist for more than two years or longer.[48] In 2017, the Singapore High Court ruled that the "worst" category of NS defaulters — those who did not serve their obligations at all — would face close to the maximum of three years' jail.[49]

---

[45] SPD, 16 January 2006, Col. 2004.

[46] ST, 17 January 2006.

[47] ST, 27 November 2005.

[48] ST, 17 January 2006.

[49] In April 2017, a NS defaulter, Ang Lee Thye, who evaded his obligation for 23 years, was accordingly sentenced to two years and nine months' jail. ST, 25 April 2017.

Where necessary, however, the SAF allowed selective deferments and disruption from NS in order to support broader SAF or national objectives. Since 1973, conscripts, for instance, were allowed to disrupt for medical studies in Singapore as there was a need for medical doctors to serve in the SAF. Upon graduation, they would be taught basic soldiering skills and normally commissioned as medical officers during their full-time NS stint. When the number of local medical graduates proved insufficient, the scheme was extended from 1981 to allow disruption of those studying medicine overseas — until 1992 when disruption from overseas medical studies was no longer allowed as the number of local medical graduates was able to meet the SAF's needs.[50] Other categories of young men who had been granted deferments or disruptions included students on scholarships administered by the Public Service Commission[51] — which were given special consideration as they served as "an important conduit for bringing key talent into the public service" — and those with exceptional talents who could bring credit and pride to Singapore like exceptionally bright "boy-wonder" Edward Teo and "star swimmer" Joseph Schooling. Teo leap-frogged his gifted-programme secondary two class at age 14 to embark on his tertiary education.[52] After obtaining his first-class honours Bachelor of Science degree in theoretical physics in 1991, the 18-year-old was granted deferment from NS to work with renowned physicist Stephen Hawking in Cambridge University for his doctoral programme which he completed in 1994, before returning to serve out his NS.[53] Schooling, on his part, broke new ground in 2013 when his enlistment was held off to allow him to focus on training for the Rio de Janeiro Olympics in 2016.[54] After Schooling scored gold in the Olympics — a historic first for Singapore in the Games — he was given a second round of deferment till after the 2020 Tokyo Games.[55]

---

[50] Between 1981 and 1992, 902 and 124 NSFs were disrupted to study medicine in Singapore and overseas respectively. See: SPD, 20 October 2011, Col. 341.
[51] Edwin Lee, *Singapore: The Unexpected Nation* (Singapore: ISEAS, 2008), 285.
[52] ST, 25 March 1990.
[53] ST, 17 September 1991.
[54] ST, 30 June 2015.
[55] ST, 15 August 2016.

Singapore's open and even-handed administration of its NS policy contributed no small part in the battle to gain broad public acceptance of military conscription as an essential part of life for Singapore's male citizens. By 1985, as the then Second Defence Minister, Dr Yeo Ning Hong, pronounced, "National Service has now become a valuable national institution ... every family in Singapore participates in national service, though a father, brother, son or cousin. No other institution is as all-pervading and all-embracing."[56] Evasion of NS was attempted only on a "negligible scale", noted Dr Goh Keng Swee in 1992.[57] Indeed, as defence minister Teo Chee Hean reported in 2006, only 185 men had been convicted for evasion the past 20 years and that in the last five years only an average of 0.5% of total liable enlistees, most of them overseas, failed to register for NS.[58] A measure of public acceptance of NS could be seen in the fact that even Singapore's opposition parties did not contest it. As opposition leader Dr Lee Siew Choh put it in 1989, NS had become "an institution that nobody can get rid of. So there is no point in continuing to oppose it."[59] During the general elections in 2011, opposition Workers' Party (WP) chief, Low Thia Khiang, held up participation in NS instead as an essential qualification for all male election candidates after it was disclosed that the PAP's new face, 38-year-old Janil Puthucheary, a Malaysian, who became a citizen in 2008, had not gone through NS.[60] Much political play was also made by the WP that its candidate, Taiwanese-born Chen Show Mao, who moved to Singapore when he was 11, and despite being away from Singapore for nearly 30 years due to studies and work, did his NS before taking up citizenship in 1986.[61]

Overcoming Resistance

When NS was first introduced, parents had legitimate concerns about sending their sons to an unfamiliar military setting of which they knew

---

[56] ST, 22 September 1985.

[57] ST, 9 February 1992.

[58] SPD, 16 January 2006.

[59] Lau, "National Service", 15.

[60] ST, 3 May 2011.

[61] ST, 26 April 2011.

little about — reinforced by fears about coping, training, safety, bad influences, and the enforced interruption to their offspring's education.[62] To allay their worries, the government mounted a publicity campaign at both the national and constituency levels to explain the necessity of NS and also obtain the support of community and grassroots leaders. Send-off dinners were organised at community centres and the narrative of the citizen-soldier lauded in heroic terms. Of great help was the public show of support by the Chinese Chamber of Commerce, which agreed to mint 5,000 souvenir National Service Medallions to be presented to the first 5,000 national servicemen. This went some way to persuade clan associations and other Chinese organisations to back NS.[63] To dispel any public misconception about army life, talks were also organised at community centres, telephone hotlines set up, and a handbook for parents produced.[64] To further allay concerns of parents that their sons were being exposed to bad influences, the SAF from 1986 prohibited smoking in its offices, meeting rooms and common areas and banned the sale of cigarettes in its camps.[65] It further conducted surveys to show that the majority of NSFs picked up the habit before enlistment and that the incidence of smoking had been declining steadily.[66] More importantly, safety procedures were established to make sure than no serviceman was exposed to unnecessary risks during training. All accidents and deaths during training were thoroughly investigated to prevent a recurrence.

In its efforts to assuage and reach out to anxious parents, MINDEF in 1993 produced a 23-minute video *The First Hundred Days* to provide a clearer idea of what happened during Basic Military Training (BMT).[67] Continuing its mission to reach out to what Defence Minister Teo Chee Hean called the "whole eco-system" that supported the defence of

---

[62] Lau, "National Service", 31.

[63] Chiang, "SAF and 30 Years of National Service", 48–51.

[64] ST, 9 March 1986.

[65] ST, 10 September 1989.

[66] According to a survey in 1991, 87.4% picked up smoking before enlistment. Of the remaining 12.6%, 5.3% were introduced to smoking by fellow soldiers. The incidence of smoking however had been declining steadily from 40.8% in 1986 to 23.1% in 1991. ST, 7 June 1992, 18 September 1992, and 12 October 1992.

[67] ST, 20 November 1993.

Singapore, MINDEF in 2010 uploaded on the YouTube video-sharing site 18 short clips that followed the progress of the recruits undergoing their nine-week stint from enlistment to completion of BMT.[68] Following its successful run, which garnered almost one million views online, the hit "reality" series *Every Singaporean Son* was reworked and converted into six episodes and broadcasted in the National Geographic Channel to allow it to reach a wider audience.[69] From 1997, parents were also invited to accompany their sons directly to the camp, tour the facilities, speak to the commanders, watch a video, and observe them taking the oath of allegiance.[70] For the SAF, the need to enlist community support behind NS was a necessary facet of its ongoing public education and engagement process to drive home the message that the defence of Singapore required the "total" participation of all Singaporeans, a notion appropriately encapsulated in the concept of "total defence" enunciated by the then defence ministry's permanent secretary, Lim Siong Guan, on 6 January 1983.[71] A year later the SAF followed up with the formation on 18 January 1984 of an Advisory Council on Community Relations in Defence (ACCORD), comprising of members of parliament, businessmen, trade unionists, civil servants, community leaders, reservists and volunteers. Its mission was not only to help "check the system"[72] but also strengthen links between the SAF and the community.[73] As each successive NS cohort completed its stint, the once feared ordeal of sons going through military service became less and less disquieting. By 1975, a shift in the attitudes of parents was already apparent: they became very concerned when their sons failed to be selected for officer cadet training or make the grade.[74] In October 1981, for instance, a survey carried out by MINDEF's Personnel Research

---

[68] ST, 1 July 2010.

[69] ST, 2 February 2011.

[70] ST, 4 September 1997.

[71] *The Singapore Monitor*, 6 January 1983. This was based on the Swiss model which saw military defence as only one component of total defence incorporating also civil, social, economic and psychological defence.

[72] ST, 18 April 1983.

[73] ST, 6 January 1984.

[74] ST, 11 July 1975.

Department on the views of 979 parents whose sons were enlisted in November and December that year confirmed MINDEF's view that, since NS was introduced in 1967, there had been a gradual but increasing acceptance and support for it, particularly from parents. An overwhelming 96% of the parents polled agreed that NS was necessary for protecting the nation.[75]

Motivating conscripts to take NS seriously was a more difficult challenge. As MINDEF Chief Psychologist, Leong Choon Cheong, noted in 1978, "As with young men in other countries, those in Singapore are averse to compulsory military service; if given the way, they would certainly avoid the Army."[76] While most eventually adapted to military life, their adjustment, according to SAF psychologists, usually followed a typical U-shaped curve — positive at the outset because of the stimulation of the new milieu, becoming "restless" in the next nine months as the novelty wore off and the training becoming more repetitious and picking up again as the end of their full-time NS approached.[77] Mindful that each new generation of soldiers was different and strategies to engage them must evolve to remain relevant, MINDEF calibrated its management of NSFs as more educated enlistees were progressively conscripted. With many young conscripts now more vocal and questioning, and had grown up in relative affluence, they had to be trained differently from their predecessors, reckoned Lieutenant-Colonel Edward Joseph, MINDEF's head of training in 1994. Whereas national servicemen in the "old days … followed their commanders unquestioningly and assumed they were right most of the time since they were more educated", Joseph observed that "more soldiers today are as educated as their commanders, and more inquisitive."[78] A more open management style was introduced and "silly things" like making recruits spend too much time polishing their boots until they shined were avoided, so that NS would not perceive by them as a "waste of time", asserted defence minister Goh Chok Tong in 1983.[79]

---

[75] ST, 6 January 1984.
[76] Leong, p. 261.
[77] ST, 18 September 1975.
[78] ST, 9 October 1994.
[79] ST, 1 April 1983.

Gone also was the "break down to build up" mentality of BMT training of old; the latter made way for a new "train hard and rest to recuperate" philosophy.[80] BMT facilities at the Pulau Tekong training centre were consequently upgraded with more comfortable living quarters and air-conditioned lecture rooms. Mattresses in the bunks were made plumper and shoes for physical training well-padded.[81] Recruits cleaned their own quarters, but common areas were maintained by contract workers.[82] To improve the level of engagement between trainers and trainees, a fourth BMT school was established in Pulau Tekong in 2010 so that class sizes could then be made smaller.[83] New systems and technologies were introduced to enhance training effectiveness, maximise mental stimulation and minimise physical injury. Computerised simulators, for instance, scored and analysed a trainee's shooting skills automatically even before he went to the live-firing range.[84] High-tech training devices like the Multiple Integrated Laser Engagement System (MILES) offered the NSF in operational units and specialist schools more realistic training by registering "kills" when sensors worn on vests were "hit" by the laser beam emitted from the enemy's rifle.[85] From November 2011, an upgraded format, dubbed Tactical Engagement System (TES), was extended to BMT as part of the SAF's ongoing drive to improve the training for its soldiers "from an early stage" by keeping electronic tabs on each recruit's agility in battle and marksmanship.[86] In March 2017, defence minister Dr Ng unveiled the development of SAFTI City, a new 88-hectare training facility, to "take our NS training to a much higher level of realism and effectiveness" by mirroring Singapore's dense urban environment and offering realistic training in homeland security and urban operations.[87] Working on the

---

[80] *My Paper*, 1 July 2011.

[81] ST, 1 July 2011.

[82] ST, 24 January 2001.

[83] ST, 17 April 2010.

[84] ST, 16 June 2004.

[85] ST, 21 July 1989.

[86] ST, 4 May 2012.

[87] Slated to be operational by 2021, SAFTI City would comprise two sectors that boast more than 200 buildings of varying heights and types, including a petrochemical complex, warehouses, container parks, industrial buildings, dense clusters of shop houses, high-rise

age-old adage that an army marches on its stomach, MINDEF from 1994 replaced the hardtack biscuits and bulky canned combat rations of old with light weight, tasty and nutritious "high tech" vacuum-sealed meals in foil pouches designed to open easily without the need for a can opener and which could be easily reheated by a flameless heat pack and eaten on the move.[88]

MINDEF's aim in its continual upgrading and innovation of training methods and equipment was not only to provide a more enriching and positive NS experience for NSFs but also to exploit their new talents and strengths, maximise their abilities, and increase their motivation to "understand their roles better, learn faster and perform better"[89] and thereby contribute to the development of the SAF's "greatest asset" — the "thinking, well-trained SAF soldier".[90] Being more educated and digitally savvy, the newer generation of enlistees, as defence minister Dr Ng Eng Hen observed in 2011, were also "very adept" at mastering new skills and operating technologically complex systems, like controlling miniature drones, which their aptitude in "video gaming somehow prepares them."[91] Building on such strengths, the SAF in December 2009 issued recruits with laptops so that trainees and commanders could discuss lessons from the field and the classroom through the SAF-wide online learning portal, LEARNet.[92] But as notebooks were bulky to lug around, lighter hand-held gadgets like iPads and tablets were eventually put into their hands from August 2011,[93] making the SAF "possibly the first military in the region to issue handheld touchscreen devices to its servicemen-in-training."[94] For Dr Ng, engaging the minds, and maximising the abilities, of its national servicemen entailed that the SAF must also work to win their hearts so that

---

and interconnected buildings, extensive road networks, basement car parks, a bus interchange and even an underground Mass Rapid Transport (MRT) station with multiple surface exits. *Pioneer* (April 2017), 20–23.

[88] ST, 15 November 1993, 13 February 2001, 19 June 2005.

[89] ST, 9 October 1994.

[90] ST, 1 July 2011.

[91] ST, 1 July 2011.

[92] ST, 17 April 2010.

[93] ST, 17 April 2010, and 1 June 2012.

[94] ST, 31 December 2011.

they might emerge from their military training with an "epiphany" about the need to protect Singapore. For this reason, the BMT centre in October 2010 moved, for the first time, its mandatory 24-kilometre route march cum graduation parade from Pulau Tekong to the heart of Singapore's Central Business District. Describing the change as designed to stir the recruits into feeling and knowing what and who they were protecting as they marched past some of Singapore's historic landmarks and skyline to the Marina Bay floating platform venue where their parents and girlfriends were waiting for them, Dr Ng noted from feedback received that the experience was "a moment of clarity for a generation that really has to find its own teaching moments."[95] From 2017, pre-enlistees entering NS would be able to express their interest in more than 30 vocations they would like to serve in although operational needs would still be the primary consideration.[96] The start of a new cyber security vocation in August 2017 would also allow "tech prodigies to receive cyber security training in incident response and forensic investigation" and kick-start Singapore's aim to develop its own "cyber defenders" for the "new battlefront".[97]

While better education had made the newer generation of NSFs more technically confident and the "right type of soldiers" for the transformation of the SAF into a high tech Third Generation or 3G army,[98] their physical robustness and combat fitness had become a key concern, especially from the late 1970s, when Singapore's growing affluence as a result of its post-independence economic transformation was reflected in youths leading more sedentary lives and the concomitant rise of obesity among school boys, which spiked six-fold from 2.4% in 1976 to 14.5% in 1989.[99] Within the SAF, a similar pattern was observed. Between 1984 and 1989, the number of overweight recruits doubled — from 5.9% to 10.4%.[100] The rate of obesity showed no sign of waning in the 1990s. Up to 2011, obese recruits

---

[95] ST, 1 July 2011.

[96] ST, 30 June 2016.

[97] ST, 9 March 2017.

[98] ST, 31 December 2011.

[99] ST, 7 December 1990. A person is considered obese if he weighed 20% more than the standard body weight for his height and age.

[100] ST, 2 June 1990.

continued to hover at around 10% of enlistees.[101] This weakness had to be compensated with greater emphasis placed on physical training.[102] Noting that few enlistees prepared themselves physically for NS, MINDEF looked to the Ministry of Education (MOE) to help boost the fitness of students. From 1982, primary and secondary schools were required to participate in the National Physical Fitness Award (NAPFA) scheme.[103] A MINDEF-MOE working committee was formed in 1987 to look into how physical education programmes in schools could be calibrated to produce youths who could meet the physical fitness requirements of the SAF. Between 1992 and 2007, a Trim and Fit (TAF) scheme was put in place to help obese students lose weight.[104] From 1999, all medically-fit students in post-secondary institutions like the polytechnics and the Institute of Technical Education were required to take the NAPFA test in their final year of study.[105]

To ensure the fitness of its servicemen, the SAF in 1979 introduced its own Individual Physical Proficiency Test (IPPT). Corresponding closely to the NAPFA, it required NSFs and regular soldiers to pass five test stations.[106] In 1991, to tackle the growing obesity problem, MINDEF linked the length of BMT to the recruits' fitness level.[107] Based on scientific studies and monitoring, the pace of physical conditioning for both less fit and obese recruits was accordingly adjusted to reduce injury and medical attrition.[108] By 2004, the programme was calibrated further: overweight

---

[101] ST, 3 September 2011.

[102] ST, 9 October 1994.

[103] Tests include sit-ups, pull-ups, sit-and reach, shuttle run, standing broad jump, and a run-walk.

[104] ST, 28 January 1992.

[105] ST, 3 February 1999.

[106] ST, 18 March 2007. The five test stations were: push-ups, sit-ups, chin-ups, half-knee bends, and a 2.4-kilometre run taken in army vests, slacks and boots. After further tweaks in 1981 and 1982, the half knee-bends and push-ups were dropped; the IPPT now consisted of sit-ups, chin-ups, shuttle run, standing broad jump, and the 2.4-kilometre run.

[107] ST, 17 July 1991. In 1991, fit recruits (those who attained a silver or gold award for their NAPFA) did a three-month BMT, with the added incentive of a month's reduction in NS liability; the less fit and obese recruits underwent a four- and five-month BMT respectively.

[108] ST, 21 April 1993, and 6 December 1997. Further refinements occurred in 1993 when MINDEF scrapped the four-month BMT for less fit recruits in favour of a two-month

recruits with body mass index (BMI) of over 27 spent 15 weeks in BMT; those with BMI above 35 required 26 weeks.[109] In 2009, BMT for obese recruits was tweaked again after an 18-month review: for the "mildly" and "moderately" obese, the training period was raised from 15 to 19 weeks; "extremely" obese recruits, however, had their stint reduced from 26 to 19 weeks, as it was found that training beyond 19 weeks did not make much difference.[110] Apart from physical toughening, NSFs, from 2012, were also given "mental coaching" under the SAF's Building Resilience in Individuals for Growth and Emotional Well-being (BRIDGE) programme where they were taught "how to talk about their emotions, think positively, manage stress during training, and overcome the adversities faced during physical or combat training." According to one local media report, those who went through the programme apparently outperformed those who did not.[111]

Developing "Frontline Soldiers"

NSFs who completed their full-time NS were required to serve a 10-year in-camp training (ICT) cycle as reservists, during which they could be mustered for up to 40 days each year. But it was not until the late 1970s — after the basic kinks in the training of the full-time national servicemen had been addressed in the course of the SAF's rapid build-up to cushion the impact of the British military withdrawal — that more attention was paid to the reserves. Years of neglect, however, had a demoralising effect on reservists. Much ICT time was "unproductive, spent in drawing

---

Physical Training Phase (PTP) conditioning programme instead — one month less if they passed the IPPT four weeks into the programme — before joining their fitter enlistees for the three-month BMT, which was made a common programme for all recruits, except for the obese conscripts who would continue with the graduated five-month BMT. In 1997, the SAF shortened the five-month BMT programme for obese recruits to four months after it found that most would have lost the required amount of weight and could be earmarked for combat roles; those who failed to do so had to attend additional training.

[109] ST, 27 March 2005.

[110] ST, 5 December 2009. The physical conditioning regime was designed by a team of exercise scientists and physiologists to ensure "proper progression" for the recruit to build up his strength, endurance and mobility. See: ST, 4 July 2008.

[111] ST, 7 March 2012.

weapons and equipment, and in waiting in between programmes".[112] Few reservists took their training seriously and their fitness was also suspect. Worse, many held the notion that they were what their name implied — "reservists" — not frontline troops.

To underline their frontline status, a number of initiatives were taken to raise the combat effectiveness of Singapore's reservists. For one, worthy reservist commanders, especially those who had also distinguished themselves in their civilian careers, were sent for upgrading courses to prepare them for senior appointments in the reserves.[113] From 1982, reserve units were assigned for standby duties lasting a week during their ICT.[114] In 1983, MINDEF increased the ICT liability from 10 to 13 years,[115] as it saw no reason to put its reservists into inactive service after only 10 years of training.[116] The week-long ICT was also made more intensive, productive, and meaningful[117] and a strict policy on deferment from ICT was also enforced to ensure that reservist units operated as a "cohesive team".[118] It was not until 2003 before MINDEF, mindful of the greater life and work commitments of reservists in later years, considered a corresponding tapering off of reservists' ICT commitments during their last three years of service, requiring them to undergo only an annual two-day ICT that focused on honing their individual soldiering skills.[119] In 2006, even this latter programme was scrapped, after ICT was shortened from 13 years to 10 years, ostensibly because of the projection of a surge of enlistees for the next 10 years, which meant that most NSmen (except officers holding key positions) would finish their NS obligations before hitting the age of 35.[120]

To ensure that no serious regression of physical standards occurred between ICTs, reservists from January 1980 were tested twice a year for their physical fitness. As an added incentive for them to train for the IPPT,

---

[112] Chiang, "SAF and 30 Years of National Service", 147.
[113] ST, 13 March 1990.
[114] Lau, "National Service", 43.
[115] ST, 17 March 1983.
[116] ST, 5 January 1982.
[117] Lau, "National Service", 51.
[118] Ibid., 42–43.
[119] ST, 29 April 2003.
[120] ST, 17 January 2006.

reservists were allowed to take the tests in T-shirts, shorts and running shoes instead of vests, slacks and boots. At the same time, a "points" system was also introduced in October 1982, requiring reservists to amass certain points to pass the test based on their age bands. Additional inducements included cash awards for fit reservists who surpassed the IPPT standards in 1993. Unfit reservists, however, faced the prospects of attending lived-in residential training (RT) programme in Pulau Tekong where they would be put through a daily physical toughening regime — that is, until 1994 when the RT regime was replaced by a more graduated remedial physical conditioning programme conducted at Khatib and Maju camps (with the addition of Bedok camp in 2003) two to three times a week spread over eight to 12 weeks. These changes seemed to have a positive outcome: in 1995, more than half of those who passed the IPPT did well enough to be exempted from a second test.[121] There was also a doubling of those who met the highest fitness standards.[122] The need to pass the IPPT had another desirable effect: it got some 63% of reservists exercising at least once a week, compared to 85% of active servicemen and 41% of the general male population.[123] Still, juggling work, family and fitness training remained very challenging for most reservists. In 2006, less fit reservists were thus encouraged to volunteer for 10 supervised fitness sessions as part of a new five-week IPPT preparatory training (IPT) programme hosted in selected army camps.[124] Giving reservists even more flexibility to participate in the programme, the sessions in 2011 were spread out over nine months instead.[125] Specially appointed outdoor parks, fitted with equipment to practise all the five test stations, including a clearly demarcated 2.4-kilometre running route,[126] and located within housing estates, were opened in 2010. From 2014, IPT classes were brought to selected parks closer to the homes and workplaces of reservists.[127] But despite these efforts, many still found the IPPT too daunting and did not even bother to train for it. In a major revamp of the IPPT in

[121] Chiang, "SAF and 30 Years of National Service", 96.

[122] ST, 10 March 1994.

[123] ST, 28 August 1995.

[124] ST, 27 October 2006.

[125] ST, 23 April 2010.

[126] ST, 4 March 2010.

[127] ST, 11 September 2014.

2014, MINDEF reduced from five to three the number of test stations — push-ups (replacing the more arduous chin-ups), sit-ups and a timed run — in a pragmatic bid to provide reservists with more attainable goals in the hope that more men might make an effort to pass them.[128]

To test the readiness of SAF units, mobilisation exercises were routinely conducted. In July 1985, an "open" mobilisation using media broadcasts was successfully implemented for the first time to recall reservists: it halved the response time that was required under the previous courier system of "silent" mobilisation.[129] Further refinements to test the recall system were carried out in subsequent exercises as reservists and the public became more familiar with the exercises. Specific dates were replaced by general advance notices and after 1987 no advance warning was given. In another first, in June 1987, recalled troops were deployed immediately for a battle exercise. In the first-ever "silent" mobilisation during office hours in 1990, 97% of the soldiers were notified using telephones and pagers and reported to their centres within eight hours of activation.[130] The scale of mobilisation was also progressively expanded. It culminated in an exercise in January 1991, where 10,000 men were recalled, the largest thus far recalled. The exercise showed that the SAF now had the capacity to mobilise thousands of troops effectively for deployment in battle.

A name change was also in order to emphasise the combat-ready status of Singapore's reservists. In January 1994, reservists became known as Operationally Ready National Servicemen — or NSmen for short — to underline their key combat-ready frontline role.[131] Further underscoring the change, the term "ROD" for "Run Out Date", which referred to the last day of training for NSFs, was replaced by "ORD" for "Operationally Ready Date".[132] In 1995, in a reorganisation of the Combined Arms Divisions, active

---

[128] ST, 3 August 2014.

[129] In a "silent" exercise, SAF units had 24 hours to recall reservists and another six hours to issue weapons and process the troops for battle. The response time for an "open" mobilization was 12 hours — six hours to report at a mobilisation centre and another six hours to get ready. *40/40: 40 Years and 40 Stories of National Service* (Singapore: Landmark Books, 2007), 133.

[130] ST, 30 June 1991.

[131] ST, 1 January 1994.

[132] *40/40*, 204.

and reservist battalions were placed in the same divisions for the first time,[133] thus breaking the "psychological barrier" of NSmen being "second-liners", observed Chief of Defence Force, Lieutenant-General Bey Soo Khiang.[134] To highlight the change in status, NSmen were given the role of parade commanders for both the SAF Day and National Day parades in 1994.[135]

Finding ways to motivate and reward NSFs and NSmen for their service to the nation remained a pressing concern and challenge for the SAF. More often than not, NS offered little by way of tangible rewards. Instead, for many able reservists, the upgrading and promotion exercises often come with high personal costs — greater responsibilities and more ICT stints — sometimes seen, ironically, as a penalty for doing well.[136] By the 1990s and early 2000s, the NS issue was brought into even sharper relief after the government's pro-immigration policy to shore up the country's low birth rate encouraged substantially more foreigners to take up permanent residency or citizenship and confronted Singapore with an emerging demographic pattern that would see a net population growth due to immigration.[137] Because of its perceived universality, NS became inevitably a bone of contention between those who fulfilled their service and those who did not. Given that first generation applicants were exempt from conscription,[138] NSmen worried about the negative effects of their own disruptive reservist liabilities on their employment and career prospects vis-à-vis the former, who posed no such liabilities, and appeared to benefit

---

[133] Chiang, "SAF and 30 Years of National Service", 120–121. Following an earlier reorganisation in 1991 which led to the creation of the Combined Arms Divisions, the 3rd Division comprised only active units while the 6th and 9th Divisions were made up of only reservist units. This gave rise to the impression that the 3rd Division was the front-line division that would go into battle first, and the other two divisions were second-line divisions.

[134] ST, 12 July 1996.

[135] ST, 30 June 1994, and 10 August 1994.

[136] Report of the Committee to Recognise the Contribution of Reservists to Total Defence (RECORD) (Singapore: The Committee, 1991), 9.

[137] Low, "Wither Conscription in Singapore", 8.

[138] To attract talented foreigners to settle in Singapore without making it even more unattractive for them to do so, the Singapore government had no choice but to exempt the first generation PRs from NS. It argued that, as an adult, the first generation PR was able to contribute effectively to Singapore. However, sons of PRs, who grew up in Singapore and enjoyed the socio-economic benefits of Singapore, like citizens, were liable to serve NS. ST, 16 March 1990, and 23 February 2008.

at their expense.[139] Sons of PRs, however, were liable for NS upon reaching 16 years of age unless they renounced their Singapore citizenship. The fact that about a third of them chose this "escape hatch"[140] prior to conscription could not but further reinforce the perceptions of locals about the commitment to Singapore of these "fair-weathered friends"[141] and raise legitimate questions about the fairness of the "universal" conscription policy that excluded the latter[142] — not only because the policy appeared to favour the children of PRs over their Singaporean counterparts, but also because the departure of the former without performing NS would not affect their parents' residency status.

Not surprisingly, against this background, NS itself came under close scrutiny, prompting urgent calls to "equalize" the "anomaly". In February 2013, MP Hri Kumar, for instance, proposed an annual "national defence duty" on PRs whose NS-liable sons renounced their PR status before enlistment. "In short, we do duty, they pay a duty," he suggested.[143] Others, responding, maintained that putting a price on NS obligations diluted its importance and would "cheapen a solemn duty."[144] MINDEF, on its part, did all it could to address such concerns and more. Besides reducing the length of conscription in 2004, it also followed through on the recommendations of the various Report of the Committee to Recognise the Contribution of Reservists to Total Defence (RECORD) committees it convened between 1990 and 2009 to recognise the contribution of reservists to total defence by giving preferential financial incentives and asset enhancement schemes and building more recreational clubhouses among others.[145] In 2010, it rolled out a further monetary incentive, the National Service Recognition Award (NSRA), to provide sustained recognition of

---

[139] There appeared to be growing disquiet, for instance, on how new citizens preferred to hire PRs and non-residents over local Singaporeans. Leong, Yang and Hong, "National Service", 314.

[140] ST, 9 May 2012.

[141] ST, 24 October 2009.

[142] ST, 9 May 2012.

[143] ST, 14 February 2013.

[144] ST, 23 February 2013.

[145] RECORD stood for Committee to Recognise the Contribution of Reservists to Total Defence. The name was subsequently amended to Committee to Recognise the Contribution of Operationally Ready National Servicemen [also NSmen] to Total Defence. Committees were convened in 1990, 1995, 2000, 2005 and 2009.

NSmen. Totalling SGD $9,000 to SGD $10,500, the award would be disbursed to servicemen in tranches across three significant milestones of their training cycle: the completion of full-time national service, the middle of the NSman's ICT cycle, and at the completion of this cycle.[146] Fully cognisant that NS had to "keep pace with changes in our society" to remain relevant, a Committee to Strengthen National Service (CSNS) was set up in March 2013.[147] Among its recommendations was the setting up of the SAF Volunteer Corps (SAFVC) that would provide a channel for more inclusive participation in national defence by those who were otherwise not eligible for NS, like women, first generation PRs and new citizens[148] and a revamping of the NSRA into the NS HOME Award to support NSmen in the areas of housing, healthcare and education.[149]

Conclusion

Since its re-introduction in 1967, NS has become the "backbone" of Singapore's rapid military build-up.[150] As a small island-state located in a strategic environment that amplifies its sense of vulnerability, Singapore's need for adequate security is obvious. "Singapore will always be small and vulnerable," reminded Prime Minister Lee Hsien Loong in February 2017. "No one owes us our sovereignty or security. These are truths we must never forget."[151] Without NS, however, there can be little doubt that the manpower base from which to build up a credible defence force to

---

[146] ST, 1 September 2010.

[147] The CSNS engaged more than 40,000 people through extensive conversations on NS. See: *Report of Committee to Strengthen National Service* (Singapore: The Committee, 2014), i.

[148] ST, 13 October 2014. Volunteers must be between the ages of 18 and 45 and would undergo a four-week basic military course (which they could spread out over several weekends if they could not stay in camp) and serve seven days a year. They could choose from 17 vocations during their stint. The first intake was in March 2015 and the 226 volunteers who completed their basic training held their first parade at Maju Camp in June 2015. Among its first military volunteers was the 43-year-old Dr Janil Puthucheary, the PAP MP for Pasir Ris-Punggol GRC, a Malaysian who became a Singapore citizenship in 2008.

[149] HOME stood for HOusing, Medical and Education.

[150] ST, 9 February 2017.

[151] ST, 16 February 2017.

undergird the young Republic's economic, social, political and diplomatic structures would remain, at best, elusive. NS contributed not insubstantially to the enlargement of Singapore's defence capability. From a mere force of two infantry battalions in 1965, the SAF, when mobilised today, according to *The Military Balance 2017*, could call to arms a force of some 72,500 active servicemen and 312,500 trained men in the reserves.[152] Indeed, as defence minister Dr Ng Eng Hean asserted in February 2017, "We can never change the fact that we are a small country, but today, after 50 years of NS, we have built an SAF capable of defending Singapore."[153]

The security Singapore desired, however, was exacted at a high price. NS imposed a severe burden on its male citizenry, more than a million of whom had served as national servicemen over the five decades.[154] While tokens of recognition and appreciation for their contributions had been dispensed from time to time, Dr Ng remarked that "nothing can replace the hours that they have spent defending Singapore".[155] Despite its burdens, support for NS, however, remained strong, as indicated in an Institute of Policy Studies (IPS) survey in 2013 which revealed that some 98% of Singaporeans believed the institution was crucial for national security.[156] This vote of confidence was possible in part because the government had kept NS equitable and universal and had come down hard on draft dodgers so as to deter them from "gaming the system", maintained *Straits Times* political correspondent, Chong Zi Liang.[157] MINDEF had also done its part to build and expand stakeholder and community support for NS and to ensure that the experience of NS remained positive and

---

[152]The International Institute of Strategic Studies, *The Military Balance 2017*, 117, 326.

[153] ST, 8 February 2017.

[154] ST, 9 February 2017. The figure includes those who served in the armed forces as well as in the police and civil defence forces. The first intake of full-time Police National Servicemen was enlisted in 1975 for peacetime and emergency functions like crime prevention patrols and protection of key installations, and preparation and training for national emergencies and disasters. The Singapore Civil Defence Force (SCDF) enlisted its first intake of NSFs in 1981 to provide emergency services during peacetime and crises. *Report of Committee to Strengthen National Service*, 12.

[155] ST, 10 April 2017.

[156]IPS, *Institute of Policy Study Report: Singaporean Attitudes to National Service* (2013), 1–5.

[157] ST, 6 April 2017.

meaningful for those who served, whether as NSFs or NSmen, while maximizing their contributions in the process.

Singapore, however, could not afford to let its guard down. "Because the city-state has deterred potential aggressors for so long, Singaporeans have to an extent been lulled into complacency, such that they now talk about 'softer' issues, be it whether PRs serve NS, and even a trimming of the defence budget," observed *Straits Times* Senior Writer William Choong.[158] In an age where many advanced states had abandoned conscription in favour of more efficient all-volunteer professional armies,[159] there will also be "increasing political pressure to justify why Singapore continues to impose two years of conscription when relations with surrounding countries are devoid of the hostility that necessitates constant military vigilance."[160] But for Singapore, there is no better alternative than NS to maintain a credible defence force capable of defending the nation-state. The Republic's economic success also means that its national servicemen would have that "much more to protect in Singapore."[161] While NS is today widely supported and deeply entrenched, the challenge is to ensure that NS continues to evolve and remain vitally relevant to future generations of Singaporeans so that its core mission of safeguarding Singapore remains unhindered. With stakes so high, MINDEF could not afford to do any less.

---

[158] ST, 15 March 2013.

[159] Kuok Hsin Chew, "Defending Singapore in an uncertain world: A force of National Service conscripts or all-volunteer professionals?" (Masters Dissertation submitted to the US Marine Corps Command and Staff College, 2012), 1; see also, Jonathan Eyal, "The return of military national service in Europe", in ST, 6 March 2017.

[160] Leong, Yang and Hong, "National Service", 322.

[161] ST, 8 February 2017.

Chapter 2

Goh Keng Swee and the Policy of Conscription

Bernard Fook Weng Loo[1]

The policy of conscription, otherwise called National Service (NS), is generally regarded as the foundation stone for the defence of Singapore. As the Ministry of Defence (MINDEF) asserts, "deterrence is provided by developing a strong and capable SAF ... through the institutions of National Service and Total Defence ..."[2] Further, MINDEF points out, "NS has been the cornerstone of our nation's defence and security since independence. Our national servicemen form the backbone of the Singapore Armed Forces (SAF), Singapore Police Force (SPF) and Singapore Civil Defence Force (SCDF) that keep Singapore safe and secure."[3]

However, conscription was not the policy option that Singapore's first Minister for Defence, Dr Goh Keng Swee, had recommended; rather, he had proposed an all-volunteer army comprising 12 battalions to be raised between 1966 and 1969. It was the first Prime Minister, Lee Kuan Yew, who had insisted on conscription as the basis for the raising of the

---

[1] This chapter is adapted from: Bernard Fook Weng Loo, "Goh Keng Swee and the Emergence of a Modern SAF: The Rearing of a Poisonous Shrimp", in *Goh Keng Swee: A Legacy of Public Service*, eds. Emrys Chew and Kwa Chong Guan (Singapore: World Scientific, 2012).

[2] http://www.mindef.gov.sg/imindef/key_topics/defence_policy.html (accessed 22 April 2016).

[3] https://www.mindef.gov.sg/strengthenNS/about_ns.html (accessed 22 April 2016).

Singapore Armed Forces (SAF).[4] As MINDEF further notes, "The need for NS became clear when Singapore gained independence in 1965. It would not have been possible to raise a regular force of a sufficient size to protect this island state given our small population."[5]

Nevertheless, it is Dr Goh who goes down in history as the architect who built the SAF.[6] It was under his tenure as Minister for Defence that the SAF implemented NS, and it was the institution of NS that allowed the SAF to build up its manpower to form the backbone of Singapore's deterrence posture through the three generations of the SAF known as the "poisonous shrimp", "porcupine" and "dolphin", respectively.[7]

This study will first examine the arguments that were raised against the NS proposition. Next it will examine Dr Goh's perceptions of the strategic environment, and how these perceptions overcame the societal and economic objections to NS. Finally, the study will briefly examine how NS became the cornerstone of the evolution of the SAF from its first-generation "poisonous shrimp" posture to its second-generation "porcupine" posture.

The Case against National Service

Popular Attitudes towards National Service

Conscription was not a popular decision. Writing in 1977, Charles Moskos argued that voluntary military service can be understood in one of three ways: as a calling, which is "legitimated in terms of institutional values, i.e., a purpose transcending individual self-interest in favor of a presumed higher good"; as a profession, which is "legitimated in terms of specialized expertise, i.e., a skill level formally accredited after long,

---

[4] Lee Kuan Yew, *From Third World to First: The Singapore Story 1965–2000* (Singapore: Marshall Cavendish and The Straits Times Press, 2000), 35.

[5] https://www.mindef.gov.sg/strengthenNS/about_ns.html (accessed 22 April 2016).

[6] See: Bernard Fook Weng Loo, "Goh Keng Swee and the Emergence of a Modern SAF: The Rearing of a Poisonous Shrimp", in *Goh Keng Swee: A Legacy of Public Service,* eds. Emrys Chew and Kwa Chong Guan (Singapore: World Scientific, 2012), 127–152.

[7] The image of a "poisonous shrimp" comes from a speech by Lee Kuan Yew: "In a world where the big fish eat small fish and the small fish eat shrimps, Singapore must become a poisonous shrimp." Cited in Amitav Acharya, ed., *The Quest for World Order: Perspectives of a Pragmatic Idealist* (Singapore: Times Academic Press, 1988), 177.

intensive, academic training"; or as an occupation, which is "legitimated in terms of the marketplace, i.e., prevailing monetary rewards for equivalent competencies."[8] But even for the volunteer, the initial experience of military life tends to end up with a self-question: "What am I doing here?"[9] For the unwilling conscript, military service, however potentially honourable it may be, is always going to be an innately unpleasant experience. The conscript, upon completing his military service, may eventually reminisce positively about his experiences in military service, and may even attribute his personal successes to the discipline he inculcated through his military service. Nevertheless, the actual experience of military service is, for the conscript, inherently unpleasant.

The experience of military life that early NS provided did not contradict the above observation. This nascent SAF, with the advice of trainers from the Israeli Defence Force, doled out a training regime that even the most rose-tinted reminiscence admits was tough.[10] As former Minister for Defence Howe Yoon Chong noted in 1979, military life for the early conscripts was characterised by "harshness and abuse."[11] Deprivation and degradation were commonplace experiences, and as news of such treatment inevitably filtered out, it no doubt strengthened popular resistance to the policy of conscription.

Furthermore, for the ethnic Chinese, the largest ethnic community in Singapore, cultural prejudices further reinforced the undesirability of compulsory NS. Dr Goh was aware of this resistance, as he noted in a speech in Parliament on 23 December 1965,

> There is a common saying among the Chinese masses which goes ...
> 'Good men do not become soldiers, good iron does not make nails' ... It

---

[8] Charles C. Moskos, Jr, "The All-Volunteer Military: Calling, Profession or Occupation?", *Parameters* 7/1 (1977), 3–4.

[9] Craig M. Mullaney, *The Unforgiving Minute: A Soldier's Education* (London: Penguin Books, 2009), 5. Also see: Colby Buzzell, *My War: Killing Time in Iraq* (New York: G. P. Putnam's Sons, 2005), 22; Nathaniel Fick, *One Bullet Away: The Making of a Marine Officer* (London: Phoenix, 2005), 10.

[10] See, for instance, Ramchandran Menon, ed., *One of a Kind: Remembering SAFTI's First Batch* (Singapore: SAFTI Military Institute, 2007), 135.

[11] Cited in: Tim Huxley, *Defending the Lion City: The Armed Forces of Singapore* (Crows Nest, NSW: Allen & Unwin, 2000), 94.

is not surprising that military service was unpopular when a soldier risked his life, not for his country or his people, but for the advantage of one contending group or other ... the position we are facing in Singapore today is, of course, completely different from that of dynastic struggles in ancient China.

The other ethnic communities did not necessarily share the Chinese cultural discrimination against military service. The ethnic Malay community, for instance, "had taken to soldiering in the Singapore Infantry Regiment with enthusiasm."[12] In 1957, "nearly 20 percent of male Malay workers were employed in the armed forces or police."[13] Of the 72 Singaporeans who were involved in the first Instructors' Preparatory Course conducted between February and May 1966, there were seven Eurasians (all commissioned officers from either the Army or the Police Force), 10 Indians (both commissioned and senior non-commissioned officers), and 23 Malays (all senior non-commissioned officers).[14] Clearly, the ethnic Chinese community, despite constituting over 70% of the population, was somewhat under-represented.

Eventually however, the policy of conscription came to be accepted as part of the Singaporean way of life because of its routinisation by the Singapore Government. Initially, Singapore's conscription policy started off as a major success, as out of 9,000 called up in the first batch of national service, more than 95% reported.[15] From 1970 to 1972, the Army, Navy and Air Force increased their numbers from 10,000 to 14,000 with approximately 8,000 reservists, from 200 to 500, and from 24 to 1,500 respectively.[16] By 1978, the size of the SAF would have increased 433% from the previous decade.[17] Even though Singapore Government faced

---

[12] Huxley, *Defending the Lion City*, 102.

[13] Huxley, *Defending the Lion City*, 103.

[14] See: Menon, *One of a Kind*, 63.

[15] Chan Heng Chee, "Singapore", in *Military-Civilian Relations in South-East Asia*, eds. Zakaria Ahmad and Harold Crouch (Singapore: Oxford University Press, 1985), 142.

[16] Wu Yuan-li, 1972, "Planning Security for a Small Nation: Lessons from Singapore", *Pacific Community* 3/4 (1972), 664–665.

[17] Sukhumbhand Paribatra and Chai-Anan Samudavanija, "Internal Dimensions of Regional Security in Southeast Asia", in *Regional Security in the Third World: Case*

civilian resistance to NS in order to achieve its domestic "fringe benefits",[18] the ruling People's Action Party (PAP) reacted to criticisms by promptly depoliticising the discussion of defence, changing the conscription policy to accommodate business interests, and prohibiting public complaints of national service.[19] By the time of the 1976 elections, conscription had ceased to be an issue of debate,[20] and remained since then as a "social rite of passage" that all able-bodied Singaporean males have had to participate in,[21] and from which "a common shared experience among the [conscripted] youth" contributed to nation-building in Singapore.[22]

Balancing between Defence and Economic Necessities

As noted earlier, conscription was not Dr Goh's first-choice policy option. Even when conscription was adopted in 1967 as the only viable approach towards building an SAF that could defend Singapore against external aggression, conscripted service was not universally applied. The original NS intake numbered 18,000 conscripts, most of who served on a part-time basis in the People's Defence Force (PDF), Vigilante Corps or Police Special Constabulary. Only the better-educated conscripts (about 10% of the intake) were conscripted into full-time military service (such

---

Studies from Southeast Asia and the Middle East, ed. Mohammed Ayoob (London: Croom Helm, 1986), 79.

[18] These benefits include the "inculcation of nationalistic values in the youth of a multiracial community and creating a pool of specialised skills," and the inspiration of a "sense of confidence among local entrepreneurs and foreign investors" from the provision of adequate security forces in Singapore. See Obaid ul Haq, "Singapore's Search for Security: A Selective Analysis", in *Leadership and Security in Southeast Asia: Institutional Aspects*, ed. Stephen Chee (Singapore: Institute of Southeast Asian Studies, 1991), 129.

[19] Norman Vasu and Bernard Loo, "National Security and Singapore: An Assessment", in *Management of Success: Singapore Revisited*, ed. Terence Chong (Singapore: Institute of Southeast Asian Studies, 2010), 462–485.

[20] Chan, "Singapore", 143–144.

[21] Ng Pak Shun, *"Why Not a Volunteer Army?" Reexamining the Impact of Military Conscription on Economic Growth for Singapore* (unpublished manuscript), 2003, 26.

[22] Elizabeth Nair, "Nation Building through Conscript Service in Singapore", in *The Military in the Service of Society and Democracy: The Challenge of the Dual-Role Military,* ed. Daniella Ashkenazy (Westport, CT: Greenwood Press, 1994), 106.

Table 1. **Singapore's defence spending, 1967–1970**

Year	Defence Spending (S$m)	Defence Spending as Percentage of Total Government Spending	Defence Spending as Percentage of GDP
1967	37	6.3	1
1968	85	12.1	2
1969	218	19.8	3.4
1970	257	21.3	4.4

conscripts were labelled National Service Full-Time or NSFs). The reason for this discrimination was economic. As Dr Goh noted, "this kind of thing [that is, full-time two year military training for all conscripts] is guaranteed to make us bankrupt."[23] However, with the introduction of the Enlistment Act in 1970, two-year military conscription became the norm in Singapore, driven principally by Britain's decision to accelerate its withdrawal "east of Suez".

In other words, Dr Goh was careful to ensure that defence spending remained economically supportable (see Table 1).[24] As he stated in Parliament on 30 December 1965, "We are a small nation and our financial resources are limited. We therefore cannot afford to raise and maintain large defence forces on a permanent basis." Singapore's economy between 1967 and 1970 was growing, but the size of the economy was still relatively small when pegged against other countries (see Table 2).[25] The amount of resources that could be dedicated towards defence spending was therefore limited. As a result, the build-up of the SAF could not happen overnight. It would have to be driven not just by the strategic imperatives of defending Singapore, but also by the economic imperatives of what was affordable. The growth of the SAF could only be undertaken in terms of

---

[23] Cited in Huxley, *Defending the Lion City*, 13.

[24] Huxley, *Defending the Lion City*, 28.

[25] Data on Singapore's gross domestic product and per capita gross domestic product come from: The World Bank, http://databank.worldbank.org/data/reports.aspx?source=2&country= SGP, accessed 25 August 2016. Singapore's economic data, in terms of gross domestic product and per capita gross domestic product, in 2015 stood as S$402,458,000,000 and S$70,704 respectively.

Table 2. Singapore's gross domestic product, 1967–1970

Year	GDP (S$m)	Per Capita GDP (S$m)
1967	3,788,000,000	6,324.6
1968	4,362,300,000	7,063.1
1969	5,078,700,000	7,912.5
1970	5,876,000,000	8,872.2

what the economy could afford. With the benefit of hindsight, seeing how excessive defence expenditures practically bankrupted the former Soviet Union in its attempt to keep pace with American defence spending, Dr Goh's prudence reflected a decision of remarkable prescience.

This reticence was not grounded solely in his concerns about economically unsustainable levels of defence spending. Dr Goh was also conscious of how the build-up of the SAF could have potentially negative ramifications for the wider strategic environment. Care was taken to match what challenges the strategic environment would throw out on the one hand with the strategic requirements of the SAF on the other:

> ... our defence forces are adequate for our present needs. Those who study the allocation of funds in the annual estimates of expenditure passed by Parliament will have noticed a levelling off in recent years of our defence expenditure ... This is as it should be. It does not make sense when everything in Southeast Asia is relatively calm and stable, to keep on spending more and more money on defence. (Goh Keng Swee, Speech to Officer Commissioning Parade, 12 July 1974)

As a consequence, the build-up of the SAF was undertaken with a constant eye towards how the strategic environment was evolving, the emergence of new strategic challenges, and the new capabilities that these new challenges would demand. As a consequence, the manner in which the SAF was built up could be described as systematic.[26] In other words, every

---

[26] Bernard Fook Weng Loo, "Maturing the Singapore Armed Forces: From Poisonous Shrimp to Dolphin", in *Impressions: The Goh Years in Singapore*, eds. Bridget Welsh,

new acquisition makes 'strategic sense': it is meant to plug an existing gap in strategic capability.

The Decision for NS

Clearly, the lack of popular support and the concerns over economic affordability were not sufficient to deter Singapore's policy makers from adopting and implementing the policy of NS. The reason for NS can be attributed to a sense of profound vulnerability from both external and internal sources in the eyes of Singapore's policy makers. NS was regarded as the only instrument that could provide Singapore with the capacity to address these profound vulnerabilities.

Leadership Perceptions of Strategic Vulnerability

The Melian Dialogue, coming from Thucydides' *The Peloponnesian War* — where "the strong do what they can and the weak suffer what they must"[27] — is the classic statement of the inherent vulnerabilities that plague small and weak countries. Its perspective of how weak states must suffer the vicissitudes of their position reflected the dominant concerns of the first generation of Singaporean leaders. Certainly it was an ever-present element in the world view of Dr Goh and former Prime Minister Lee.

At the point of its independence, Singapore existed in a strategic environment that could be regarded as far from ideal. There were a number of potential externally derived challenges to Singapore's existence. The Cold War was the order of the day, and it manifested itself in Southeast Asia in the form of the so-called Vietnam War. From the moment of independence, there was the history of *Konfrontasi* with Indonesia[28] and threats

James Chin, Arun Mahizhnan and Tan Tarn How (Singapore: National University of Singapore Press, 2009), 188–197.

[27] Robert B. Strassler, ed., *The Landmark Thucydides: A Comprehensive Guide to The Peloponnesian War* (New York: Touchstone, 1996), 352.

[28] Felix Chang, "In Defense of Singapore", in *Orbis* (Winter 2003), 108; Lau Teik Soon, "National Threat Perceptions of Singapore", in *Threats to Security in East Asia-Pacific: National and Regional Perspectives*, ed. Charles Morrison (Lexington, MA: Lexington

from Malaysia to cut off the island's water supply. It is difficult to not conclude that the dominant image was one of potential trouble that could directly or indirectly affect the security of Singapore.[29] Up to 1970, British troops were stationed in Singapore to safeguard the island's external defence, but the SAF had only two infantry battalions "for [her] protection in normal times."[30] By itself, the SAF was clearly not in a position to do very much in terms of defending the island-state against external aggression. However, when the British Government announced on 15 January 1968 its plan to withdraw all British forces east of Suez by December 1971, the Singapore Government had to begin plans to build up the SAF, since the island would no longer come under a British defence umbrella. As a consequence, a central element in Singapore's strategic culture was a pervasive discourse of vulnerability:[31]

There is a geostrategic element that underpins this strategic culture of vulnerability. In contrast to its immediate neighbours, Singapore suffers from a natural geostrategic asymmetry — simply put, the island lacks geostrategic depth, stemming from its small geophysical size. Tim Huxley also makes the point that the territorial waters of Singapore are completely surrounded by the territorial waters of Indonesia and Malaysia.[32] There

---

Books, 1983), 122; Lee, *From Third World to First*, 20; Michael Leifer, *Singapore's Foreign Policy: Coping with Vulnerability* (New York: Routledge, 2000), 2.

[29] Lee, *From Third World to First*, 24; Leifer, *Singapore's Foreign Policy*, 53. Also see: Chin Kin Wah, "Reflections on the Shaping of Strategic Cultures in Southeast Asia", in *Southeast Asian Perspectives on Security*, ed. Derek da Cunha (Singapore: Institute of Southeast Asian Studies, 2000), 7; Alom Peled, *Soldiers Apart: A Study of Ethnic Military Manpower Policies in Singapore, Israel and South Africa* (Ann Arbor: University Microfilms International, 1994), 60–65; Bilveer Singh, "Singapore's Management of Its Security Problems", *Asia-Pacific Community* 29 (Summer 1985), 85.

[30] "Military spending modest and purely for defence", *The Straits Times*, 6 December 1967.

[31] See, for instance, Derek da Cunha, "Defence and Security: Evolving Threat Perceptions", in *Singapore in the New Millennium: Challenges Facing the City-State*, ed. Derek da Cunha (Singapore: Institute of Southeast Asian Studies, 2002), 133–153; Kwa Chong Guan, "Relating to the World: Images, Metaphors, and Analogies", in *Singapore in the New Millennium: Challenges Facing the City-State,* ed. Derek da Cunha (Singapore: Institute of Southeast Asian Studies, 2002), 108–132; Bilveer Singh, *The Vulnerability of Small States Revisited: A Study of Singapore's Post-Cold War Foreign Policy* (Yogyakarta: Gajah Mada University Press, 1999).

[32] Huxley, *Defending the Lion City*.

was also a geopolitical element to this that pervades to this day. Singapore's position lies astride the trade routes connecting the Pacific and Indian oceans.[33] This location places Singapore in a position to control maritime trade in Asia, and this makes the island a potentially attractive target.

It is not that the Singapore Government identified a specific country as a threat. Rather, the strategic problems for Singapore stemmed from the simple fact of its small size and the absence of a self-defence capability. As Dr Goh noted in Parliament on 23 December 1965,

> Our army is to be engaged in the defence of the country and our people against external aggression. This task we are unable to do today by ourselves. It is no use pretending that without the British military presence in Singapore today, the island cannot be easily overrun by any neighbouring country within a radius of a thousand miles ...

Later, on 13 March 1967, Dr Goh reiterated this strategic narrative of inherent vulnerability:

> If you are in a completely vulnerable position anyone disposed to do so can hold you to ransom, and life for you will become very tiresome.

There was also a subtle shift in the strategic narrative. Now, it was less the idea of another state invading simply because of Singapore's weaknesses. Rather, it was the idea that other states might want to intervene in the event that Singapore's domestic political environment disintegrated into turmoil. In the same speech, Dr Goh noted,

> Small states are likely to be a great source of trouble in the world if they cannot look after themselves. If the management of their domestic affairs is so bad as to invite civil war and disorder, there is always the risk that larger states may be tempted to intervene ...

---

[33] See: Richard A. Deck, "Singapore: Comprehensive Security — Total Defence", in *Strategic Cultures in the Asia-Pacific Region*, eds. Ken Booth and Russell Trood (Houndmills: Macmillan Press, 1999), 248–249; Huxley, *Defending the Lion City*, 31–33.

In other words, there was a potential problem that derived from domestic political conditions. One source of domestic threat came from the communist threat emanating from the Malayan Communist Party (MCP). Up to 1960, the MCP had perpetrated various acts of civil and political unrest and violence in an attempt to undermine the Singapore Government, with the ultimate aim of unseating the legitimately constituted authority.[34] Even after 1967, the MCP continued its campaign of terrorism and subversion.[35] A second source of instability and insecurity emanated from communal politics. Indeed, communal politics was considered to be "the gravest threat" prior to independence.[36] There had already been two major incidents of communal violence in Singapore, the Maria Hertogh riots and the 1964 riots.[37] While these threats were largely domestic, they were nevertheless part of a symbiotic relationship with the external strategic environment. A constant image that has run through Singapore's strategic culture of vulnerability is that of a "Chinese island in a Malay sea".[38] Being located within an essentially Malay and Muslim archipelago, Singapore was extremely mindful that "Chinese chauvinism" could adversely affect its relations with Malaysia and Indonesia and give both countries an excuse to intervene on behalf of the Malay-Muslim population in Singapore.[39] Similarly, "Malay chauvinism" represented a potential threat to Singapore in the form of Islamic fundamentalist movements.[40]

The "Problem" of Malaysia

It has to be noted that Indonesia was the only country to have directly threatened Singapore's security by its initial refusal to recognise the

---

[34] Lau, "National Threat Perceptions of Singapore", 116; Singh, "Singapore's Management of Its Security Problems", 81.

[35] Wu, "Planning Security for a Small Nation", 663.

[36] Chan Heng Chee and Obaid Ul Haq (eds.), *The Prophetic and the Political: Selected Speeches and Writings of S. Rajaratnam* (New York: St. Martin's Press, 1987), 105.

[37] Jürgen Haacke, *ASEAN's Diplomatic and Security Culture: Origins, Development and Prospects* (New York: RoutledgeCurzon, 2003), 39.

[38] da Cunha, "Defence and Security", 134; Lee, *From Third World to First*, 15.

[39] Singh, "Singapore's Management of Its Security Problems", 83–84.

[40] Lau, "National Threat Perceptions of Singapore", 120.

Federation of Malaysia, which Singapore had joined from 1963 to 1965. The then-Indonesian President Sukarno had launched a policy of *Konfrontasi* (Confrontation), which sought to mount a low-intensity challenge to the international legitimacy of the Malaysian Federation. Singapore became a target of Indonesian sabotage and bombing, and there were apparently plans to even invade the island. Post-*Konfrontasi* throughout the 1970s, while relations between Singapore and Indonesia had stabilised, it is possible to argue that Singapore policy elites never completely lost any lingering concerns about potential threats arising out of Indonesia.

Nevertheless, it seems clear that between Indonesia and Malaysia, it was the latter that tended to occupy the attention of the policy elites, and Dr Goh in particular. To be fair, Malaysia never actually threatened military conflict with Singapore. Still, complications arose out of three problematic aspects to the Singapore-Malaysia relationship. Malaysia, it seemed at the time, held all the vital strategic cards against Singapore. The strategic levers that Malaysia apparently held over Singapore are a theme that runs through the memoirs of former Prime Minister Lee.[41]

One such lever was the initial refusal of a Malaysian battalion stationed in Singapore to vacate its barracks and return to Malaysia. Malaysia had refused to evacuate its troops stationed in Singapore and to release Singaporean troops then serving in Malaysian Army battalions. It took fairly intense British pressure to finally resolve this issue.[42] As Dr Goh noted in Parliament on 23 February 1966, "a disagreement of such a nature could have arisen in the way it did is symptomatic of a deeper malaise in the relations between the two governments on defence matters. This issue is but one of the many outstanding issues which had arisen between us."

Alternatively, other Malaysian leaders less moderate than Tunku Abdul Rahman, the Malaysian Prime Minister, might persuade "Brigadier Alsagoff (the commander of Malaysian forces stationed in Singapore at the time of separation) it was his patriotic duty to reverse separation."[43] Throughout the 1970s, even though relations with Malaysia would never

---

[41] Lee, *From Third World to First*, 663.

[42] Peled, *Soldiers Apart*, 63–65.

[43] Lee, *From Third World to First*, 31.

again reach such levels of crisis, the Singapore policy elites could not overcome "its sense of innate vulnerability."[44]

Several outstanding issues drove this concern over the relationship with Malaysia. The first was the acrimonious manner in which Singapore and Malaysia became separate states and the subsequent strained relations across the Causeway — the connecting north-south bridge between Malaysia and Singapore across the Straits of Johor separating the two countries — resulted in a situation where Singapore's policy makers could not rule out the possibility of a threat to the island-state emanating from Malaysia.[45] Malaysian politicians had felt that Kuala Lumpur had a natural right to ensure that Singapore would not undertake any policies prejudicial to Malaysian interests. One such policy perceived by Kuala Lumpur as prejudicial to its interests was the Singapore decision to rapidly expand the SAF through conscription. To circumvent these Malaysian obstacles, the first NS call-ups were sent via post rather than through television broadcasts. Given that the Malaysian Prime Minister Tunku Abdul Rahman's decision to expel Singapore from the Federation was not popular within Malaysia itself, there were concerns in Singapore about the possibility of the Malaysian Army invading Singapore to "take Singapore back into the Federation forcibly."[46] Another scenario revolved around the fear that "Malay ultras ... in [Kuala Lumpur would] instigate a coup by the Malaysian forces in Singapore and reverse the independence we had acquired ... If anything were to happen to Tunku Abdul Rahman, Tun Abdul Razak would become the Prime Minister and he could be made to reverse the Tunku's decision by strong-minded ultra leaders."[47]

Related to this issue of pressuring Singapore was the issue of water. Not only was it physically much larger, but more importantly, Singapore's vital water supplies came largely from Malaysia. There were apparent threats from Malaysia to use Singapore's dependence on Malaysia for its potable water supplies as a lever against Singapore adopting policies that

---

[44] Haacke, *ASEAN's Diplomatic and Security Culture*, 48.

[45] Chin, "Reflections on the Shaping of Strategic Cultures in Southeast Asia", 7; Singh, "Singapore's Management of Its Security Problems", 85.

[46] Lee, *From Third World to First*, 24; Leifer, *Singapore's Foreign Policy*, 53.

[47] Lee, *From Third World to First*, 22.

would be "prejudicial to Malaysia's interests."[48] In his memoirs, former Prime Minister Lee referred to this scenario as "rash political acts" from Malaysian political elites[49] and "random act of madness."[50] Water was therefore the potential *casus belli* in Singapore's relations with Malaysia.[51]

This "concern" with Malaysia was, however, tempered by an admission that neither country was powerful enough to undertake military action of any kind in the early years of their existence. If Malaysia was a major concern for Dr Goh and his colleagues, it seems to have stemmed from the simple fact that Malaysia remains significantly larger, with a similarly larger population, than Singapore. As Dr Goh noted in Parliament on 23 February 1966,

> Both Malaysia and Singapore do not have adequate defence forces at their command to deter aggression from their larger neighbours nor are they able successfully to fend any major assault mounted upon us. For some time until our defence forces are substantially increased, we have to depend on the military shield provided by our Commonwealth Allies ... if the Governments of Singapore and Malaysia are unable to cooperate in their common defence, this must surely adversely affect the efficacy of the defence arrangements with Britain, Australia and New Zealand ... So cooperate we must, but this cooperation must be as between two sovereign States and not as between big brother and his satellite. It is therefore necessary that the Malaysian Government should revise its attitude towards the Singapore Government in defence matters.

There was, as such, an explicit recognition of the need to cooperate with Malaysia on strategic issues. This cooperation was best manifested in the form of the Five Power Defence Arrangement (FPDA), a structure

---

[48] Kwa Chong Guan, "Introduction", in *Beyond Vulnerability? Water in Singapore–Malaysia Relations*, ed. Kwa Chong Guan (Singapore: Institute of Defence and Strategic Studies, 2002), 4.
[49] Lee, *From Third World to First*, 46.
[50] Lee, *From Third World to First*, 276.
[51] Leifer, *Singapore's Foreign Policy*, 19.

that bound the SAF with their Malaysian counterparts, along with Australian, British and New Zealander participation. It is worth noting, however, that this was by no means a defence alliance or pact; rather the arrangement merely promised that the member countries would consult in the event of security problems emerging. Bilateral cooperation between Singapore and Malaysia remained rudimentary, although given the fact that neither armed forces was well-developed at that point, this rudimentary cooperation throughout the 1970s was about all that either side could afford.

Conscription and Nation-Building

Finally, there was the issue of how a national identity could be built. The internal security concerns discussed earlier stemmed from the absence of a national identity. NS was regarded as an instrument that could help to build such a national identity in a newly independent state without any sense of its own identity. As Dr Goh noted in Parliament on 13 March 1967,

> There is another important aspect of our defence effort. This is a contribution it can make to nation-building. Nothing creates loyalty and national consciousness more speedily and more thoroughly than participation in defence and membership of the armed forces.

This nurturing of a national identity through conscription was deemed to be a necessary element of broader national policy. In a speech on 29 November 1969, Dr Goh noted,

> In Singapore, we are not yet a close-knit community; so many of our people are of recent migrant origin. All of this goes towards creating a sense of values which is personal, self-centred with anti-social tendencies where a conflict arises between personal interest and social obligations. There are the values of a rootless parvenu society. We cannot hope to remove them overnight, but in the process of creating a stronger national consciousness among our people, we will find that military service will play an increasingly important role, as it has played in other nations and in other ages.

It was part of a broader national objective of survival. National survival was simply a function of the military capacity to defend oneself; it was also a function of the extent to which the population at large felt connected to the island. This sense of connection was absolutely necessary, if the population was to be successfully mobilised to undertake not only the military tasks of nation-building, but the other aspects discussed elsewhere in this volume. In a sense, therefore, Dr Goh was conscious of not only the defence and security needs, but how answering these needs plugged into wider concerns within the overall project of nation-building.

Growing the SAF

Rearing the "Poisonous Shrimp"

Given these uncertainties in the internal and external strategic environment, Singapore needed to develop its capacity to defend itself. The construction of an SAF capable of achieving these objectives was, however, not an easy task. At the point of independence, the SAF was a very small force of two infantry battalions with no significant armoured or artillery forces, let alone credible air or naval capabilities. As a first step, manpower resources had to be increased. The solution that was arrived at was conscription.[52] This was absolutely critical for the task of developing an indigenous capacity to defend the nascent state. As Dr Goh noted in Parliament on 23 December 1965,

> British military protection today has made quite a number of our citizens complacent about the need to conduct our own defence preparations. These people assume that this protection will be permanent. I regard it as the height of folly ... the only rational basis on which we, as an independent country, can plan its future is on the opposite assumption, i.e., the removal of the British military presence at some time in the future. Nobody, neither us nor the British, can say when this will be ... whatever the time may be, it would be useless then to think about building up your defence forces. The time to do so is now.

---

[52] Chan Heng Chee, *Singapore: The Politics of Survival 1965–1967* (Oxford University Press: Singapore, 1971), 48.

Dr Goh acknowledged that there was no indigenous expertise in this enterprise. External advice and assistance was absolutely necessary. Attempts to seek defence assistance from India and Egypt were — as former Prime Minister Lee recalls — rebuffed.[53] The only state to react favourably to Singapore's requests for defence advice and assistance was Israel. Not surprisingly, the build-up of the SAF in its formative years emphasised the development of land and air power, reflecting the Israeli experience and pattern of defence development. From November 1965, only three months into Singapore's independence, Singapore started inviting the first batch of Israeli military personnel to advise on her build-up of defence capabilities.[54] For the next 10 years, Singapore developed its military's training syllabi and produced trained military instructors with the help of the Israeli military mission.[55]

Besides conscription, Singapore also pledged to support a relatively high level of military spending in its government budget to acquire sophisticated weaponry and develop its own defence industry so as to address Singapore's foreign uncertainties. At the end of 1968, Singapore's defence budget was announced to target 6% of gross domestic product (GDP) annually.[56] By 1972, Singapore's military expenditure was nearly comparable with that of Indonesia and Malaysia in terms of per capita figures.[57] Especially in face of the withdrawal of British troops in Singapore to reduce its military commitments "east of the Suez",[58] the SAF needed a generous military budget to arm itself from scratch. Also, by committing a substantial amount of the government budget on defence, the Singapore Government signalled its resolve to address Singapore's external vulnerabilities. A high level of military spending not only allowed Singapore to acquire sophisticated weaponry abroad, it also allowed Singapore to develop a local defence industry in order to "enhance the defence capability of the country and make it credible by meeting its operational needs in

---

[53] Lee, *From Third World to First*, 15.
[54] Lee, *From Third World to First*, 15.
[55] Chan, "Singapore", 141; Huxley, *Defending the Lion City*, 11.
[56] Huxley, *Defending the Lion City*, 27.
[57] Charles Morrison and Astri Suhrke, *Strategies of Survival: The Foreign Policy Dilemmas of Smaller Asian States* (New York: St. Martin's Press, 1979), 183–184.
[58] Leifer, *Singapore's Foreign Policy*, 63.

peacetime and in crisis."[59] Therefore, a sustained high level of military spending could fund both foreign and local military acquisitions to reduce Singapore's external uncertainties.

Dr Goh was always insistent on an intelligent approach towards learning from others. Hence, throughout the first two decades of statehood, Singapore had also shown itself to be discriminating in applying Israeli policies and associating itself with Israel. For example, unlike Israel, Singapore did not extend NS to female citizens. Although former Prime Minister Lee recognised that NS could "reinforce the people's will to defend themselves" by incorporating the participation of women,[60] the Chinese cultural bias against military service noted earlier precluded a truly universal application of NS. Furthermore, Singapore had always known the possible repercussions of associating itself with Israel, and had thus tried hard to distant itself from any overt Israeli connection. Although Singapore maintains full diplomatic relations with Israel, it maintains a Consulate-General in Tel Aviv while Israel maintains an Embassy in Singapore.[61] In addition, Singapore had always been aware that its position as a Chinese enclave in a Muslim-concentrated Malay archipelago would be a prime target for nationalistic criticisms from its Muslim neighbours, because where "religious prejudices have to be stirred up against Singapore then Singapore is Israel."[62] Instead, Singapore had tried to compare itself with other small states, such as Switzerland or the city-state of Venice.[63] As Dr Goh said in a speech on 19 July 1971,

> Because the Swiss make such conscientious preparations for their defence, they have left a potential aggressor in no doubt that any intrusion into Swiss territory will effectively be resisted. As a result, when three major European wars broke out in 1870, 1914 and 1939, the Swiss were able to preserve their neutrality. The reason was that they had the

[59] Bilveer Singh, "Singapore's Defence Industries", in *Canberra Papers on Strategy and Defence*, No. 70, 1990, 42.

[60] Lee, *From Third World to First*, 17–18.

[61] Leifer, *Singapore's Foreign Policy*, 65.

[62] Quoted in *The Mirror* 4/5 (29 January 1968), 7; Singh, "Singapore's Management of Its Security Problems", 87.

[63] Chan and ul Haq, *The Prophetic and the Political*, 494–495.

arms and the will to defend themselves ... If history has one lesson to teach us, it is that we can hope to live in peace if we maintain strong defences. Small countries generally have no other desire than to be left in peace to develop their potential. But until a new international order is created whereby small nation states can have an assurance that their territory and independence will always be respect[ed], there is no other choice than the example of Switzerland and Sweden.

Morphing into the "Porcupine"

The "poisonous shrimp" defence posture postulated a scenario where the SAF would defend the island at the water's edge first, to be followed by a "Stalingrad-style of close combat" in urban areas, aiming to make the human and material costs of aggression against Singapore to unacceptable levels.[64] This posture was necessitated by the then poor state of the SAF, its lack of manpower, firepower and mobility — basically, an armed force incapable of offensive operations.[65]

The "poisonous shrimp" strategy was, however, deficient because it was essentially defeatist. Clearly, the strategy envisaged the eventual defeat of Singapore and its disappearance. Its deterrent value lay in the promise of great pain that the potential aggressor would suffer in the process of defeating the SAF, but that defeat was virtually guaranteed. Singapore would, in a "poisonous shrimp" strategy, eventually cease to exist as an independent political entity. As early as 1971, Dr Goh had implicitly recognised this, when he said in his Armed Forces Day speech,

> ... the highest priority must be given to raising the technical capacity of the SAF in all arms and services. It is not merely a question of improving quality. It is also a matter of quantity. We must get enough men in the several hundred categories of skilled vocations and at all levels — artisan, technician, engineer and scientist.

The "poisonous shrimp" also did not allow Singapore to address its perceived geopolitical and geostrategic vulnerabilities — namely its lack of

---

[64] Deck, "Singapore: Comprehensive Security — Total Defence", 249.
[65] Huxley, *Defending the Lion City*, 56.

self-sufficient water resources and lack of strategic depth. In tandem with the changing nature of the SAF's equipment, organisation and training throughout the 1980s, it was hard to escape the conclusion that doctrinal emphasis was increasingly placed on the offensive as part of a pre-emptive deterrent strategy. This was in line with what the Israeli military advisors had been arguing for, the building up of a more offensive capability — what Huxley calls the "only strategy which made sense if Singapore, bearing in mind its peculiar geostrategic vulnerabilities, was to base its deterrent on national military resources: strategic pre-emption of potential adversaries."[66]

In any case, by the late 1970s, the SAF's build-up of capabilities had resulted in a situation that increasingly contradicted the "poisonous shrimp" strategy and made pressing the need to reformulate its basic defence doctrines. Even during its "poisonous shrimp" years, the long-term vision was clearly oriented towards the acquisition of capabilities that strongly suggested a defence strategy of offensive pre-emption.[67] Furthermore, Singapore's conscription policy was becoming a major success. Between 1965 and 1978, the size of the SAF had increased 433%.[68] The SAF was, even now, a highly regarded and potent military force in Southeast Asia. High levels of economic growth allowed Singapore's defence spending as a percentage of its GDP to remain fairly constant, while increasing military expenditure 114% over the 1969–1978 period.[69] The SAF had better and more modern weapons systems than its Malaysian and Indonesian counterparts. A new strategic formulation was needed to rationalise the SAF.

Conclusion

NS, and the accompanying policy of sustained high level of military spending, was Singapore's immediate response after independence to reduce its strategic uncertainties. By judging the state of Singapore

---

[66] Huxley, *Defending the Lion City*, 56.

[67] Huxley, *Defending the Lion City*, 56–58.

[68] Paribatra and Samudavanija, "Internal Dimensions of Regional Security in Southeast Asia", 79.

[69] Huxley, *Defending the Lion City*, 28; Paribatra and Samudavanija, "Internal Dimensions of Regional Security in Southeast Asia", 79.

politics and the SAF by the mid-1970s, this policy seems to have achieved its objectives. Internally, NS directly and indirectly engendered social cohesion among Singaporeans and produced an increasing sense of camaraderie among conscript youths regardless of race and religion, which was crucial in addressing the societal rifts that the policy makers had perceived. Externally, NS provided Singapore with the manpower, and the sustained high rates of military spending provided them with the weaponry, to pose a reasonable deterrence towards its two historically hostile neighbours. Indeed, in a speech on 20 September 1973, Dr Goh recognised this new set of problems derived from the relative success of building the SAF from scratch:

> In 1968 there was widespread anxiety over our future ... In 1973, when we have achieved some success, there is increasing evidence of complacency ... Whereas previously many thought they were being overwhelmed by problems, now too many believe they are on top of them.

This fear of complacency setting in, as early as 1973, is already a remarkable statement, that within a decade of its inception, the SAF should begin to display signs of complacency. Ironically, it is a testament to the success that Dr Goh and his colleagues had achieved in growing the "poisonous shrimp". The SAF would not morph into its "porcupine" phase under Dr Goh's stewardship, but in retrospect, it is possible to see the mid-1970s as the very early stages of this process.

Successive Singapore governments have espoused the argument that a stable and secure country, the result of a strong and capable SAF, has been key to allowing the Singapore economy to grow. In other words, there is a positive, linear progression between establishing a strong defence capability on the one hand, and experiencing economic growth and development on the other.[70] However, the historical record suggests that economic growth and the growth of the SAF through high levels of defence spending

---

[70] Muthiah Alagappa, "Military Professionalism and the Development Role of the Military in Southeast Asia", in *Soldiers and Stability in Southeast Asia,* eds. J. Soedjati Djiwandono and Yong Mun Cheong (Singapore: ISEAS, 1988), 33; Harold Crouch, "The Military Mind and Economic Development", in *Soldiers and Stability in Southeast Asia,* ed. J. Soedjati Djiwandono and Yong Mun Cheong (Singapore: ISEAS, 1988), 54–55.

occurred in parallel. Singapore's economic success can be divided into three phases: the infusion of foreign capital, talent and technology, and the steady advance up the value-chain from low-technology textiles in the late 1960s; the high-technology manufacture of semiconductors and memory chips in the late 1980s; and the present re-engineering of the economy towards greater knowledge-intensive technology such as IT and biotechnology.

The SAF today is almost totally unrecognisable from its first incarnations. This difference is not simply a function of technological change. Certainly technological change has a big part to play: from SLR rifles to the indigenous SAR-21, hand-me-down Hawker Hunters left behind by the British to the current F-15SGs, the RSS Panglima to today's "stealth" frigates, the SAF has indeed grown beyond all recognition. Operationally, the SAF is similarly unrecognisable from its early days: today's SAF speaks of doctrines like IKC2 (integrated knowledge-based command and control), a far cry from the highly centralised command and control systems that characterised its earliest incarnations. Today's SAF engages with the concept of Revolutions in Military Affairs (RMA), best exemplified by the so-called Military Transformation that the United States military had engaged in throughout the 1990s and early 2000s.[71]

It is of course potentially fallacious to attribute the peace and security that Singapore has experienced throughout its existence as a sovereign state to its deterrence postures afforded by NS and high levels of defence spending. Furthermore, as noted earlier, Singapore's economic growth occurred in tandem with the growth of the SAF, which makes problematic the argument that security and stability attracted the foreign investments that drove economic growth. Nevertheless, it is also plausible to at least hypothesise a correlation between the build-up of the SAF and Singapore's peace and security. As the basic condition for Singapore's deterrence posture, NS may plausibly be the underlying condition that facilitated Singapore's peace and security and economic growth, continuing to do so today.

---

[71] It is widely held that such RMA-inspired transformation agendas are possible only for military organisations with mature conventional war fighting capabilities. See, for instance, Robin F. Laird and Holger H. Mey, "The Revolution in Military Affairs: Allied Perspectives", *McNair Paper* 66 (April 1999), 19–23.

Chapter 3

In the Service of the Nation Too:
An Early History of National Service
Outside the Singapore Armed Forces

Ho Shu Huang

National Service (NS)[1] can presently be served in the Singapore Armed
Forces (SAF), Singapore Police Force (SPF) and Singapore Civil Defence
Force (SCDF) — the latter two key services in the Ministry of Home
Affairs' operational arm known as the "Home Team". National servicemen
are recognised as being instrumental to ensuring Singapore's peace and
security. At a dinner reception held to commemorate the 50th anniversary
of NS in independent Singapore (NS50), Prime Minister Lee Hsien Loong
noted that over a million Singaporeans have served national service in the
SAF and the Home Team since 1967.[2] The SPF "work hard to maintain law
and order daily, and are prepared to deal with any threat." The SCDF
"respond to all types of emergencies, big and small and they do this not just
when war comes, but everyday in peace time, around the clock … a source
of comfort … because they are there for us at the time of our greatest
need."[3] PM Lee emphasised national servicemen, and not just regulars,

---

[1] The acronym NS refers to National Service as a government policy. The act of serving it,
national service, will be in lowercase in this chapter.

[2] Lee Hsien Loong, "PM Lee Hsieng Loong at the NS50 Dinner Reception" (Singapore,
30 October 2017), http://www.pmo.gov.sg/newsroom/pm-lee-hsien-loong-ns50-dinner-
reception (accessed 5 April 2018).

[3] Ibid.

enable the Home Team to secure Singapore. Minister for Home Affairs K. Shanmugam earlier noted over 260,000 national servicemen have served in the Home Team.[4] National servicemen there now wear the same uniforms as their regular counterparts and fill similar roles as them. Some SPF units, such as the Public Transport Security Command, comprise mainly national servicemen. In a four-man fire engine crew, two or three are national servicemen. In an ambulance crew, one out of three is a national serviceman.[5] When Minister for Finance Heng Swee Kiat collapsed during a Cabinet meeting in May 2017, one of the four ambulance first responders was indeed a full-time national serviceman.[6] PM Lee subsequently wrote to the Commissioner of the SCDF a letter of appreciation acknowledging the competency and confidence displayed by the crew of both regulars and a national serviceman.[7] As a matter of policy, national servicemen in the Home Team are as instrumental to protecting Singapore's security as their counterparts in the SAF.

This chapter argues this recognition that Home Team national servicemen play as important an operational role to Singapore's security as those in the SAF occurred only gradually despite the importance of policing and civil defence duties to Singapore's security being acknowledged at independence. In fact, from 1965 to 1970, internal and external security came under a single Ministry of Interior and Defence. National service could also be served part-time outside the SAF in the Special Constabulary (SC) and Vigilante Corps (VC). Yet the notion of "national defence" was still widely regarded as being primarily the responsibility of the SAF. In its early years, national service outside the SAF occurred because of practical necessity and political expediency. Amongst the security services then, the

---

[4] K. Shanmugam, "Speech by Mr K Shanmugam, Minister for Home Affairs & Minister for Law, at the Official Opening Of HomeTeamNS Tampines Clubhouse on Monday, 13 February 2017, 1.00 pm" (Singapore, 13 February 2017), https://www.hometeamns.sg/wp-content/uploads/2016/12/Speech-by-Min-HA-at-Opening-of-HTNS-Tampines-Clubhouse-13-Feb.pdf (accessed 5 April 2018).

[5] Ibid.

[6] "PM Lee thanks SCDF for 'excellent job' in tending to Heng Swee Keat," *Channelnewsasia.com*, 14 May 2016, https://www.channelnewsasia.com/news/singapore/pm-lee-thanks-scdf-for-excellent-job-in-tending-to-heng-swee-kea-8021944 (accessed 5 April 2018).

[7] Ibid.

SAF was clearly the first amongst equals. For example, in 1971, the SC was well under its intended strength because the rapid expansion of the SAF had absorbed most national servicemen.[8]

This early history of national service outside the SAF proceeds in three sections. Rather than offer a chronology of key events in the evolution of national service in the Home Team which other publications have already ably done, it approaches the evolution thematically.[9] The first section examines the notion of "national service". It looks at how the British conceived it, how Singapore inherited the policy, and how in practice it predominantly centred on military defence against an external aggressor in the early post-Independence years. The second section then outlines how and why NS was implemented in the SC and VC. As much as NS was seen as a means to quickly raise a credible military, enlisting national servicemen entirely into the SAF was not feasible. Part-time national service in the SC and VC accommodated these constraints. The third section explores how NS in the Home Team gradually expanded. This happened initially for practical reasons but gained momentum subsequently for larger strategic ones as Singapore formalised its "whole-of-government" approach to national defence, culminating in Total Defence in the early 1980s. This journey sheds light on how the idea of national security, and the means to ensure it, expanded beyond being a primary military concern to one where "everyone has a part to play."[10] National servicemen, regardless of where they served, would be acknowledged as being equally important not only in public discourse, but in actual operations and deployments.

The Origins of NS: What Is "Service" to the "Nation"?

The SAF presently comprises an estimated 350,000 personnel.[11] The majority are national servicemen either in full-time service or in operationally-ready

---

[8] "SCs will serve more than 4 years", *New Nation*, 16 August 1971.

[9] A comprehensive chronology can be found in Koh Buck Siong, *Everyday Guardians: 50 Years of National Service in the Home Team* (Singapore: Marshall Cavendish International (Asia) Pte Ltd, 2017).

[10] "Driving home message of Total Defence", *Business Times*, 3 April 1984.

[11] Fred Wei-Shi Tan and Psalm B. C. Lew, "The Role of the Singapore Armed Forces in Forging National Values, Image, and Identity", *Military Review* (March–April 2017), 15.

units which train annually. They constitute about 10% of Singapore's resident population.[12] While the exact distribution of national servicemen across the SAF, SPF and SCDF has not been publicly stated, the SAF enlists the bulk of the Malay full-time NS cohort, an indication of how the majority of national servicemen serve in the SAF.[13] For a policy commonly associated with the military, it is curious why NS was so-named and did not reference the military, and defence, more specifically, as is the case elsewhere. For example, the pieces of conscription legislation in South Korea and Israel are the Military Service and Defense Service laws, respectively.[14] The key reason for its name was NS was never intended to limit service to just the military, even if such service was privileged in the policy's actual implementation.

NS has British origins. It was conceived at the turn of the 20th century with the founding of the National Service League. This organisation campaigned for universal military service as a means to raise a large land force by a traditionally maritime power to counter perceived German militancy. Though the term "national service" was frequently used in discussions, conscription was introduced in the World War I through the specifically worded Military Service Act of 1916. The National Service (Armed Forces) Act, the successor of the Military Service Act, was only introduced in 1939 at the start of World War II. The policy survived the war before ending in 1963.

"National service", however, had a larger conceptual basis that extended beyond mere service in the military. Although contemporary thought dictated that a successful national defence was still largely contingent on the ability to field a large, trained military, and thus NS was mainly implemented to meet this objective, there was also recognition that other areas crucial to a nation's defence also had to be served. As early as 1916, upper house parliamentarian Lord Alfred Milner declared "I should [not] hesitate to perform any duties for which I was fit which

---

[12] Ibid.

[13] *Hansard Singapore Parliamentary Debates*, Parl. No. 12, Session No. 1, Vol. No. 88, Sitting No. 20, Sitting Date 6/3/2012, "Committee of Supply — Head J (Ministry of Defence), page 2005.

[14] "Landmarks", *Military Manpower Administration* website, http://www.mma.go.kr/eng/contents.do?mc=mma0000843; and "Basic Laws of Israel: Defense Service Law (1986)", *Jewish Virtual Library: A Project of AICE*, http://www.jewishvirtuallibrary.org/israel-defense-service-law-1986 (accessed 5 April 2018).

might be allotted to [me] if the Government thought well at a crisis like this to commandeer the whole nation, to apply the principle of National Service not only for military but for all purposes."[15] Ironically, for most of the World War I, there was no shortage of volunteers for the British military, precluding the need to conscript soldiers until the latter part of the war as casualties mounted. In fact, Sir Auckland Geddess, the first Minister of National Service suggested its main function was to "prevent the … young men of the country flocking in excessive numbers into the fighting services to the detriment of essential civilian activities."[16] As British historian Richard Vinen observes, NS "was about keeping men out of the army as much as getting them in because the voluntary recruitment campaigns that took place early in the war had stripped factories of their workers."[17]

This is a crucial point. Even in an era where large armies were a key measurement of national power and therefore defence capability, the British Government recognised that a successful defence policy had to also factor in roles in non-military, but equally important, areas. These included service in so-called strategic industries crucial to the war effort. Vinen notes that the implementation of the 1939 National Service (Armed Forces) Act in Britain during the World War II "extended beyond the purely military. Men of military age were permitted (or required) to work in war industries and could, indeed, be forbidden to join the armed forces. Men and women were directed to take civilian jobs of national importance."[18] There was a clear understanding that national defence and the roles within it had to be more broadly understood given the industrialised character of war and how it afflicted the whole of British society.[19] National service could encompass much more than military service alone. These other

---

[15] *UK Hansard Parliamentary Debates*, Lords Sitting, Series 5, Vol. 21, Sitting date 18/4/1916, "National Service", Column 769.

[16] *The Times*, 8 November 1938, as cited in Richard Vinen, *National Service: Conscription in Britain 1945–1963* (London: Penguin Group, 2014), 36.

[17] Vinen, *National Service*, 35.

[18] Vinen, *National Service*, 37.

[19] For a fuller exploration of how NS was interpreted in the United Kingdom during the period, see Paul Horsler, "National service or conscription? Bolton debates", *International History Group 28th Annual Conference*, 8–10 September 2016, Edinburgh, UK; and Brendan Maartens, "To Encourage, Inspire and Guide: National Service, the People's War

interpretations of national service would, however, only manifest themselves in voluntary national service schemes, not compulsory ones. They had government-supported but grassroots-initiated recruitment campaigns.[20] As far as legislation went, the association of NS with military service would be intertwined. The full name of the Act already explicitly referenced the "armed forces". In its implementation, NS was overwhelmingly served in the military with only a minority directed to serve in strategic industries.[21] This focus remained when the National Service Act was amended in 1948. "Armed forces" was removed from its title as it was superfluous — national servicemen would be exclusively conscripted into the British armed forces.[22]

Colonial Singapore adopted the same terminology for the provision of national service in Singapore when the National Service Ordinance was passed in 1952 and implemented in 1954. The Ordinance, however, differed from the British version in that it explicitly included service in police forces and civil defence forces in addition to the armed forces. The National Service Ordinance defined civil defence forces as those providing "measures not amounting to actual combat for affording defences against any form of hostile attack" before or after it occurs.[23] The local context of Singapore's experience during the World War II and post-war political turbulence was the impetus for this internal security dimension to Singapore's National Service Ordinance.

Referencing this context, the colonial government assured Singapore the legislation was merely a "precautionary measure to ensure that men will be available for the orderly and prompt expansion of the forces, and especially of civil defence, to meet any emergency, local or international."[24] Yet seeing how NS in the United Kingdom was essentially conscription into the British armed forces to provide the manpower it needed to maintain its global

and the Promotion of Civil Defence in Interwar Britain, 1938–1939", *Media History* 21/33 (2015).
[20] Maartens, "To Encourage, Inspire and Guide", 332.
[21] Vinen, *National Service,* 37–38.
[22] See *National Service Act,* 1948 (Chapter 64), "Part I: Service in the Armed Forces".
[23] The 1952 National Service Ordinance used the definition of "civil defence forces" provided by the 1951 Civil Defence Ordinance.
[24] "The Service Bill", *The Straits Times,* 17 April 1952.

presence, the rationale for its introduction in Singapore was assumed to be similarly military-focused. Some opposed needing to contribute to this effort. In the words of the Singapore Labour Party's General Secretary Peter M. Williams, it was "immoral to expect [Singapore residents] to shoulder arms in defence of interests not identical with their own."[25] After all, Singapore was still a British colony with limited say in the direction of British colonial policy. As Singapore's political master, the British should logically be solely responsible for the defence of Singapore.[26] The counter-argument was acknowledging the importance of defence by accepting the proposed law was necessary for Singapore to progress towards self-rule.[27] Following its implementation in 1954, protests broke out. These culminated in the National Service Riots of 1954 staged mainly by Chinese high school students, many of whom were liable for national service under the law. The heart of the protest remained opposition to the idea that Singapore residents should take on the British responsibility of military defence without accompanying political rights. If the British could not defend Singapore, they should leave.[28] The connection between national service, the military and defence was implicit.

Singapore inherited the National Service Ordinance at independence. Amended in March 1967, the first batch of Singapore full-time national servicemen enlisted into the SAF in July that year to significant fanfare and adulation.[29] They would eventually form the third and fourth battalions of the Singapore Infantry Regiment to augment the then regular first and second battalions. This initial cohort of 900 full-time national servicemen is often commemorated as a symbol of the start of national service as Singaporeans presently know it — two years of full-time service, followed by service as operationally-ready national servicemen (formerly known as "reservists") and usually served in the SAF.

[25] "Labour to be asked to oppose call-up bill", *The Straits Times*, 7 March 1952 as cited in National Library Board Singapore (NLB), "National service: Early years", http://eresources.nlb.gov.sg/infopedia/articles/SIP_692_2005-02-01.html (accessed 5 April 2018).
[26] Mickey Chiang, *SAF and 30 Years of National Service* (Singapore: Armour Publishing, 1997), 18, as cited in NLB, "National service: Early years".
[27] "Call-up is 'wise insurance, not war-mongering'", *The Straits Times*, 18 April 1952, as cited in NLB, "National service: Early years".
[28] "The Service Bill".
[29] "Dinner to honour S'pore's first batch of soldiers", *The Straits Times*, 18 August 1967.

The parliamentary debate at the second reading of the National Service (Amendment) Bill in 1967 certainly assumed this close association of NS with military service. While a broader recognition of security beyond military defence was hinted at, a dominant theme in the speeches given then was still how NS was needed to quickly fill the ranks of the fledgling SAF to defend Singapore's sovereignty in a geopolitically dangerous region. In his parliamentary speech, Minister for Interior and Defence Dr Goh Keng Swee noted "if small States can manage their affairs efficiently and can raise sufficient defence forces to deter others from risky adventures by making them costly, then they would add to the stability and security of the whole region."[30] Dr Goh also stressed national service in the military was a priority. While acknowledging national service could be served part-time in the SAF's People's Defence Force (PDF), VC and SC because of individual circumstances, national servicemen could still be posted to the SAF for full-time national service should this change and their talent there be needed.[31]

In support of the Bill, other Members of Parliament (MPs) referenced NS similarly. In many instances, the notion of "national service" was used interchangeably with "military training" or "military service". Teong Eng Siong spoke of how NS would "educate and train our citizens and future generations in military consciousness and preparedness and defence responsibility [because] the Bill provides various forms of military training on a full-time or part-time basis."[32] Similarly, Fong Sip Chee, Bernard Rodrigues, Dr Chew Chin Han, Ang Nam Piau among others spoke in support of NS as a means to provide the military means for defending Singapore by putting its citizens through "military training" without needing to incur the cost of a standing army.[33] Yeoh Ghim Seng was particularly single-minded about this need to focus on military training. "I am not particularly happy," he remarked, "to see the division of national service

---

[30] *Hansard Singapore Parliamentary Debates*, Parl. No. 1, Session No. 1, Vol. No. 25, Sitting No. 16, Sitting Date 13/3/1967, "National Service (Amendment) Bill", Column 1160.

[31] Ibid., Column 1163.

[32] Ibid., Column 1165.

[33] Ibid., Columns 1174–1180; *Hansard Singapore Parliamentary Debates*, Parl. No. 1, Session No. 1, Vol. No. 25, Sitting No. 17, Sitting Date 14/3/1967, "National Service (Amendment) Bill", Columns 1220, 1224.

into four kinds, as I feel our young citizens should be given equal treatment. They should all undergo the same form of service, namely, military training — part-time for two years."[34]

Only a few MPs acknowledged non-military national service in the VC and SC during the parliamentary debate. Teo Hup Teck, for example, declared "to those who join the Army, Navy and Air Force, the Police Force, the Vigilante Corps, and the Special Constabulary, great glory goes to them."[35] R. A. Gonzales reminded the House that "as in the past, a larger number will be asked to serve [national service] on a part-time basis in the People's Defence Force, the Special Constabulary and the Vigilante Corps."[36] Just as his fellow MPs did, Teo, however, concluded by situating the need for NS as part of "the setting up of the Armed Forces ... with a view to defending our country."[37] Similarly returning the focus to the military, Gonzales only spoke of the PDF, and not the SC or VC, when stressing the importance of part-timers in NS and not forming the impression that they will be "less capable as SAF regulars or full-time national servicemen."[38]

Part-Time NS and the SC and VC

While MPs readily suggested NS was the solution to raising a credible military for Singapore's defence in lieu of a standing military, achieving this quickly was difficult. Despite the overwhelming connection of NS with the military in public discourse then, many in early cohorts of national servicemen did not, in fact, serve their national service full-time in the SAF, presumably the quickest way to raise a credible SAF. Only 10% of the 9,000 who were eligible for NS in 1967 were called up for

---

[34] *Hansard Singapore Parliamentary Debates*, Parl. No. 1, Session No. 1, Vol. No. 25, Sitting No. 17, Sitting Date 14/3/1967, "National Service (Amendment) Bill", Column 1227.

[35] *Hansard Singapore Parliamentary Debates*, Parl. No. 1, Session No. 1, Vol. No. 25, Sitting No. 16, Sitting Date 13/3/1967, "National Service (Amendment) Bill", Column 1171.

[36] *Hansard Singapore Parliamentary Debates*, Parl. No. 1, Session No. 1, Vol. No. 25, Sitting No. 17, Sitting Date 14/3/1967, "National Service (Amendment) Bill", Column 1246.

[37] *Hansard Singapore Parliamentary Debates*, Parl. No. 1, Session No. 1, Vol. No. 25, Sitting No. 16, Sitting Date 13/3/1967, "National Service (Amendment) Bill", Column 1171.

[38] *Hansard Singapore Parliamentary Debates*, Parl. No. 1, Session No. 1, Vol. No. 25, Sitting No. 17, Sitting Date 14/3/1967, "National Service (Amendment) Bill", Column 1246.

full-time service in the SAF.[39] This "elite batch" was selected by educational qualifications and physical fitness to help create an army envisioned by Dr Goh to have "both brawn and brain."[40] Despite the urgent need to expand the SAF, it could not enlist more full-time. It was too administratively challenging and expensive for the government. Training infrastructure and suitable instructors were lacking. At the time, Dr Goh even declared that full-time military training for all eligible national servicemen would "bankrupt the nation" in a decade's time.[41] Additionally, although NS had been in force since 1954, the British only implemented the policy tentatively with a degree of hesitance given the resistance the policy had faced. There was also no need for additional manpower despite the on-going Emergency. While many were registered for national service, most were not actually called up to serve.[42] Ironically, British national servicemen played a far bigger role in Malayan (and Singapore's) defence against the Communist insurgency. At least 119 British national servicemen were killed in action in Malaya.[43] In contrast, the sudden call up of those liable for NS by the Singapore Government in 1967 would invariably disrupt the lives of a sizeable portion of the population. This presented a politically challenging situation considering earlier NS protests which Albert Lau discusses in his earlier chapter. The government therefore initially allowed a degree of flexibility in its implementation of NS. Those who would face financial hardship (such as sole breadwinners) or who were still in school could apply to defer their national service, or serve it part-time.[44] For these reasons, of those liable for national service in these early years, a sizeable number successfully

---

[39] *Hansard Singapore Parliamentary Debates*, Parl. No. 1, Session No. 1, Vol. No. 25, Sitting No. 16, Sitting Date 13/3/1967, "National Service (Amendment) Bill", Column 1163.

[40] "Call-up: 'Elite' youths for a full-time Army", *The Straits Times*, 17 March 1967.

[41] *Hansard Singapore Parliamentary Debates*, Parl. No. 1, Session No. 1, Vol. No. 25, Sitting No. 17, Sitting Date 14/3/1967, "National Service (Amendment) Bill", Column 1253. Dr Goh, however, would be proven wrong when full-time NS became the norm with the introduction of the Enlistment Act in 1970. Full-time national service would not bankrupt the government.

[42] NLB, "National service: Early years".

[43] Vinen, *National Service*, 318.

[44] "All set for call-up of first batch", *The Straits Times*, 14 March 1967. *Hansard Singapore Parliamentary Debates*, Parl. No. 1, Session No. 1, Vol. No. 26, Sitting No. 2, Sitting Date 7/9/1967, "Registration for National Service (Particulars)", Column 98.

deferred it and a majority of those who eventually served did so part-time. In 1967, of the 9,000 who were liable for NS, 4,900 were selected to serve — 900 full-time in the SAF, with 2,000 serving part-time in the SC and VC each.[45] None were sent to the PDF, presumably because military resources were already stretched training the pioneer batch of full-time SAF national servicemen. Part-time national service was administratively the best way to ensure the universality of NS within the constraints of limited resources and assuaging public concerns.

Enlistment for part-time NS occurred from 1967 till 1970 when the Enlistment Act became law. Under the Act, NS from 1 January 1971 would begin with a full-time service period for all. Exemption from full-time national service was still possible but became increasingly difficult to attain.[46] Part-time national servicemen, however, would continue to serve for many years after because those enlisted under the preceding NS legislation could serve it part-time for 12 years or until 40 years of age, whichever was later.[47] Part-time national servicemen would receive up to eight hours of basic training per week, as well as one full-time weekend in-camp training a month for the first six months. Thereafter, three hours of duty had to be served a week, and a week-long full-time in-camp training a year. This would be conducted after office hours except for the residential in-camp trainings.[48]

Those selected for military training during their part-time national service were posted to the PDF. It was thought that they could accelerate the build-up of a credible SAF and be equal to their full-time peers and regulars in the SAF as MP Gonzales had hoped. This, however, proved challenging. When it was first constituted in 1965 to recruit volunteers into the

---

[45] "Toh: Call-up to cushion pull-out", *The Straits Times*, 1 September 1967.

[46] The issue of transferring from full-time to part-time national service was debated in Parliament in 1979. Then Minister for Defence Howe Yoon Chong noted as an MP he received many such requests from his constituents but the government policy was national service would have to be served full-time save rare exemptions granted on "medical grounds or some other special grounds that are permitted by the Advisory Committee." *Hansard Singapore Parliamentary Debates,* Parl. No. 4, Session No. 2, Vol. No. 38, Sitting No. 14, Sitting Date 22/3/1979, "Budget, Ministry of Defence", Column 1097.

[47] *National Service (Amendment) Bill*, Part VIIB, 16K, 1(b).

[48] *National Service (Amendment) Bill*, Part VIIB, 16K, 2.

military to defend newly independent Singapore, the enthusiasm of the large numbers who volunteered for the PDF belied the difficulty in raising a force of part-timers that could competently conduct complicated military operations. Although generally organised into infantry battalions, the part-time nature of PDF volunteers limited the extent of their training in modern warfare. Part-time national servicemen in the PDF trained for similarly short hours. Even an amendment to legislation in 1969 allowing for 12 hours of continuous training a month (instead of just three-hour blocks once a week) was still insufficient.[49] With the SAF seeking to quickly establish itself as a modern fighting force, the learning curve for part-time national servicemen in the PDF was too steep. Integrating with the rest of the SAF comprising full-time national servicemen and regulars who trained daily was difficult. Minister for Defence Lim Kim San alluded to these difficulties when he spoke of "new demands" that had rendered the 1952 National Service Ordinance inadequate when the Enlistment Bill, its proposed replacement, was debated in Parliament in 1970.[50] In practice, volunteers and part-time national servicemen in the PDF were therefore mainly assigned narrowly defined internal security responsibilities to assist the police force with maintaining law and order during emergencies. By 1972, these PDF part-time national servicemen were transferred to the SC and VC.[51] It was apparent that the VC and SC could better train and deploy part-time national servicemen because the short hours of duty lent themselves more easily to training and deployment for police work than military service.

As with the PDF, the SC and VC were volunteer organisations before the introduction of NS in 1967. The SC was established in October 1945 as an organisation of volunteer policemen led by regulars.[52] Members of

---

[49] *Hansard Singapore Parliamentary Debates,* Parl. No. 2, Session No. 1, Vol. No. 29, Sitting No. 1, Sitting Date 11/6/1969, "National Service (Amendment) Bill", Column 28.

[50] *Hansard Singapore Parliamentary Debates,* Parl. No. 2, Session No. 1, Vol. No. 30, Sitting No. 2, Sitting Date 21/5/1970, "Enlistment Bill", Column 48.

[51] Ho Shu Huang, "The Formation: People's Defence Force (1965–1985)", in *The 2nd People's Defence Force, Steadfast We Stand, Guardian of Our Homeland* (Singapore: The 2nd People's Defence Force, 2015), 28.

[52] National Library Board Singapore (NLB), "Volunteer Special Constabulary", http://eresources. nlb.gov.sg/infopedia/articles/SIP_1141_2010-05-07.html (accessed 5 April 2018).

the SC had police powers similar to their regular counterparts.[53] Although the earlier National Service Ordinance allowed for national service to be served in the police force, the SC remained a largely volunteer organisation until part-time national servicemen were directed there when the Police Force Act was amended in 1967 to provide for their management.[54] Part-time national servicemen would serve basic police duties.[55] The VC began as a community network of volunteers that was involved in anti-crime neighbourhood patrols in the 1950s and early 1960s. In 1964, during *Konfrontasi*, these existing arrangements were formally recognised by the government with the establishment of the VC. The VC augmented internal security by guarding key installations and "providing vigilance in congested public areas" during a period of attacks by Indonesian saboteurs, hence its name.[56] In 1967, the National Service (Amendment) Bill added national service in the VC alongside the armed forces and police force. Later in the year, the Vigilante Corps Bill formally constituted the VC as a government statutory organisation tasked with domestic security. It was to "assist the Police Force in the maintenance of law and order, the preservation of public peace, the prevention and detection of crime and the apprehension of offenders." While VC members were affiliated with the police, they were not given full policing powers.[57] In its early years, the VC even departed significantly from its original security role to prevent "internal subversion."[58] National service in the VC then was a "youth movement aimed at keeping Singapore's youths off the streets and organising them for more useful civic and cultural activities."[59] The VC found it difficult to deploy its large cohort of national servicemen with lower education qualifications for security operations.[60]

---

[53] *Hansard Singapore Parliamentary Debates,* Parl. No. 1, Session No. 1, Vol. No. 26, Sitting No. 5, Sitting Date 2/11/1967, "Police Force (Amendment) Bill", Column 338.
[54] Ibid.
[55] "Call-up today: Part-time service as Special Police", *The Straits Times*, 30 August 1967.
[56] "Security Corps guards vital plants", *The Straits Times*, 15 April 1964.
[57] *Vigilante Corps Bill*, Section 7 (1).
[58] "Vigilante Corps takes on new role in Singapore", *The Straits Times*, 22 February 1970.
[59] Ibid.
[60] Ibid.

This would gradually change. In 1971 the VC would formally take on a civil defence role, and in 1974, proper policing duties.[61] Thereafter, the VC would provide a vast body of manpower for general policing or other duties associated with domestic security. Together with the SC, they were to be the "boots on the ground" in domestic security where numbers mattered more than in depth specialist training. Under SPF command, the SC and VC would play an important role when crime rates began to soar with increased urban development in Singapore as more public housing estates were set up. In 1974, with the regular police force stretched, the SC was deployed more intensively to support it, providing manpower the equivalent of 400 extra regular policemen.[62] Concurrently, the VC's Community Security Force launched that year allowed for more frequent anti-crime patrols.[63] The generality in their duties suited the brevity of part-time national service training and deployments. Less time was needed to train national servicemen for general policing duties, and they could be deployed in shifts matching their national service obligations. The almost 15 years of part-time national service in the SC and VC, and their visible contributions to community policing, raised the profile of national service outside the SAF. This was not plain sailing. Aspersions over the ill-discipline, the dubious character of some in its ranks and their ineffectiveness were regularly cast.[64] Reassurances that the benefit of both schemes outweighed the trouble the black sheep in their ranks caused were repeatedly given in the 1970s.[65] The standing of national service outside the SAF consequently would improve slowly, but surely,

---

[61] "VC's vital role", *The Straits Times*, 5 November 1973.

[62] "Gov't acts to help the police", *New Nation*, 1 December 1974.

[63] "VC's vital role", *The Straits Times*, 5 November 1973.

[64] See, for example, the discussion of the ill-discipline of the VC and in Parliament. *Hansard Singapore Parliamentary Debates,* Parl. No. 3, Session No. 2, Vol. No. 35, Sitting No. 7, Sitting Date 22/3/1976, "Budget, Ministry of Home Affairs"; and "The 'bad' SC influence", *New Nation*, 23 April 1976.

[65] See, for example, *Hansard Singapore Parliamentary Debates,* Parl. No. 2, Session No. 1, Vol. No. 16, Sitting No. 5, Sitting Date 24/3/1971, "Budget, Ministry of Home Affairs", Column 1234; and Minister for Home Affairs and Education Chua Sian Chin's illustration of the effectiveness of SC and VC community patrols. *Hansard Singapore Parliamentary Debates,* Parl. No. 4, Session No. 1, Vol. No. 37, Sitting No. 12, Sitting Date 17/3/1978, "Budget, Ministry of Home Affairs", Column 113.

encouraged by an equally gradual broadening of how national security was understood.

Implementing a Broader Understanding of National Security and the Expansion of National Service in the Home Team

Today, the importance of national service in the Home Team is closely associated with the "civil" pillar of Singapore's Total Defence strategy. The strategy, however, was only officially introduced in 1984. Under it, national security, and therefore defence, is understood in five areas — military, civil, economic, social, and psychological. Up to that point, the SAF was still assumed to be the dominant pillar of Singapore's defence. As the previous section describes, NS was still closely associated with building up the SAF. It commanded most resources and drove NS policy. In 1985, then Minister for Defence Goh Chok Tong explained the comprehensive national security strategy of Total Defence was only introduced then because the government had to first spend "many years to educate the general public concerning military defence," particularly national service in the SAF.[66]

Be that as it may, a broader notion of "national defence" which transcended the military had always existed. In contrast to the UK's NS legislation, Singapore's version did include service in the police and civil defence forces, and not just the military. It was just typically backgrounded in public discourse with the foregrounding of the importance of military defence. Yet while the parliamentary debate on the National Service (Amendment) Bill in 1967 was predominantly focused on how NS could raise a credible military force to protect Singapore's sovereignty, how "security" was presented during the debate on the Vigilante Corps Bill held just half a year later was more nuanced. The importance of "law and order", "public security", "racial harmony" and "resilience", terms all closely associated with what would be eventually identified as elements of Total Defence, was highlighted. MP Teong Eng Siong observed members of the VC would, "after strict semi-military training … become the pillars of our

---

[66] *Hansard Singapore Parliamentary Debates,* Parl. No. 5, Session No. 1, Vol. No. 43, Sitting No. 10, Sitting Date 16/3/1984, "Budget, Ministry of Defence", Column 1118.

rugged society and become model citizens of our multi-racial society ...
[They should] also be inculcated with a spirit of patriotism and loyalty to
our country."[67] "The [VC] organisation," he continued, "can be further ...
strengthened ... making it more effective in the preservation of our social
order and in carrying out their task in serving the country and protecting
the lives and property of [Singaporeans]."[68]

MP Ang summarised Total Defence more than 15 years before it was
unveiled. He first spoke of "economic defence". "All those people who are
concerned with security and who pay attention to current affairs," Ang
noted, "will agree with me that the economy of a nation is a basic factor in
contributing towards its stability. Our people work very hard in contributing towards Singapore's economic stability."[69] He then acknowledged the
importance of organising for "military defence".[70] Finally, he alluded to
"civil", "psychological" and "social defence" when he described the establishment of the VC as a means to "preserve order in [Singapore]" and
"smash up the intrigues of our enemies who wished to disrupt our social
order and, at the same time, to unite our people so that the various races in
Singapore could understand the importance of racial harmony in the
State."[71] Curiously, Teong and Ang had spoken of NS in largely military
terms during the earlier National Service (Amendment) Bill debate. Yet
their passionate speeches illustrated how the value of national service outside the SAF to Singapore's security could also be quickly identified and
acknowledged if the focus of the discussion shifted there.

Shifts in policy direction, however, could not happen as quickly. While
a broader idea of "national security" and consequently the importance of
national service outside the military had been easily acknowledged in
public discourse, actual changes on the ground reflecting this could only
happen gradually. Goh Chok Tong's explanation of why Total Defence
was only unveiled in the 1980s is particularly instructive. Priority was
given to military defence even though the principles of a broader approach

---

[67] *Hansard Singapore Parliamentary Debates,* Parl. No. 1, Session No. 1, Vol. No. 26,
Sitting No. 3, Sitting Date 8/9/1967, "Vigilante Corps Bill", Column 219.
[68] Ibid., Column 220.
[69] Ibid., Column 222.
[70] Ibid., Column 223.
[71] Ibid.

to national defence had long been recognised. The expansion of national service outside the SAF would therefore also happen incrementally.

A key milestone was the introduction of full-time national service in the SPF. This was crucial to the elevation of the standing of national servicemen there. Part-time national service would invariably always be viewed as less significant than full-time service. When the Enlistment Act came into force in 1971, full-time national service became the norm in the SAF. Full-time national service in the SPF, however, was only introduced in 1975, and with a much smaller pioneer batch of 200.[72] The rationale for introducing full-time national service in the SPF was entirely practical. The crime rate in the preceding five years had risen yet there was a shortage of police manpower.[73] Domestic law and order was threatened and enlisting full-time national service policemen to remedy this was a "direct response" to this.[74] The national security implications of not addressing rising crime rates were wide-ranging. Socially and psychologically, high crime made Singaporeans feel insecure in their own homes and affected the fabric of Singapore society. Economically, the presentation of Singapore as an attractive stable country worth investing in because the rule of law was effectively enforced would be undermined. The SPF particularly needed manpower to combat crime during the day in high-rise public housing estates through a "vertical policing" strategy of having officers patrol all floors and lift lobbies of high-rise buildings. Regular officers could not be released for such duty as they had other responsibilities. Moreover, part-time national servicemen were only able to serve at night. Full-time national servicemen were therefore the solution to securing neighbourhoods by providing much needed manpower.[75] The hijacking of the *Laju* ferry and attempted terrorist bombings by the Japanese Red Army and Popular Front for the Liberation of Palestine in 1974 also prompted the enlargement of the SPF for internal security duties.[76] Without the time constraints imposed by part-time service, full-time

---

[72] Koh, *Everyday Guardians*, 10.

[73] "NS in the police for now", *New Nation*, 18 July 1975.

[74] Ibid.

[75] "Police — NS men for HDB estates", *The Straits Times*, 21 July 1975.

[76] John Drysdale, *In the Service of the Nation* (Singapore: Federal Publications (S) Pte Ltd, 1985), 46.

national servicemen could be more broadly trained and therefore deployed in more roles. They would also continue to serve short full-time stints in the police reserves thereafter as part of their "in-camp training". In 1981, part-time national service in the SPF ended.[77] National service in the SPF would thereafter comprise an initial period of full-time service followed by several years in the reserves, similar to the SAF. Today, national service Special Constables in the SPF serve in 11 vocations alongside their regular counterparts in leadership, specialist and front-line roles.[78]

The introduction of national service in the SCDF was more complicated than in the SPF. To begin with, unlike the SPF and SAF which were formed at independence, the present SCDF is far younger. The evolution of the concept and administration of "civil defence" underwent several iterations that straddled several police and civil defence organisations. While the SPF and SCDF are today complementary but independent services under the Home Team, the structural and command clarity in the division of labour only emerged with the establishment of the independent SCDF. The merging of the Singapore Fire Service (SFS) with the SCDF into the Singapore Joint Civil Defence Force in 1989 finally consolidated all civil defence forces into a single entity. It reverted to the SCDF in 1992. Up till then, national service in a non-policing civil defence role could be served in the VC (1971–1981), the Singapore Fire Brigade (1976–1980), its successor the SFS (1980–1989) or with the end of part-time national service in the VC, the SPF's Civil Defence Command (CDC, 1981–1986) and the first iteration of the independent SCDF (1986–1989).

Although the importance of civil defence was recognised early on, there was ambiguity in how exactly it should be organised, and how national servicemen should be deployed for it. In the early years, national servicemen serving a civil defence role came from the VC. In 1971 it was announced part-time national servicemen would serve in the VC in three phases — an initial four years of policing duties, four years in civil defence and a final four years in the reserves.[79] Those in the civil defence phase would be posted to the Civil Defence Organisation (CDO) and not

---

[77] "End of SC and Vigilante Corps no surprise", *The Straits Times*, 9 September 1981.

[78] Koh, *Everyday Guardians*, 6.

[79] *Hansard Singapore Parliamentary Debates,* Parl. No. 2, Session No. 2, Vol. No. 31, Sitting No. 1, Sitting Date 21/7/1971, "Addenda, Ministry of Home Affairs", Column 44.

deployed in specific front-line roles. This partly stemmed from how the VC was constituted. Whereas the tasks of the specific policing role of the VC was clearly spelt out in the Vigilante Corps Act, its civil defence function fell under the ambiguous catch-all clause of performing "such other functions and duties as may be assigned to the Corps by the Minister."[80] While policing could be intuitively understood and grasped, civil defence, non-specifically defined as non-combat "measures" to protect the safety of the public in times of national emergency, was on the other hand comparatively abstract.[81] A contemporary newspaper report wondered where the CDO, "Singapore's largest-ever civil defence organisation", would "fit into the present police–military set up?"[82]

The VC civil defence phase included general training in "fire fighting, rescue techniques, mechanical aids, first aid and other training relevant to civil defence." VC members would thereafter serve as "wardens" in times of crisis.[83] The Auxiliary Fire Service scheme was launched in 1972 to train selected members of the VC in firefighting specifically to equip them with a more specific civil defence skillset.[84] When part-time national service was phased out in 1981, the majority of part-time national servicemen ended their tours in a civil defence role.[85] The enlistment of full-time national servicemen for civil defence began earnestly, with an initial plan to enlist 100 into the SFB over two years beginning in 1978.[86] National service firefighters, however, would play only supporting roles for their regular counterparts up till the late 1980s.[87] Training in specific civil defence roles would only be extended to more national servicemen with the introduction of the National Civil Defence Plan in 1982. The detailed plan was premised on

---

[80] *Vigilante Corps Bill*, Section 5(a) & 5(b).

[81] Both the 1951 Civil Defence Ordinance and 1986 Civil Defence Act defined "civil defence" similarly.

[82] "Home guards? But where to fit them in the present set-up", *New Nation*, 26 February 1971.

[83] *Hansard Singapore Parliamentary Debates*, Parl. No. 2, Session No. 2, Vol. No. 31, Sitting No. 1, Sitting Date 21/7/1971, "Addenda, Ministry of Home Affairs", Column 44.

[84] Koh, *Everyday Guardians*, 28.

[85] National Library Board Singapore (NLB), "Vigilante Corps", http://eresources.nlb.gov.sg/infopedia/articles/SIP_2016-03-29_151550.html (accessed 5 April 2018).

[86] "First batch of full-time NS men for fire service", *The Straits Times*, 22 January 1976.

[87] Koh, *Everyday Guardians*, 31.

developing civil defence capabilities for the worst-case scenario of war in Singapore.[88] The plan explicitly identified the CDC as being complementary to the SAF in protecting Singapore's national security, elevating the importance of the national servicemen who served in civil defence.[89] National servicemen in Civilian Co-ordination Units would liaise with community volunteers to coordinate civil defence activities in times of crisis. More significantly, the Emergency Response Groups would comprise national servicemen trained in urban rescue and emergency re-construction. The latter came mainly from the Construction Brigade of full-time national servicemen trained in construction and the operation of heavy machinery. Up to 2,000 national servicemen were enlisted into it annually making it one of the most "active" full-time national service vocations in civil defence.[90] Even with this sharpened clarity on what civil defence entailed conceptually and operationally, a single independent civil defence entity, the SCDF was not formed till four years later in 1986 with the passing of the Civil Defence Act. The large number of national servicemen involved in civil defence, including the intended transfer of over 30,000 reservists from the SAF to the SCDF, necessitated the creation of a single civil defence force and the enactment of accompanying legislation to manage them.[91] The integration and administration of different civil defence functions undertaken by national servicemen from different organisations would take time to be streamlined. In 1988 and 1989, then Senior Minister of State for Home Affairs Lee Boon Yang outlined the breadth of civil defence responsibilities that the newly independent SCDF had to design training packages for, as

---

[88] Koh, *Everyday Guardians*, 32.

[89] *Civil Defence Handbook* (Singapore: Singapore Police Force, 1982), 6.

[90] Koh, *Everyday Guardians*, 33. The Construction Brigade is also an example of how national defence resources could be used for national development purposes. National servicemen serving in the Brigade spent much of their training on construction jobsites, could have competency in their construction skills certified and find employment in the construction industry after their national service. They would provide the skilled labour required during the construction boom of the 1980s fuelled by the rapid construction of public housing. See Tan Feng Qin, "The Security Sector in Singapore: Contributions and Challenges", *The Brenthurst Foundation Discussion Paper 3/2017* (Johannesburg: E Oppenheimer & Son (Pty) Ltd, 2017), 12–14.

[91] *Hansard Singapore Parliamentary Debates*, Parl. No. 6, Session No. 2, Vol. No. 48, Sitting No. 7, Sitting Date 22/9/1986, "Civil Defence Bill", Columns 722–726.

well as the challenge of integrating the SFS with the SCDF.[92] Parliamentarians were concerned over the progress being made given the breadth of integration required. These teething problems and the late start as an independent unified organisation meant that the expansion in the roles of civil defence national servicemen could play would come later than in the SPF or SAF. The SCDF did, however, catch up. SCDF national servicemen presently serve alongside regulars in 11 vocations, the same as the SPF.[93]

Conclusion

This chapter has offered an early history of national service outside the SAF. When NS was first introduced in independent Singapore in 1967, a coherent 'whole-of-government' approach to defending Singapore did not exist to the extent it does now. Although a wider notion of national defence had been publicly acknowledged, NS was still widely associated with the military despite the fact significant numbers of national servicemen actually served part-time outside the SAF. Greater recognition only began when day-to-day police manpower needs increased from the mid-1970s and national servicemen began to be deployed for front-line policing roles. A broader national defence strategy, culminating in the concept of Total Defence launched in in the early 1980s, also began to develop then. At the same time, an operational National Civil Defence Plan organised national servicemen who had hitherto played loosely defined civil defence roles into specific units with clear tasks defined. These developments collectively resulted in the wider deployment of national servicemen outside the SAF to the extent seen today. Their importance to Singapore's peace and security has been duly recognised by the government.

Yet the legacy of national service as being military service may still linger in the public's consciousness. *Straits Times* Journalist Fabian Koh, who serves his national service in the SPF, laments:

---

[92] *Hansard Singapore Parliamentary Debates*, Parl. No. 6, Session No. 2, Vol. No. 50, Sitting No. 16, Sitting Date 23/3/1988, "Budget, Ministry of Home Affairs", Column 1285; and Parl. No. 7, Session No. 1, Vol. No. 53, Sitting No. 11, Sitting Date 27/3/1989, "Budget, Ministry of Home Affairs", Column 888.

[93] The list of the 11 national service vocations in the SCDF can be found behind the cover of *Everyday Guardians*.

When most Singaporeans think of national service (NS), they see the colour green. Green for the uniforms won by soldiers. Green for their trucks and tanks. Green for the paint they streak across their faces. Me? I see green too — for the colour of envy. You see, I serve my NS in the Singapore Police Force … But I feel left out when all the talk on NS seems to focus only on the familiar military arm as that leaves me out of the NS narrative … My NS experience is as legitimate as any other Singaporean son's.[94]

An online post by another full-time national serviceman in the SCDF also eloquently even if colloquially encapsulates this sentiment:

I wish the public knew the risks that some [full-time national servicemen in the Home Team] take each day. We might not be as fit as the [Naval Diving Unit] or as garang [daring] as commandos, but we put our lives on the line literally every day.

As a [full-time national serviceman] I can say I have contributed to Singapore. No play acting or training for a war that will never happen (though I understand the incredible need for an armed military). I love my job, I love NS and wouldn't trade it for anything else (maybe an [Emergency Medical Technician] vocation).

*I am still amazed that many members of public still associate NS with the army. I wish more people would know … Take a look at every fire or major rescue/ambulance incident in the news. **Chances are 70% of the people that responded to that incident are [full-time national servicemen].** Whenever I get my haircut … the [hair-dresser] always asks me "boy you army ah?" and I've run out of effort to correct her.[95]*

The author received much support for his observations. He subsequently clarified the intention of his post was not to "bash [disparage] the SAF" but "to raise awareness for the often overlooked and under-praised

---

[94] "We serve too, but in blue", *The Straits Times*, 3 June 2018.
[95] Reddit member "longtailbutterfly", "A Rant on National Service from an NSF", *Reddit: self.singapore*, https://www.reddit.com/r/singapore/comments/4iexp5/a_rant_on_national_service_from_an_nsf/ (Last accessed 5/4/2018).

'little brother' [full-time national servicemen] in SCDF/SPF. So many of our kind deserve recognition for what they deal with."[96]

Despite the great strides made over the years in elevating national service in the Home Team and securing its due recognition in official discourse, closing this perception gap in the general public is seemingly one challenge that still remains.

---

[96] Ibid.

Part 2
NS in Practice

Chapter 4

Conscripting the Audience: Singapore's Successful Securitisation of Vulnerability

Chang Jun Yan[1]

Contours of the Chapter: Introduction

When the first-ever independent study on Singaporeans' perception of Singapore's National Service (NS) was conducted by the Institute of Policy Studies[2] (IPS), *The New Paper*, a Singaporean tabloid, ran a headline titled "Results So Positive, They Had to Relook NS Study".[3] The news article highlighted how the extent of the support for NS amongst those surveyed took even the researchers themselves by surprise. This chapter examines the puzzle of this "surprising" support for NS through the lens of Copenhagen School securitisation theory. Copenhagen School securitisation, which analyses how issues become a matter of security, is most apt here as it is able to examine how the vulnerability Singapore

[1] I am grateful to Dr Alan Chong, Angela M. Y. Poh and Ho Shu Huang for their comments on earlier drafts of this chapter. Thanks also to Lee Xiao Wen for her help in proofreading. Any errors remain solely my own.
[2] Leong Chan-Hoong, Yang Wai Wai, and Henry Ho, "Singaporeans' Attitudes to National Service" (Singapore: Lee Kuan Yew School of Public Policy, 2013). The Institute of Policy Studies is part of the Lee Kuan Yew School of Public Policy (LKYSPP), National University of Singapore (NUS).
[3] Foo Jie Ying, "Results so positive, they had to relook NS study", *The New Paper*, 9 October 2013.

faced upon independence in 1965 became a security issue which necessitated the establishment of NS. I contend that the strong support for conscription is due to the securitisation of vulnerability by the Singapore policy elites. This was successful because the audience (the citizens of Singapore) of the securitising move was itself co-opted and mobilised by the policy of National Service. Even though females do not serve NS, they are still part of the social institution of NS. This success of the securitisation of vulnerability is subsequently further demonstrated by the entrenchment of the discourse of vulnerability in Singapore, something which permeates all aspects of society.

There have been very few treatments of NS in the literature — and hence the impetus for this edited volume — partly because of the lack of public information. Case in point, this study originally started as a chapter on the crewing of warships in the Republic of Singapore Navy (RSN) by Operationally-Ready NSmen,[4] but I had to change the topic eventually since I was denied access to information. Nevertheless, there have been some studies variously examining the need for NS, or its impact on society, or the effectiveness of NS.[5] My treatment of NS here is novel, however, in that it analyses conscription as a function of the securitisation of vulnerability — making vulnerability itself a security issue — as well as the success of this securitisation thereafter. Previous studies have simply taken vulnerability and securitisation for granted.[6] In so doing, I examine the links between conscription and vulnerability in Singapore, as well as consequent inductive insights for Copenhagen School securitisation theory. Towards these ends, this chapter is divided into three main sections. The first explicates Copenhagen School securitisation in order to give

---

[4] See: Jermyn Chow, "NSmen fill every post on some warships", *The Straits Times*, 8 May 2015.

[5] For instance, Chan Ching Hao, "The Citizen-Soldier in Modern Democracies: The Case for Conscription in Singapore", *Pointer* 39/1 (2013), 42–50; Derek da Cunha, "Sociological Aspects of the Singapore Armed Forces", *Armed Forces and Society* 25/3 (1999), 459–475; Elizabeth Nair, "Conscription and Nation-Building in Singapore: A Psychological Analysis", *Journal of Human Values* 1/1 (1995), 93–102.

[6] See for instance, Norman Vasu and Bernard Loo, "National Security and Singapore: An Assessment", in *Perspectives on the Security of Singapore*, eds. Barry Desker and Ang Cheng Guan (Singapore: World Scientific, 2016), 21–43.

background to the argument of this chapter. The second briefly examines the historical context of Singapore's vulnerability. The third part illustrates how said vulnerability was subsequently securitised, and with the establishment of NS as an exceptional measure to safeguard against vulnerability, goes on to demonstrate the success of such securitisation before the chapter is concluded.

Copenhagen School Securitisation

The Copenhagen School, a loose grouping of scholars centred upon the old Centre for Peace and Conflict Research established in 1985,[7] theorised the concept of "securitisation". Securitisation is "a move that takes politics beyond the established rules of the game and frames the issue either as a special kind of politics or as above politics"; securitisation is political, but is "a more extreme version of politicization."[8] Any issue could potentially be placed on a "spectrum of securitisation"; ranging from non-politicisation/ non-securitisation, a non-issue that need not be dealt with at one end; to varying stages of politicisation along the spectrum, a political issue to which resources need to be devoted; to the other end of securitisation, "meaning that the issue is presented as an *existential* threat, requiring *emergency* measures and *justifying* actions outside the *normal* bounds of political procedure."[9]

Copenhagen School securitisation thus examines how security is constructed, and can therefore be used as an analytical tool to investigate how vulnerability was formed as a security issue in Singapore. It takes the "process of securitisation" as a "speech act" in which "the utterance itself is the act"[10] — labelling an issue as security and acting upon it thereafter causes it to *become* a security issue. Securitisation has six crucial components: (1) the existential threat, (2) the referent object, to which the existential threat applies, (3) the securitising speech act, (4) the securitising actor which applies the

---

[7] See: Jef Huysmans, "Revisiting Copenhagen: Or, On the Creative Development of a Security Studies Agenda in Europe", *European Journal of International Relations* 4/4 (1998), 479–505.

[8] Barry Buzan, Ole Wæver, and Jaap de Wilde, *Security: A New Framework for Analysis* (Boulder, Colorado: Lynne Rienner, 1998), p. 23.

[9] Buzan, Wæver, and de Wilde, *Security*, 23–24; emphasis added.

[10] Buzan, Wæver, and de Wilde, *Security*, 26.

speech act, (5) the audience for whom the speech act is uttered, and (6) the required security practices, the practical measures, which are often extreme or exceptional in order to deal with the emergency of the existential threat.

Given the social constructivist bent of securitisation, the question which follows is "what determines the success of securitisation?" This question sparked the first key debate in securitisation theory: between the traditional first-generation Copenhagen School scholars maintaining that securitisation is self-referential, whereby branding an issue a matter of security causes it to actually become a security issue; and the second-generation securitisation scholars viewing securitisation as intersubjective, dependent upon the context of the securitising move, in particular the receptivity of the audience.[11] Two approaches to this key debate have been formulated. The first, in the tradition of the classical scholars, proposed that securitisation be judged upon the actions of security practitioners and actors rather than a "sanctioning audience" as "there simply is no conclusive relationship between audience acceptance and the 'success' of securitization"; securitisation would be successful thus if it follows the logic of an identification of a threat, a securitising move (the illocutionary speech act), and a consequent action of security practice in response.[12] The second, in the mould of second-generation securitisation scholarship, emphasises the audience, conceiving of successful securitisation as involving two distinct parts: the first "stage of identification", using the rhetoric of security to frame the issue in order to get audience buy-in to the narrative of the existential threat; whilst a further second "stage of mobilisation" additionally seeks the audience's support and acceptance of the exceptional measures enacted in response to the threat.[13] If only one stage is fulfilled, then securitisation is only partly successful.

---

[11] See: Thierry Balzacq, "The Three Faces of Securitization: Political Agency, Audience and Context", *European Journal of International Relations* 11/2 (2005), 171–201; Holger Stritzel, "Towards a Theory of Securitization: Copenhagen and Beyond", *European Journal of International Relations* 13/3 (2007), 357–383.

[12] Rita Floyd, "Extraordinary or Ordinary Emergency Measures: What, and Who, Defines the 'Success' of Securitization?", *Cambridge Review of International Affairs* 29/2 (2015), 679 and 691, emphasis removed.

[13] Paul Roe, "Actor, Audience(s) and Emergency Measures: Securitization and the UK's Decision to Invade Iraq", *Security Dialogue* 39/6 (2008), 615–635.

One brief example serves to highlight securitisation and its success (or lack thereof). As this is being written, crime is being securitised in the Philippines under new President Rodrigo "The Punisher" Duterte. His "war on crime" has dominated headlines throughout the world. Duterte, the securitising actor, deems crime, in particular drugs, as an existential threat to the referent object of Philippine society, claiming that the "sons of whores [drug traffickers] are destroying our children," so people should "kill them yourself as getting their parents to do it would be too painful."[14] Exceptional measures invoked consequently included vigilantism (Duterte promised medals), urging "Congress to restore the death penalty by hanging", and extrajudicial killings, with 465 recorded drug-related killings by 1 August 2016 since Duterte assumed office on 30 June 2016.[15] The audience in this case is the Philippine population and this "sense of security" resulted in his "landslide" victory, as Duterte explained in a speech.[16] Duterte's securitisation of crime and drugs in the Philippines is thus successful, ticking all the boxes in the two approaches highlighted earlier. The audience was persuaded and mobilised, electing him to the Presidency. Furthermore, a section of the audience even took up his call to conduct extrajudicial killings.

I contend in this chapter that when the audience is co-opted and furthermore *fully mobilised* as part of an exceptional security practice enacted as a response to the existential threat enunciated in the securitising move, securitisation becomes exceptionally successful. This argument is subsequently demonstrated in the following case study of Singapore and National Service.

Concerning Singapore's Vulnerability

This section briefly examines the objective and subjective conditions of Singapore's vulnerability. Oxford Dictionaries defines "vulnerability" as

---

[14] Quoted in "New Philippine President Duterte vows deadly crime war", *Channel NewsAsia*, 1 July 2016.

[15] Euan McKirdy, "Philippines' Rodrigo Duterte: Public 'can kill' criminals", *CNN*, 6 June 2016; Tiffany Ap, "Philippines' Duterte: I'll bring back the death penalty", *CNN*, 16 May 2016; Euan McKirdy, "Dead or alive: Is The Philippines' war on drugs out of control?" *CNN*, 4 August 2016.

[16] Quoted in McKirdy, "Dead or alive".

the "quality or state of being exposed to the possibility of being attacked or harmed."[17] The concept of "vulnerability" is thus often linked to the concept of "small states" because in the assumed anarchical international system with no overarching authority,[18] small states are deigned to be more susceptible to the possibility of being attacked or harmed in relation to its survival and security.[19] Christopher Easter further specified that "vulnerability" refers to the state's "exposure to economic, environmental, political and social shocks, over which they have little, if any, control."[20] Singapore's vulnerability, both internal and external, can be cast in these four categories.

In terms of the economy, Singapore has a small domestic market. It imports most of its necessities since it lacks natural resources, with the common refrain being: "the only natural resource Singapore has is its citizens." Despite this, Singapore's geostrategic location at the crossroads between the Indian and Pacific oceans is a significant economic advantage. Historically, Singapore prospered as "a trading and business centre of Southeast Asia possessing the deepest harbour and dock facilities within a thousand-mile radius", enabling successful entrepôt trade. Today, Singapore "is a major financial and banking centre" which "depends on world trade for its economic viability and buoyancy."[21] Singapore's "open" nature therefore makes it highly susceptible to international and regional economic shocks and changes, similar to other small states. It was the "first East Asian country to fall into a recession" from the Global Financial Crisis of 2008, reflecting "the greater

---

[17] Oxford Dictionaries, http://www.oxforddictionaries.com/ (accessed 1 September 2016).
[18] See for instance, Karen A. Mingst, *Essentials of International Relations*, Second ed. (New York: W. W. Norton & Company, 2003).
[19] For small states and vulnerability, see for instance, Commonwealth Secretariat, *A Future for Small States: Overcoming Vulnerability* (London: Commonwealth Secretariat, 1997); Andrew F. Cooper and Timothy M. Shaw, eds., *The Diplomacies of Small States: Between Vulnerability and Resilience* (Houndsmill, Basingstoke: Palgrave Macmillan, 2009); Bilveer Singh, *The Vulnerability of Small States Revisited: A Study of Singapore's Post-Cold War Foreign Policy* (Yogyakarta: Gadjah Mada University Press, 1999).
[20] Christopher Easter, "Small States Development: A Commonwealth Vulnerability Index", *The Round Table: The Commonwealth Journal of International Affairs* 88/351 (1999), 403.
[21] Singh, *The Vulnerability of Small States Revisited*, 15–21.

vulnerability of the Singapore economy to global economic shocks."[22] Furthermore, in order to attract foreign trade and investment, Singapore needs stability and security, be it against military invasion, terrorism or criminal activities.[23]

With regard to the environment, unlike other small states which are "situated in regions which are highly susceptible to natural disasters,"[24] Singapore's geographical location at the tip of peninsula Malaysia gives it a measure of shelter against natural disasters such as typhoons or earthquakes. However, it is not entirely safe, especially from the rising threat of climate change. Singapore's economy and security could also be threatened indirectly by natural disasters upon neighbouring states. For example, flooding in Bangkok increased the prices of rice sold in Singapore.[25] Perhaps the greatest geostrategic disadvantage is Singapore's small size. At about 700 square kilometres, the island state lacks any sort of strategic depth, "the ability to trade space for time if necessary, especially so if the state is caught by strategic surprise."[26] Furthermore, as Tim Huxley put it, "Singapore's population and its civilian and military infrastructure are necessarily highly concentrated and thus vulnerable to physical attack, further weakening Singapore's overall strategic position."[27]

---

[22] Shandre M. Thangavelu, "Riding the Global Economic Crisis in Singapore", *East Asian Bureau of Economic Research Newsletter*, January 2009.

[23] See: Singapore Ministry of Defence, *Defending Singapore in the 21st Century* (Singapore: Ministry of Defence, 2000), 16–25; Singapore Ministry of Foreign Affairs, "Remarks by Minister for Foreign Affairs K Shanmugam, Second Minister for Foreign Affairs Grace Fu, and Senior Minister of State for Foreign Affairs Masagos Zulkifli in Parliament during the Committee of Supply Debate on 5 March 2015", 2015, https://www.mfa.gov.sg/content/mfa/overseasmission/geneva/press_statements_speeches/2015/201503/press_20150305.html (accessed 5 June 2018).

[24] Easter, "Small States Development", 405.

[25] Karen W. Lim, "Singapore not safe from natural disasters: Scientist," *AsiaOne*, 28 February 2012.

[26] Bernard Fook Weng Loo, "Explaining Changes in Singapore's Military Doctrines: Material and Ideational Perspectives", in *Asia in the New Millennium*, eds. Amitav Acharya and Lee Lai To (Singapore: Marshall Cavendish, 2004), p. 363.

[27] Tim Huxley, *Defending the Lion City: The Armed Forces of Singapore* (St Leonards, Australia: Allen & Unwin, 2000), 32; see also, Derek da Cunha, ed., "Defence and Security: Evolving Threat Perceptions", in *Singapore in the New Millennium: Challenges Facing the City-State* (Singapore: Institute of Southeast Asian Studies, 2002), 148.

Political vulnerability is an amalgamation of the geopolitical position of the island state as well as its size. Small states, whether defined in terms of physical size, population size, economic size, power, or such other measures,[28] are generally deemed to be politically vulnerable as their sovereignty could more easily be challenged by larger neighbours due to the size disparity. Sandwiched by Malaysia and Indonesia, Singapore is "wedged between the sea and airspace of two larger neighbours with which Singapore has *never been politically at ease*."[29] These maritime and air borders continue to be sensitive and difficult issues. For instance, maritime borders in the eastern part of the Singapore Strait (SS) were only agreed upon between Singapore and Indonesia in 2014; Singapore and Malaysia have yet to agree upon maritime boundaries around Pedra Branca, Middle Rocks and South Ledge, a territorial dispute between these two littoral states settled by the International Court of Justice (ICJ) in 2008; and the control and use of the airspace above the Indonesian Riau islands continue to be a source of conflict as well.[30]

Last but not least, Singapore's society is vulnerable to social shocks. Not only does the island state have a small population, the ethnic make-up of this resident population, the majority ethnically Chinese (74%) with sizeable Malay (13%) and Indian (9%) minorities in 2014,[31] makes for the basis of what J. S. Furnivall called a "plural society" — "a society in which distinct social orders live side by side, but separately, within the same political unit" — one which would be unstable and conflict-prone.[32] In addition, this predominantly ethnic Chinese composition is unique to the region. The state's two closest neighbours are primarily Muslim, Indonesia at 87.2% and

---

[28] Matthias Maass, "The Elusive Definition of the Small State", *International Politics* 46/1 (2009), 65–83.

[29] Michael Leifer, *Singapore's Foreign Policy: Coping with Vulnerability* (London: Routledge, 2000), 1; emphasis added.

[30] Zakir Hussain, "Singapore, Indonesia sign treaty on maritime borders in Eastern Singapore Strait," *The Straits Times*, 3 September 2014; Francis Chan and Wahyudi Soeriaatmadja, "Singapore 'respects Indonesia's sovereignty'", *The Straits Times*, 30 September 2015.

[31] Cited in Ho Shu Huang and Samuel Chan, *Singapore Chronicles: Defence* (Singapore: Institute of Policy Studies and Straits Times Press Pte Ltd, 2015), 29.

[32] See J. S. Furnivall, *Netherlands India: A Study of Plural Economy* (Cambridge: Cambridge University Press, 1939; repr., 1967), xv.

Malaysia at 61.3% in 2010.[33] Such a picture of regional ethnic and religious difference, and hence insecurity, has been captured by the oft-heard phrases: "a Chinese nut in a Malay nutcracker" or "a little red dot amidst a sea of green". The latter was a comment made in 1998 by B. J. Habibie, then-President of Indonesia, in an interview with *The Wall Street Journal* where he singled out Singapore for its tardiness in sending him a congratulatory letter when he assumed office.[34]

Nonetheless, these objective conditions for vulnerability form only a part of the equation as to whether such vulnerabilities create problems thereafter. In this, there are two other important factors. The first is the subjective conditions of vulnerability, or the threat perception, especially as perceived by the elites deciding policy. This is arguably more vital to this study of the securitisation of Singapore's vulnerability as the objective conditions by themselves do not guarantee instability. Rather, these are only the "operating environment", and any perceived insecurity is also informed by the "psychological environment" of the policy maker, which consists of "ideas derived from his perception of conditions and events interpreted in the light of his conscious memories and subconsciously stored knowledge," and which together with the "heredity" (genetic) of the individual, informs all human activities.[35]

What might affect the psychological environment of Singapore's policy makers, or what are the subjective conditions of vulnerability? Whilst this chapter does not seek to examine in depth the psychological environment of Singapore's first generation of leaders who shaped the policies of the newly independent state, the important factors in this calculation are arguably Singapore's history and the experiences of these policy makers with the past.[36] Significant historical events include British colonial policies

---

[33] Cited in Chang Jun Yan, "Essence of Security Communities: Explaining ASEAN", *International Relations of the Asia-Pacific* 16/3 (2016), 346.

[34] Richard Borsuk and Reginald Chua, "Singapore strains relations with Indonesia's President", *The Wall Street Journal*, 4 August 1998.

[35] For more on "heredity", "operating environment" and "psychological environment", see: Harold Sprout and Magaret Sprout, *Foundations of International Politics* (New York: D. Van Nostrand Company, 1962), 44–58.

[36] For more on Singapore's history, see: Ernest C. T. Chew and Edwin Lee, eds., *A History of Singapore* (Singapore: Oxford University Press, 1991); Kwa Chong Guan, Derek Heng

such as encouraging immigration to meet labour demands yet managing different ethnic communities through "divide-and-rule", generating separate ethnic enclaves and consequently a plural society; the brutal Japanese Occupation between 1942–1945 due to the failure of the British in defending Singapore as the British priority then was the defence of its own homeland, the British Isles[37]; the long-running Malayan Emergency against the communists (1948–1960), *Konfrontasi* (Confrontation) against Indonesia (1963–1966), as well as communal tensions emblematised by the Maria Hertogh riots of 1950 and race riots of 1964 and 1969 and the difficult merger followed by a painful separation with Malaysia leading to independence being thrust upon the city-state in 1965. All these episodes taught enduring lessons to Singapore's first generation of leaders. These lessons are further reiterated to subsequent generations through the government's policy of national education (NE), which consists of five key messages: (1) "Singapore is our homeland"; (2) "Singapore is worth defending" because of "our heritage and our way of life," of which a pillar is the multiethnic character of its society; (3) "Singapore can be defended," despite its vulnerabilities; (4) "We must ourselves defend Singapore" since "[n]o one else is responsible for our security"; and (5) "We can deter others from attacking us."[38]

The second important factor is the other side of the vulnerability coin: "resilience", the "ability of a country to resist the impact of shocks and to recover from their consequences."[39] In this regard, the Commonwealth Vulnerability Index (CVI), which takes into account both vulnerability and resilience through measuring 30 variables "representing the economic features, remoteness and susceptibility to natural disasters" of a state in an

---

and Tan Tai Yong, *Singapore: A 700-Year History, From Early Emporium to World City* (Singapore: National Archives of Singapore, 2009).

[37] For a detailed analysis, see: S. Woodburn Kirby, *Singapore: The Chain of Disaster*, Foreword by Admiral of the Fleet the Earl Mountbattern of Burma, Supreme Allied Commander, South-East Asia, 1943–6, (New York: The Macmillan Company, 1971).

[38] Huxley, *Defending the Lion City*, 25; see also the account of "History" syllabi in Singapore's schools in Michael D. Barr and Zlatko Skrbiš, *Constructing Singapore: Elitism, Ethnicity and the Nation-Building Project* (Copenhagen: Nordic Institute of Asian Studies Press, 2008), 187.

[39] Easter, "Small States Development", 404.

"econometric modelling procedure," found Singapore of low vulnerability (albeit in 1999 and not 1965);[40] although other environmental, political and social aspects of resilience are clearly not as easily quantifiable.

The objective and subjective conditions of vulnerability, plus the obvious need therefore to build resilience, shaped the existential threat posed by vulnerability a newly-independent Singapore faced for its survival. This led the Singapore elite to securitise "vulnerability", placing "vulnerability" as transcending "normal" politics. The following section analyses how this was done, and its consequent success. Therein, the section demonstrates the existential threat of vulnerability against the referent object of the sovereign Singapore state through focusing on the discourse (securitising moves) of the securitising actors, the policy makers. As others have noted, securitisation is a state-centric and elitist enterprise, particularly in Singapore.[41] I further contend that the audience of the securitising discourse of vulnerability is, itself, furthermore a part of the exceptional security practice of NS required to counter the threat to Singapore's survival upon independence, leading to a more successful securitisation of vulnerability. A caveat ought to be noted here as well. Since the referent object is the sovereign state, the securitisation I examine is therefore purposely limited to the period after Singapore's independence (except where it relates directly to the pre-independence period), even though vulnerability existed before 1965 and overt recognition of it was also part of the drive towards self-government prior to full independence.

Constructing Singapore's Securitisation of Vulnerability

In the second part of his memoirs which began from Singapore's independence, Singapore's first prime minister, Lee Kuan Yew, wrote on the very first page: "We faced tremendous odds with an improbable chance of survival. Singapore was not a natural country but man-made, a trading post the British had developed into a nodal point in their world-wide maritime empire. We inherited the island without its hinterland, a heart without

---

[40] Easter, "Small States Development", 407–408.
[41] See: Ken Booth, *Theory of World Security* (Cambridge: Cambridge University Press, 2007), 166; Vasu and Loo, "National Security and Singapore", 21–43.

a body."[42] Indeed, the speech by the *Yang Di-Pertuan Negara* (Head of State), Yusof bin Ishak, to the first post-independence Singapore Parliament on 8 December 1965, opened with a grisly reminder that the Japanese first bombed Singapore on that exact date in 1941, and thereafter paralleled the internal and external vulnerabilities facing Singapore as a newly independent state underscored earlier, particularly the threats from the "Communalists" and the "Communists", whilst further highlighting the assumption of "two new responsibilities" as an independent state, "Defence and Foreign Affairs", which were "closely related" to Singapore's survival.[43]

Accordingly, another of the earliest securitising moves was by Dr Goh Keng Swee, then-Minister for Interior and Defence, and widely acknowledged as "the policy architect of Singapore's national defence".[44] Dr Goh, in a speech to Parliament on the second reading of the Singapore Army Bill on 23 December 1965 (and reported in the state's main newspaper, *The Straits Times*, the following day), asserted that:

> Our army is to be engaged in the defence of our country and people against external aggression. Today, we are unable to do this task by ourselves. It is no use pretending that without the British military forces in Singapore today, the island cannot be easily overrun within a matter of hours by any neighbouring country ... if any of these countries care to do so ... British military protection today has made quite a number of our citizens complacent about the need to conduct our own defence preparations. These people assume that this protection will be permanent. I regard it as the height of folly to plan our future on this assumption. And

---

[42] Lee Kuan Yew, *From Third World to First: The Singapore Story: 1965–2000* (Singapore: Times Media Private Limited, 2000), 19.

[43] "*Yang Di-Pertuan Negara*'s Speech", 8 December 1965, Parliament of Singapore Official Reports. All citations from the Parliament of Singapore Official Reports in this chapter can be accessed from https://www.parliament.gov.sg/publications-singapore-official-reports

[44] Bernard Fook Weng Loo, "Goh Keng Swee and the Emergence of a Modern SAF: The Rearing of a Posionous Shrimp", in *Goh Keng Swee: A Legacy of Public Service*, eds. Emrys Chew and Kwa Chong Guan (Singapore: World Scientific, 2012), 144; see also, Ang Cheng Guan, "Singapore's Conception of Security", in *Perspectives on the Security of Singapore*, eds. Barry Desker and Ang Cheng Guan (Singapore: World Scientific, 2016), 8.

if there is a basis on which we, as an independent country, can plan our future, it will be on the opposite assumption, that is, the removal of the British military preserve at some time in the future.[45]

This securitising move in securitising the existential threat of Singapore's vulnerability to military attacks, without specifying a likely aggressor, went hand in hand with the security practice of the Singapore Army Bill, passed to provide for the establishment and maintenance of an armed force to safeguard national defence for when the British withdraw. The People's Defence Force (PDF) Bill was further introduced on 30 December 1965 to complement the regular armed forces with a volunteer force.

Vulnerability then was perceived even more intensely by the policy makers. Specifically, there was the presence of a Malaysian regiment occupying the empty Camp Temasek barracks of the Second Singapore Infantry Regiment (2SIR) — 2SIR had been sent to Sabah upon the request of the Malaysians to fight in *Konfrontasi* — as under the Separation agreement, "Malaysia had retained the right to the use of military facilities in Singapore."[46] The Malaysians thereafter refused to move out even upon the return of 2SIR in February 1966 until they finally withdrew "on their own accord in November 1967."[47] In addition, the communist threat also loomed large internally as the opposition Barisan Sosialis was linked to the communists. In support of the Singapore Army Bill, Inche Mahmud Awang, the Member of Parliament for Kampong Kapor, emphasised that "Our Republic must be defended at all costs and by all means against our external and internal enemies ... not only do the Barisan Sosialis have no interest at all to defend the Republic of Singapore, but they intend to surrender our sovereignty to their foreign masters, like the Communist Party of Indonesia."[48] Lee repeatedly underscored the communist threat as well as the subsequent need for Singapore to defend itself against such threats in speech after speech, such as the one given at the fifth anniversary celebrations of the Sims Avenue community centre in November 1965,

---

[45] "Singapore Army Bill", 23 December 1965, Parliament of Singapore Official Reports; "Dr Goh: If it isn't for the British bases in Singapore...", *The Straits Times*, 24 December 1965.

[46] Kwa, Heng and Tan, *Singapore: A 700-Year History*, 186.

[47] Lee, *From Third World to First*, 32.

[48] "Singapore Army Bill", 23 December 1965, Parliament of Singapore Official Reports.

which *The Straits Times* reported as "yet another 'survival' speech."[49] To make matters worse, the British decided to accelerate its withdrawal "east of Suez" as it was unable to sustain its policy of maintaining overseas bases beyond Europe.[50] Thus, from an original plan to withdraw from Singapore in 1975, it was suddenly announced in January 1968 that "all British forces would withdraw from Southeast Asia by March 1971", a deadline which Singapore only managed to delay to December 1971.[51]

Further securitisation of Singapore's vulnerability thereby took place with the second reading of the National Service (Amendment) Bill in 13 March 1967. Dr Goh's securitising move in his speech to Parliament deserves to be quoted extensively here:

> A useful starting point to ask oneself, why bother defending Singapore at all? I am not being facetious in asking this question, for there are people ... who say that we should not. They tell you that the island is quite indefensible, and if there is a sustained major attack upon it, it is unlikely that, without major assistance from outside, Singapore can hold out ... There are, however, excellent reasons why we should bother about defence ... If you are in a completely vulnerable position, anyone disposed to do so can hold you to ransom and life for you will then become very tiresome ... I consider it to be wrong to believe that there is nothing we can do or should do about defending ourselves, even though we cannot achieve complete invulnerability by our unaided efforts ... There is another aspect to our defence effort. This is a contribution it can make to nation-building. Nothing creates loyalty and national consciousness more speedily and more thoroughly than participation in defence and membership of the armed forces ... The nation-building aspect of defence will be more significant if its participation is spread over all strata of society. This is possible only with some kind of national service.[52]

---

[49] "Jakarta teaching Barisan a lesson: Lee", *The Straits Times*, 11 November 1965.

[50] See Malcolm H. Murfett *et al.*, *Between Two Oceans: A Military History of Singapore from First Settlement to Final British Withdrawal* (Singapore: Marshall Cavendish Academic, 2004), chapters 10 and 11.

[51] Ho and Chan, *Singapore Chronicles: Defence*, 38.

[52] "National Service (Amendment) Bill", 13 March 1967, Parliament of Singapore Official Reports; "National Service Bill passed in Singapore Parliament", *The Straits Times*, 14 March 1967.

The extreme and wide-ranging security practice of NS — making military service compulsory — legitimised as a result therefore killed two birds with one stone. It was directed towards both external vulnerabilities in the form of military defence, as well as internal vulnerabilities in the form of nation-building. Dr Goh has always recognised such a dual purpose of an army, such as when he had required all "new employees of Government and statutory bodies who are of military age" to "undergo military training" from 1 January 1967 since "it links a privileged status in society obtained through a secure and well-paid occupation with the most fundamental responsibility owed to society — its defence against external enemies"; and also because Singapore "is not yet a close-knit community" as "many of our people are of recent migrant origin," thus the "aspect of military service" in "creating a stronger national consciousness among our people" is "at least as important as the purely defence considerations."[53] The Enlistment Act of 1970, following the British decision to withdraw from Singapore, further expanded full-time military training from the previous 10% provided for under the 1967 NS (Amendment) Bill and accelerated the development of "the SAF's order of battle, particularly its reservist component."[54] Other security practices, extreme or otherwise, rationalised by vulnerability were to follow, including the Total Defence doctrine introduced in 1984.

Have the exceptional policy of NS and the consequent securitisation of vulnerability been successful? From a functional point of view, NS can be said to have been extremely successful as a security practice response against the existential threat of vulnerability. Although "certain key weaknesses which could be critical in time of crisis or war" exists, such as being untested in combat, or an aversion to casualties, which would further affect the "credibility" pillar of the SAF's deterrent; as Huxley affirmed, "the SAF is in many ways the most impressive military force in contemporary Southeast Asia."[55] Other than the quantitative indicators of the SAF's capabilities which are skewed in the SAF's favour, including the capability of

---

[53] Quoted in Gabriel Lee, "Army training for new civil servants", *The Straits Times*, 30 November 1966.

[54] Huxley, *Defending the Lion City*, 13.

[55] Huxley, *Defending the Lion City*, 65, 98, 249 and 252. For more on deterrence theory, see Richard K. Betts, "The Concept of Deterrence in the Postwar Era", *Security Studies*, 1/1 (1991), 25–36.

fielding a force as large as 350,000; qualitatively, "its soldiers are highly-educated, well-trained and technically proficient," in large part due to the policy of NS.[56] Moreover, with regard to NS addressing internal vulnerability, whilst it may be difficult to isolate and directly measure the impact NS had on nation-building as there were a lot of other mechanisms at work, various indicators have indicated that NS had indeed played a part. For instance, a 1994 study by Elizabeth Nair highlighted that "seventy-six per cent of a sample of undergraduate males who had completed two and a half years of conscript service reported that the experience helped to forge stronger ties and links between different racial groups in Singapore."[57] Whilst the SAF and NS policy have often been criticised for discrimination against the Malays in Singapore, progress has been made towards ameliorating this, illustrated by the appointment of Malays to various leadership positions and other sensitive postings, such as the commandos.[58] Indeed, the IPS survey mentioned at the start of this chapter further corroborates the nation-building role of NS, showing that out of a scale of 6, from 1 as least important and 6 as most important, that NS was: for national education achieved a score of 4.65, to "build a unique Singaporean identity" 4.61, and to "promote understanding between people of different backgrounds" 4.55.[59]

As for securitisation, Singapore's policy elites have successfully securitised vulnerability through articulating various securitising moves and implementing consequent security practices. More distinctly, however, is the acceptance of NS as an exceptional measure to guard against vulnerability, fulfilling both the stages of identification and mobilisation. Right from the start, the population of Singapore had no military tradition or motivation to speak of, neither "ideology, culture nor outright coercion."[60]

---

[56] Huxley, *Defending the Lion City*, p. 65.

[57] Quoted in Nair, "Conscription and Nation-Building in Singapore", 94.

[58] See Huxley, *Defending the Lion City*, 102–104; Sean P. Walsh, "The Roar of the Lion City: Ethnicity, Gender, and Culture in the Singapore Armed Forces", *Armed Forces and Society*, 33/2 (2007), 265–285; Alan Chong and Samuel Chan, "Militarizing Civilians in Singapore: Preparing for a 'Crisis' within a Calibrated Nationalism", *The Pacific Review*, 30/3 (2016), 373.

[59] Leong, Yang and Ho, "Singaporeans' Attitudes to National Service", 1.

[60] Ooi Kee Beng, *In Lieu of Ideology: An Intellectual Biography of Goh Keng Swee* (Singapore: Institute of Southeast Asian Studies, 2010), 130–131.

Rather, it was accepted by Singapore's leaders such as Lee and Dr Goh that there was a "traditional dislike for soldiering", particularly amongst the Chinese, encapsulated in the Chinese phrase "好铁不打钉，好汉不当兵" (*hao tie bu da ding, hao han bu dang bing*), meaning one would not use good iron to make nails, just as good men do not become soldiers. Dr Goh explained that this impression was a result of China's warring years where people were either "press-ganged" or bullied by invading armies.[61] As Lee had also pointed out in his memoirs, "people's minds" had to be reoriented to "accept the need for a people's army"; and to make people "admire military valour," "national cadet corps and national police cadet corps" were set up in "all secondary schools so that parents would identify the army and police with their sons and daughters," which would cause "people to regard our soldiers as their protectors — a reversal from the days when army and police uniforms aroused fear and resentment as symbols of colonial coercion."[62] The securitising moves of the existential threat of vulnerability caused the audience to buy in to the need for survival and accept the required exceptional measures and there was therefore "full public support" when the NS (Amendment) Bill was passed, and there were "no problems getting 9,000 young men registered in the first batch" of NS as Lee emphasised, highlighting that he was "right about the changed public attitude."[63] Admittedly, it could possibly be true that even after 50 years of NS, "conscription and reservist service are still only grudgingly accepted as necessary evils by Singapore's predominantly ethnic Chinese population."[64] Yet, grudgingly or not, Singaporeans are still mobilised and can identify with the need to address vulnerability, with the aforementioned IPS survey further highlighting that there is an "ingrained perception of National Service as a rite of passage for the Singaporean male," as well as for National Defence.[65] The successful securitisation of vulnerability thus accounts for the support for conscription.

---

[61] Lee, *From Third World to First*, 33; "Singapore Army Bill", 23 December 1965, Parliament of Singapore Official Reports.

[62] Lee, *From Third World to First*, 33.

[63] Lee, *From Third World to First*, 36.

[64] Huxley, *Defending the Lion City*, 251.

[65] Leong, Yang and Ho, "Singaporeans' Attitudes to National Service", 1.

Indeed, conscripting the audience in the exceptional measure of NS has so successfully securitised Singapore's vulnerabilities that various monikers have been coined for this "ingrained perception" of vulnerability across Singaporeans from all walks of life, from the policy elites, such as prime ministers after Lee, to the citizens. These appellations include "the pervasiveness of the discourse of vulnerability" in Singapore's strategic culture, a "siege mentality", the "militarised civilian" or Singapore as a "garrison state".[66] After all, as Tan See Seng put it: "Philosophically, the institutions of National Service and Total Defence amounted to putting the entire citizenry on a permanent 'war footing'."[67] Even what have been emphasised as some of Singapore's unique identifiers, Singaporeans as being "*kiasu*" (from the Hokkien "scared to lose") and "*kiasi*" (from the Hokkien "scared to die") — also called Singapore's "national habit of fear" — is linked to, and part of this "siege mentality", with the Singapore government repeatedly highlighting "potential scenarios of political instability, economic decline, religious or ethnic conflict, and even foreign intervention," such that these "alleged threats to survival promote the imperative of political solidarity."[68] Goh Chok Tong, Singapore's second prime minister, concluded in a 2002 speech commemorating the 35th anniversary of NS that "the reasons for a National Service armed forces are as relevant and valid today as 35 years ago," and over "the last 35 years, National Service has helped us build a country, and bond our people," without which "Singapore may not have survived, let along prospered," or "forged the solidarity" which it currently possesses.[69] Lee Hsien Loong, Goh Chok Tong's successor and the current incumbent, declared in 2012 in a speech to the Economic Society of Singapore, that "We must always

---

[66] Loo, "Explaining Changes in Singapore's Military Doctrines", 362; Ho and Chan, *Singapore Chronicles: Defence*, 23; Chong and Chan, "Militarizing Civilians in Singapore"; Tan See Seng, "Mailed Fists and Velvet Gloves: The Relevance of Smart Power to Singapore's Evolving Defence and Foreign Policy", *Journal of Strategic Studies*, 38/3 (2015), 335–336.

[67] Tan, "Mailed Fists and Velvet Gloves", 335–336.

[68] David Martin Jones and David Brown, "Singapore and the Myth of the Liberalizing Middle Class", *The Pacific Review*, 7/1 (1994), 86; Justin Ong, "Singapore should kill '*kiasu*' culture: NMP Kuik Shiao-Yin", *Channel NewsAsia*, 5 April 2016.

[69] "Speech by Prime Minister Goh Chok Tong at the 35 Years of National Service Commemoration Dinner", 7 September 2002 (accessed 19 September 2016), https://www.mindef.gov.sg/imindef/press_room/official_releases/sp/2002/07sep02_speech.html

fend for ourselves. No one will bail us out if we falter. In a rapidly changing world, this is one fact that will not change for Singapore."[70] Despite the
success in the securitisation of vulnerability, the policy makers do not rest
on their laurels and the securitising moves continue.

Conclusion: The Next 50 Years?

Singapore's policy elites were faced with both objective and subjective
conditions of vulnerability, internal and external, in the economic, environmental, political and social realms upon Singapore becoming an independent sovereign state in 1965. In order to mitigate these vulnerabilities
and build resilience, vulnerability itself was placed above politics and
securitised, with the introduction of conscription as an exceptional security practice as a consequence of such securitising moves. That debates
during election campaigns for Singapore's parliament may focus on the
size of the defence budget or the length of conscription, but not the *need*
for conscription, speaks volumes about the securitisation of vulnerability
and its placement above politics. This securitisation of vulnerability was
thereafter triply successful: first in the success of conscription in providing for national defence and nation-building, thereby successfully com-
bating the emergency of vulnerability; second in the co-option and
subsequent mobilisation of its audience, the Singapore public; and third in
the entrenchment of vulnerability in the fabric of society itself.

The pervasiveness of the vulnerability narrative has further repercussions
on civil-military relations in Singapore. Tan Tai Yong calls Singapore a
civilian-military fusion model, "in which the military, both in leadership
and in structural terms, functions as an integral part of a centralized, bureaucratic state."[71] Derek da Cunha highlights the civilianisation of the
Singapore military since "the universality of national service ... makes
enlistees part of a citizens' armed force, with the stress first on 'citizens'."[72]
Both thereby underscores the civilian supremacy of civilian-military relations in Singapore in essence, albeit in a nuanced manner. However, if

---

[70] Quoted in Tan, "Mailed Fists and Velvet Gloves", 334.
[71] Tan Tai Yong, "Singapore: Civil-Military Fusion", in *Coercion and Governance: The
Declining Political Role of the Military in Asia*, ed. Muthiah Alagappa (Stanford: Stanford
University Press, 2001), 276.
[72] da Cunha, "Sociological Aspects", 469.

Singaporeans are "living under siege" all the time, or are on a "permanent war footing", as the dominance of vulnerability suggests, then Alan Chong and Samuel Chan arguably are more accurate with their emphasis on the "militarised civilian".[73] Although there is civilian supremacy in Singapore on the surface, Singapore is actually being run like a garrison state (though not a military state), with military norms and expectations, with constant reminders of being under threat, and the continuous securitisation of vulnerability and all that it entails.

This case study of Singapore's triply successful securitisation of vulnerability has additional inductive implications for Copenhagen securitisation theory. It would appear that when the exceptional measure involves conscripting the audience, securitisation becomes even more successful since the audience, not only accepts the securitising move and supports the consequent security practice, but further *partakes* of it, thus reifying the securitisation that has taken place. In Singapore, this is furthermore helped along by a continuous securitising process. Having said that, Ole Wæver's emphasis about security also needs to be borne in mind: "security and insecurity do not constitute a binary opposition."[74] The former situation is a threat which calls for and has a response, whilst the latter shares the threat problematique but has no response. When there is no threat and therefore "complete security", it is no longer "security", but "asecurity".[75] Hence, since the securitisation of existential threats exacts exceptional security practices as responses to mitigate the threat, a logical follow-on question is whether overly successful securitisation thereafter leads to "asecuritisation", wherein the perception of threat is masked even if the objective sources of threat remain. This might then ironically imply a failure of securitisation. Where would "asecuritisation" be placed on the securitisation spectrum thereafter? Before or after non-securitisation?

---

[73] Chong and Chan, "Militarizing Civilians in Singapore".

[74] Ole Wæver, "Securitization and Desecuritization", in *On Security*, ed. Ronnie D. Lipschutz (New York: Columbia University Press, 1995), 56, emphasis removed.

[75] See: Ole Wæver, "Insecurity, Security and Asecurity in the West European Non-War Community", in *Security Communities*, eds. Emanuel Adler and Michael Barnett (Cambridge: Cambridge University Press, 1998), 69–118.

Whilst the scope of this chapter prohibits me from a longer examination of these questions, they are directly related to Singapore's securitisation of vulnerability. Singapore's policy elites have already warned of the dangers of failing to treat vulnerability as an existential threat in light of Singapore's successes. Bilahari Kausikan, one of Singapore's better known public intellectuals and Ambassador-at-Large at the Ministry of Foreign Affairs (MFA) at the time of writing, warned: "Young Singaporeans who have *known only* a prosperous Singapore do not understand how unnatural a place this is; they are sceptical when we speak of our vulnerabilities, regarding it as propaganda or scare tactics designed to keep the Government in power."[76] Younger generations of Singaporeans do not share the exact same psychological environment as Singapore's founding fathers after all. As Singapore becomes more and more successful, and its securitisation of vulnerability more and more entrenched, would vulnerability eventually be "asecuritised"? Thus lies the biggest challenge for the future of National Service.

---

[76] Bilahari Kausikan, "Foreign policy is no laughing matter", *The Straits Times*, 8 June 2015, emphasis added.

Chapter 5

Numbers Matter and Number Matters: National Service and Singapore's Quest for Military Deterrence

Samuel L.W. Chan

"… the strong do what they have the power to do and the weak accept what they have to accept."[1]

— The Melian Dialogue

Introduction

National Service (NS), or conscription, is a major milestone in the life of every male Singaporean citizen and certain male permanent residents (PRs). Full-time service is today rendered in the Singapore Armed Forces (SAF), the Singapore Police Force (SPF) or the Singapore Civil Defence Force (SCDF). The majority are enlisted for military service with the SAF under the ever watchful eyes of the Ministry of Defence (MINDEF). The priority of NS, in both active and reserve service, is to develop conscripts to fill billets across Singapore's formidable war machine. In visual terms, this means an army of brigades and divisions, a fleet of squadrons and flotillas, and an air force of squadrons and commands. These are the fruits of the consistent and sacrosanct commitment of land, labour, and capital to national defence.

---

[1] Rex Warner (trans.) with an Introduction and Notes by M. I. Finley, *Thucydides: History of the Peloponnesian War* (London, UK: Penguin Books, 1972), 402.

NS is undoubtedly the cornerstone that has provided independent Singapore with a credible defence force in terms of manpower, technology, organization, and preparation. The raison d'être for NS is to provide adequate manpower within budgetary constraints to ensure the military meets the primary goal of deterring potential aggression in peace and, should this fail, to fight and win in war. As *The Straits Times* declared in 1970 "national service — or a citizen's army — was the cheapest form of an expensive business."[2] Yet it is essential to take a holistic look beyond mere monetary terms to appreciate the NS system. Conscription is a security covenant where the majority of men who call Singapore home are called to sacrifice a portion of their youth so that the national collective is better off in the long term. It is only from this vantage point that conscripts and their respective families can appreciate NS as more than just "a discharge of duty imposed on him."[3] This chapter covers two finer points of NS namely the conception of the conscript system, and the concomitant force structure on which Singapore's military deterrence rests.

All-Volunteer Professional or Conscript Citizen-Soldier?

NS was never a given when Singapore suddenly found itself independent on 9 August 1965. Indeed the question of national defence seemed foreign since the British had long held responsibility for the island's security since 1819. Yet, if Singapore was to determine its destiny then its inhabitants had to cease behaving and thinking like a colony. The early leadership was cognisant of this and pushed hard to impress the facts upon the rather indifferent population. Parliament worked overtime to pass the necessary legislature before the new calendar year. The Singapore Army Bill was introduced in Parliament on 13 December 1965, publicly released on 15 December, and contained provisions for the establishment and maintenance of the army "along lines of the British military forces."[4] The 150-page document

---

[2] Yeo Toon Joo, "Students in U.K. get a N-Service reminder", *The Straits Times*, 10 August 1970, 30.

[3] Vanessa Paige Chelvan, "SAF officers in NSF death have 'statutory immunity': Judicial Commissioner", *Channel NewsAsia*, 28 June 2016.

[4] "Bills, from Army to infants, for House", *The Straits Times*, 14 December 1965, 6; and "150-page Army bill for establishment", *The Straits Times*, 16 December 1965, 6.

outlined the Army Board for administration purposes, detailed service conditions, disciplinary code, and provided adequate scope for the formation of maritime and air components as and when required. The initial political intent was to raise a small and well-trained regular army augmented with a larger force comprised of part-time volunteers.[5] The latter was addressed in the People's Defence Force (PDF) Bill passed on 30 December 1965. The PDF was to be "a part-time fighting force" of volunteer men and women who received "military training without seriously interfering with their normal lives" — meaning a commitment of no more than 20 hours a month or 16 continuous days annually — to augment the regular army.[6]

Singapore's political leaders recognized they had to act immediately to address defence needs even though the British still maintained a sizable military presence in the Far East. Dr Goh Keng Swee, then Minister of the Interior and Defence, moved for the second and third reading of the Singapore Army Bill before 1965 drew to a close and made very clear that:

> British military protection today has made quite a number of our citizens complacent about the need to carry out our own defence preparations. These people assume that this protection will be permanent. I regard it as the height of folly to plan our future on this assumption and, indeed, the only rational basis on which we, as an independent country, can plan our future is on the opposite assumption, that is, the removal of the British military presence at some time in the future. Nobody, neither we nor the British, can say when this will be. It may be five, 10, 15 years; maybe more, maybe less. Whatever the time may be, it would be useless to then to think about building up out defence forces. The time to do so is now."[7]

Dr Goh proved prescient as the British military umbrella folded quickly soon after as London withdrew forces east of the Suez Canal which reflected

---

[5] "Yusof charts way ahead and warns of twin dangers", *The Straits Times*, 9 December 1965, 14.

[6] "Volunteers drive in Singapore", *The Straits Times*, 7 November 1965, 8; and "Spore to have volunteer fighting force", *The Straits Times*, 31 December 1965, 4.

[7] "Dr Goh: If it isn't for the British bases in Singapore ..." *The Straits Times*, 24 December 1965, 22.

geo-political realignments after the World War II, and with the onset of the
Cold War. Ethnic fault-lines together with the concomitant effects of separation from Malaysia further emphasised the need for indigenous defence
capabilities. Yet both provided no favours for the undertaking.

Defence planners faced two immediate challenges as they approached
the question of self-defence. First, the military assets Singapore possessed
were vastly inadequate in terms of quality and quantity. The Order of
Battle (ORBAT) listing in 1963 on the eve of what would be a short-lived
merger with Malaysia counted the following: two professional battalions
(1st and 2nd) of the Singapore Infantry Regiment (SIR) which were supported by part-timers in two Volunteer Infantry Battalions (10th and 11th
battalions, Malaysian Territorial Army), one Volunteer Artillery Battery,
one Volunteer Armoured Car Squadron, one Volunteer Signals Squadron,
one Volunteer Field Engineer Squadron, one General Transport Company,
and the Women's Auxiliary Corps.[8] The Singapore Naval Volunteer Force
had three ships — *Singapura*, *Panglima*, and *Panji* — and the 1967 parade
state counted only "89 mobilised personnel and 278 volunteer officers and
men."[9] There was no air force to speak of. It did not help that the treasury
could ill-afford a credible defence force with a dozen professional battalions at its core. The question of adequate manpower has persisted as Goh
Chok Tong, the then Minister for Defence, reiterated in 1988:

> As reservists, you all know that you are the front-line troops in the
> defence of Singapore. We are a small country. We cannot sustain a large
> regular army without affecting the economy. We, therefore, have to fall
> back on the citizen-soldier.[10]

---

[8] Ramachandran Menon (ed.), *One of a Kind: Remembering SAFTI's First Batch*
(Singapore: SAFTI Military Institute, 2007), pp. 15, 30; and John Abisheganaden and
Adrian Koh (eds.), *Medical Corps: The Story of the SAF Medical Corps* (Singapore: HQ
Medical Services, Singapore Armed Forces, 1992), 63–64.

[9] "National Service in Singapore", *The Straits Times*, 28 February 1967, 10; and "Back
Paddle", *Navy News* 4 (2005), 14.

[10] Speech delivered by Mr Goh Chok Tong, First Deputy Prime Minister and Minister for
Defence, at the 6th Reservist Officers' Staff Course Graduation Ceremony at the Istana on
4 December 1988. Full text of speech reproduced in "SAF is 'a factor for peace, not a force
for war'", *The Straits Times*, 5 December 1988, 28.

Dr Goh shelved his predilection for a professional defence force built around 12 battalions as conscription seemed the only path forward. Prime Minister Lee Kuan Yew favoured universal conscription for both males and females but later agreed with Goh that compulsory conscription for males only was adequate.[11] NS would provide the manpower and create awareness of national defence as the burden would eventually be shared among most households. This would in time forge a symbiotic relationship between the armed forces and the society that it serves to protect.

Once the idea of NS was agreed upon, the next step was to enact policy and secure public acceptance. The latter seemed insurmountable at times given the societal disdain for soldiering, and the experiences under British colonialism and Japanese imperialism. There were certainly pockets of eagerness to serve evident by the first recruitment of volunteers on 8 November 1965.[12] The recruitment drive for the first local intake of regular officers later in June 1966 also attracted more than 500 applications with "Senior Cambridge School Certificates" by April 1966.[13] Yet these individuals were by no means reflective of wider society. There were certainly those who viewed NS negatively on the grounds of state-sanctioned forced labour that impinged on civil liberties, and the associated effects of a subservient and servile male population. The mass media went into overdrive in explaining the need for self-defence and the cost-effectiveness of NS. The *Straits Times* took a holistic view beyond the initial active full-time service of how Singapore would grow its armed forces:

> After their tours of duty these national servicemen will be on reserve for 10 years, with periodical retraining. Thus, the number of people in Singapore with fairly extensive military training will grow by the year. At the present proposed rate of recruitment, there will be a self-renewing reserve of 20 army and police battalions at the end of 10 years, while

---

[11] "Singapore call-up: Military training for the girls, too", *The Straits Times*, 26 February 1967, 1; Lee Kuan Yew, *From Third World to First: The Singapore Story: 1965–2000* (Singapore: Times Media and The Straits Times Press, 2000), 35; and Ooi Kee Beng, *In Lieu of Ideology: The Intellectual Biography of Goh Keng Swee* (Singapore: Institute of Southeast Asian Studies, 2010), 135.

[12] "Volunteers drive in Singapore", *The Straits Times*, 7 November 1965, 8.

[13] "500 apply to join up as cadet officers", *The Straits Times*, 5 April 1966, 8.

annually recurrent costs will be kept to the sum required to support four new battalions. As the Ministry of Interior and Defence has admitted, an enlarged standing army would be better from the point of view of combat efficiency. But it would be beyond Singapore's means to maintain anything like 20 extra professional battalions. Nor would it make sense for the island to have such a large force on active duty."[14]

NS would begin piecewise but when it reached full swing, assuming an annual intake of 16,000 recruits annually, Singapore would have 100,000 trained soldiers within a short span of six to seven years.[15] Political leaders recognised that they had to match the words in the press and lead with their deeds in uniform. Jek Yeun Thong (Minister for Labour), Othman Wok (Minister for Culture and Social Affairs), Ong Pang Boon (Minister for Education), Wee Tong Boon (Minister of State for Defence), Fong Sip Chee (Parliamentary Secretary to the Ministry of Culture), and Members of Parliament such as R. A. Gonzales, S. V. Lingam, Rahmat Kenap, Toh Weng Cheong, and Ho Cheng Choon all stepped forward to volunteer service in the PDF.[16] Even Dr. Goh himself donned the olive greens periodically as the honorary colonel of the 20th Regiment, PDF (Artillery) (20 PDF (Arty)).[17]

NS came to fruition after the necessary legislature was passed in Parliament and 9,000 males born between 1 January and 30 June 1949 were swiftly called up. Registration reminders were received on 17 March 1967 and four NS registration centres operated from 28 March to 18 April.[18] It was uncertain how the inaugural enlistment exercise would turn out even after political leaders worked tirelessly to convince their electorates of the

---

[14] "National Service in Singapore", *The Straits Times*, 28 February 1967, 10.

[15] "Military training target: A pool of 100,000", *The Straits Times*, 10 April 1967, 1.

[16] "Day and night of joy and fun in S'pore", *The Straits Times*, 10 August 1966, 1; "Ministers in uniform", *The Straits Times*, 25 August 1966, 11; "Ministers on parade ..." *The Straits Times*, 30 November 1966, 4; Cheong Yip Seng, "Vital role of Republic's new citizen soldiers", *The Straits Times*, 6 September 1967, 8; "Singapore soldiers get 'no service in Vietnam' pledge", *The Straits Times*, 3 November 1967, 11; "The heroes catch the eye at a passing out parade", *The Straits Times*, 12 October 1969, 6.

[17] "Ministers in uniform", *The Straits Times*, 25 August 1966, 11.

[18] "All set for call-up of first batch", *The Straits Times*, 14 March 1967, 20.

pressing need. There was much fanfare and a celebratory atmosphere with send-off reception dinners and specially minted mementos to mark the occasion.[19] Dr Goh cogently and continually stressed the importance of defence and warned that reliance on others for defence meant "that Singapore must revert to a colony or satellite of whoever wishes to afford it protection." The Defence Minister continued saying:

> If you are in a completely vulnerable position anyone disposed to do so can hold you to ransom and life for you will become very tiresome. I consider it wrong to believe that there is nothing we can or should do about defending ourselves, even though we cannot achieve complete invulnerability by our unaided efforts.[20]

Of the 9,000 males called up, all eyes were on the almost 900 who were selected for two years of active service in the army. The pioneer batch of 200 full-time national servicemen (NSFs) reported on 14 August 1967 where they began their journey in the rank of recruit (REC).[21] Others followed and the collective soon filled the ranks of the 3rd and 4th battalions of the SIR (3 and 4 SIR). The remaining 8,000-plus conscripts were apportioned according to manpower requirements in the PDF, the Special Constabulary (SC), and the Vigilante Corps (VC). Each scheme differed in service lengths and designated allowances (see Table 1).

Various issues cropped up even as the initial batches registered and enlisted for NS. There were those who tried to evade service using almost any means necessary and those who questioned the fairness of the various schemes. The Vietnam War raging against the backdrop did not help. Member of Parliament Fong Sip Chee emphasized at a NS send-off ceremony in November 1967 that: "The only things we will send to Vietnam are eggs, meat, pork, plywood and other goods. We will not send you ... You cannot go anywhere. This is our land and this is where we fight for

---

[19] R. Chandran, "Call-up youths report for training", *The Straits Times*, 27 December 1967, 11.
[20] "All set for call-up of first batch", *The Straits Times*, 14 March 1967, 20.
[21] "200 recruits for new battalions", *The Straits Times*, 4 August 1967, 4.

Table 1.   Schemes for the first intake of 9,000 national servicemen enlisted in 1967[22]

Scheme	Full-Time	Part-Time	Reserve	Allowances
SAF	2 years	—	10 years	Same as SAF regulars. $118.50 (REC) to $321.50 (WOII).
PDF	—	12 years First six months: 2 × 3-hour training periods per week and 1 × In-Camp Training (ICT) per month. Subsequently: 1 × 3-hour training period per week and 1 × 1-week ICT per year.	—	$2.50 (REC) to $4 (officers) per parade.
SC	—	12 years First six months: 2 × 4-hour training periods per week (at one of five training centres) and up to a fortnight of ICT. Subsequently: 4 days of duty per week and up to a week of ICT annually.	—	$2 to $3 each parade.
VC	—		—	Nil.[23]

our survival."[24] The legislations passed in late 1965 were also streamlined. The Singapore Armed Forces Bill (1972) passed on 23 March 1972 replaced various acts — the key ones being the Singapore Army Act (1965) and People's Defence Force Act (1965) — and established the SAF as a tri-service outfit with the addition of the maritime and air commands.[25] A seven-member Armed Forces Council comprised of the

---

[22] "Call-up: 4,000 youths have registered", *The Straits Times*, 6 April 1967, 4.

[23] Call-up: 4,000 youths have registered", *The Straits Times*, 6 April 1967, 4. Members of the VC were not eligible for allowances because "Their training is done close to homes, and much of the activity consists of playing games and learning useful things such as first-aid, law and self-defence."

[24] "Singapore soldiers get 'no service in Vietnam' pledge", *The Straits Times*, 3 November 1967, 11.

[25] Chia Poteik, "SAF-the army navy and the air force", *The Straits Times*, 10 March 1972, 11; "It's stricter discipline now in the armed forces", *The Straits Times*, 24 March 1972, 21.

Defence Minister (chairman), Permanent and Second Permanent Secretaries (Defence), and Directors of General Staff, Manpower, Logistics, and Security and Intelligence also replaced the Army Board.[26] Measures were taken to enforce discipline and prevent the SAF from degenerating "into a rabble of indisciplined (sic) soldiers" and bring the institution into disrepute.[27] A million men have since enlisted for NS in the SAF as the nation marks this Golden Jubilee milestone.[28]

Numbers Matter

The numbers game is the most important consideration when it comes to NS. Conscription provides an impressive quantitative estimate of available manpower to deter state-en-state aggression. It is worthwhile to remember that the cornerstone of the SAF's deterrence factor is not solely reliant on the technologically advanced frontline of air and naval assets. Any potential aggressor bent on waging masse-en-masse conventional war will be taking on a live city — Singapore has no hinterland to retreat and trade space for time — prepared through a whole-of-society approach to defence where every man and every volunteer woman has received a degree of military training. After all, it is people who are the living soul of any armed forces. Without conscription there will be no deterrence of numbers, no impressive entry in the annual publication of *The Military Balance*, and Singapore's defence ecosystem would inevitably be much reduced in form and content. Thanks to conscription, the SAF's magic numbers for both friend and foe alike are 70,000 in peace and up to 350,000 when fully mobilised for war. This numerically significant force is further enhanced by civilian members of the Defence Technology Community at the Defence Science and Technology Agency, Defence Science Organisation (DSO) National Laboratories, and Centre for Strategic Infocomm Technologies.

For this deterrence of numbers to be effective, NS is and must be managed equally in the sense that every conscript does his time when it is his turn. Exemptions from service are extremely rare with certain exceptions

---

[26] "Six top defence men for forces council", *The Straits Times*, 15 June 1972, 5.

[27] "It's stricter discipline now in the armed forces", *The Straits Times*, 24 March 1972, 21.

[28] Danson Cheong, "As NS turns 50, what is its future?", *The Straits Times*, 31 July 2017.

such as those in full-time religious ministry and the physically and mentally disabled.[29] Deferments for education are clearly stipulated with allowances usually favouring the completion of pre-tertiary studies only. MINDEF more recently has sought to assuage concerns through its transparent handling of any exceptional cases. A list of individuals granted deferments is published annually and normally consists of local medical students (who subsequently render full-time NS as medical officers), government scholarship recipients, and rare sporting talents such as Olympic gold medallist Joseph Schooling.[30]

Despite the line being drawn clearly in the sand, there were those who considered themselves above the law to their own detriment. For example, Wang Yinchu was one month shy from completing NS when he went AWOL on 8 October 2008 after his application for disruption from NS was turned down. He returned to Singapore on 2 July 2015 after his medical studies and surrendered himself to authorities. Wang was initially charged with three weeks in detention but the successful appeal by military prosecutors resulted in an 18-month sentence.[31] In another case, Brian Joseph Chow ignored authorities to return for NS when his March 2009 application for deferment to pursue university studies was rejected. He returned to Singapore in May 2013 after graduating and completed NS in August 2015. He was initially fined S$4,500 for evading NS for four years but the successful appeal by military prosecutors resulted in a 1.5-month jail sentence in 2016.[32] The sentences may seem harsh to those who chose to flaunt the rules or to self-righteous foreign observers. For the Singapore Government, it was clear that the very foundation of NS will be seriously eroded should the rules prove partial. The bottom-line for every NS-liable male is clear-cut: serve when it is time or face the consequences.

---

[29] "Dilemma of the conscientious objector", *The Straits Times*, 7 June 1968, 14.

[30] "Press Release on Joseph Schooling's NS Deferment till the 2020 Olympics — Statement by Defence Minister", *MINDEF Website*, 15 August 2016. https://www.mindef.gov.sg/imindef/press_room/official_releases/nr/2016/aug/15aug16_nr.html (accessed 19 August 2016).

[31] Shaffiq Alkhatib, "Longer detention for doctor who went AWOL", *The Straits Times*, 16 June 2015.

[32] Valerie Koh, "NS evader gets 1.5 months' jail", *TODAY*, 11 February 2015; "Court urged to set four months' jail benchmark for NS dodgers", *The Straits Times*, 26 October 2015; Selina Lum, "NS evader jailed 1½ months; judge gives sentencing guidelines", *The Straits Times*, 12 February 2016.

Number Matters

The strict adherence to policy realised through statutory law and its concomitant enforcement has provided the major uniformed agencies — namely the SAF, the SPF, and the SCDF — with a steady self-renewing stream of manpower. The deployment and employment of conscripts vary within the services of the SAF. Most vocations are opened to national servicemen with few exceptions such as air force pilots (manned and unmanned), submariners, and certain specialties in engineering, intelligence, and communications. The limited length of service also equips conscripts with only basic competency in most combat vocations especially those requiring specialised skills such as sniper, sapper, diver, and commando. Military skills invariably atrophy without practice and operationally-ready national servicemen (NSmen) — who despite changes in nomenclature are often referred to as "reservists" — require periodic refreshers in the form of ICT. A large proportion of NSmen render a 10-year ICT cycle subjected to suitable physical employment status and age limitations (50 for officers and 40 for other ranks).

The conscript system is essential for the SAF to generate adequate units to maintain its current force structure. This is nowhere more evident than in the six-division army that is most reliant on conscripts for manpower. All-regular units in the army have been far and few between, and are normally battalion-sized or smaller. In the early days, this meant 1 and 2 SIR which were raised in 1957 and 1962, respectively. At present, the only all-regular units include the Special Operations Task Force (SOTF) and few others within the commando and guards formations.[33] The role of NS in populating the army's ORBAT commenced with infantry units. The first conscripts of 3 and 4 SIR (both raised in April 1967) enlisted in August 1967 and after their two-year tours became the first NSmen. The first reserve battalion, 50 SIR, was formed on 1 August 1969 and was soon joined by sister battalions (51 and 52 SIR) under the command of

---

[33] See "Urban Operations Feature", *Army News* 127 (February–March 2006), 3; "Ex Maju Bersama 2006", *Army News* 132 (July–August 2006), 3; *40/40: 40 Years & 40 Stories of National Service* (Singapore: Landmark Books, 2007), 250–253, 296; "Passing on the Baton", *Army News* 144 (July–August 2007), 7; and "Passing on the Baton", *Army News* 157 (August–September 2008), 11.

the first reserve brigade, Headquarters (HQ) 5th Singapore Infantry Brigade (5 SIB), which was established on 23 June 1970. New active infantry battalions and brigade HQs were raised in quick session to accommodate the increased numbers of NSFs allocated to the army: HQ 2 SIB (October 1968), 5 SIR (November 1968), 6 SIR (April 1969), HQ 3 SIB (June 1969), 7 SIR (August 1970), and 8 SIR (April 1974). The number of reserve infantry units had grown to a point that necessitated the creation of HQ Reserve Infantry in December 1971 for administrative purposes. The SAF fielded division HQs soon after with 3 Division formed from Area III Command (May 1976), HQ Reserve Infantry reflagged as 6 Division (October 1976), and 9 Division (October 1978).

The infantry formation grew rapidly but the SAF was cognisant of the need to develop combined arms capabilities. The Israeli Defence Force was instrumental in the creation of the armour formation. A core group of 36 SAF officers formed the pioneering cadre to raise successive mechanised infantry units. The 40th Battalion, Singapore Armoured Regiment (40 SAR), was first in 1968 followed by 41 SAR (1969), 42 SAR (1972), and the divisional reconnaissance battalion in 46 SAR (1976). HQ 4th Singapore Armoured Brigade (1970) was formed as an active headquarters with the first reserve brigade in 8 SAB (1977). As a conscript force, the SAF could not afford attrition and had to win quickly. The sharp end of land manoeuvres would consist of the triumvirate of rapid moving armour, commando, and guards units. The SAF commandos started out as the SAF Regular Battalion in December 1969 with an emphasis on unconventional warfare. The airborne capable red berets were reflagged as the 1st Commando Battalion in 1972 and the first intake of NSF commandos took place a year later. The Guards commenced as a project to form an elite heliborne and amphibious capable infantry outfit with HQ 7 SIB established in January 1975 specifically for the task. Units were transferred and reflagged in quick succession with the 1st Battalion, Singapore Guards (1 Guards) formed from the SAF Guards Unit (1977), 2 Guards formed from 8 SIR (1978) and 3 Guards formed from 9 SIR (1980).

The infantry, armour, commando, and guards units may have the highest visibility as combat units but conscripts also man critical combat support units. The artillery with its linage to colonial outfits redesignated the 20 PDF (Arty) to form the 20th Singapore Artillery Battalion (20 SAB) in September

1967.[34] A General Artillery HQ was established (December 1969) for administration as numbers grew and provided fires capabilities for the General Staff. Units proliferated in quick succession thereafter with 21 SAB (1970), 22 SAB (1971), 24 SAB (1972), and 23 SAB (1973). In 1974, a change in nomenclature witnessed the renaming of General Artillery HQ to HQ Singapore Artillery. The "SAB" suffix was also replaced so that, for example, 20 SAB became 20th Battalion, Singapore Artillery (20 SA). A mere decade after the first conscript gunners joined the formation, the SAF fielded artillery brigades to the land divisions with 3 Division Artillery (3 DIV ARTY) in 1976 followed by 6 DIV ARTY (1976) and 9 DIV ARTY (1978).

The combat engineers and their expertise required by the army also generated battalions quickly thanks to NS. The first was the 30th Battalion, Singapore Combat Engineers (30 SCE) in 1968 with the task of clearing and creating obstacles on the battlefield. This was followed by the bomb disposal expertise of 36 SCE (1969), the bridging unit in 35 SCE (1970), and 38 SCE (1972) that addresses the requirements of supporting armoured units.[35] Over in the signals formation, conscripts were introduced into battalions depending on the sensitivities of the unit. NS nevertheless proved essential in the 1st SAF Signals Corps which was reflagged as the MID Signal Battalion (1967) and later renamed the 1 Signal Battalion (1 Signals) in 1982, the Static Radio Relay Unit (1970) which became 2 Signals (1984), Area III Signal Battalion (1972) that was reflagged 3 Signals (1974), 6 Signals (1977), 9 Signals (1978), and the 2 PDF Signals Unit (1985).[36]

The utility of NS in the rapid build-up of the most visible army units in the First Generation SAF (1G SAF) from independence until the mid-1980s is undeniable. The previously mentioned battalions certainly overshadow Dr Goh's initial suggestion of 12 and this is only the tip of the

---

[34] *Singapore Artillery Centenary Special Edition* (Singapore: Pointer: Journal of the Singapore Armed Forces, January 1988), 57–75; "Artillery", *Army News* Special Supplement 7 (April 2011).

[35] Lim Kheng Sing (ed. Chairman), *Singapore Combat Engineers Celebrates XXV Anniversary, 1967–1992* (Singapore: Headquarters Singapore Combat Engineers, 1992), 19, 29–30, 51; "Singapore Combat Engineers", *Army News* Special Supplement 9 (June 2011).

[36] *The Spirit of Signals: SAF Signals' 30th Anniversary* (Singapore: Pointer, December 1996); *The Signal Journey: Of Command & Systems* (Singapore: HQ Signals, 2006), 34–35; "Signals", *Army News* Special Supplement 8 (May 2011).

proverbial iceberg. The combat and combat support units could not function without the numerous combat service support brethren who provide essential logistical (such as medical, transport, engineering, ammunition, maintenance) or provost (such as the Dog Unit, Detention Barracks, or Military Police units that support brigades and divisions) functions. Conscription also provides the flexibility of raising and closing units quickly according to organisational requirements. Take the following examples. 42 SAR was non-generating between 1983 and 1991.[37] 2 Guards stood down in 1995. The same fate awaited 46 SAR in 2011.[38] On the other hand, fresh conscript manpower could be directed where and when units were required quickly. For example, in 2001, 39 SCE with its expertise in Chemical, Biological, Radiological, and Explosives (CBRE) became the fifth active SCE battalion.[39] The army raised the 1st Military Intelligence Battalion (1 MI Bn) in 2004 to specialise in field intelligence, 8 Signals in 2005 to support the army's command and control systems and networks, and 48 SAR in 2008 to operate variants of the Leopard 2 main battle tank.[40] Two dedicated battalions were established in 2010 for "Protection of Installation" (POI) duties due to the clear-cut spectre of terrorism. 8 SIR provides security troopers at all SAF installations.[41] 9 SIR in turn guards key civilian locations at Sembawang Wharves, Jurong Island, Changi Airport, and the Exxon Mobil Refinery.[42] In 2010, a majority of the signals battalions were also reconfigured and enhanced as Command, Control, Communications, Computers and Intelligence (C4I) battalions.

---

[37] See "Unit Profile — 42 SAR", *Army News* 7 (August 1995), 6.

[38] "3rd Singapore Division", *Army News* Special Supplement 11 (September 2011), 1.

[39] "Singapore Combat Engineers", *Army News* Special Supplement 9 (June 2011). For more on SAF CBRE, see Presentation by COL Ho Kong Wai on "Singapore Armed Forces Chemical Biological Radiological & Explosives Defence Group" (27 June 2006). http://www.dtic.mil/ndia/2006cbrn/wai.pdf

[40] "Welcome 8 Signals" and "1st Intelligence Battalion Ready for Action", *Army News* 123 (October–November 2005), 2; and "Armour", *Army News* Special Supplement 1 (September 2010).

[41] Samuel Cheam, "Protecting Our Camps and Vital Installations", *Army News* 186 (March 2011), 6–7; Rachel Lim, "Robust Security", *Pioneer* (December 2012), 11–13.

[42] Samuel Cheam, "Protecting Our Camps and Vital Installations", *Army News* 186 (March 2011), 6–7.

Conscription has bestowed the army with an impressive active service ORBAT. Yet military deterrence in the form of numbers is only seen when the active and reserve components are taken into account. The 2006 revision in NS policy emplaced NSmen on a shortened 10-year (down from the previous 13) ICT cycle. This means each active battalion that runs on a two-year training/operational cycle exists for a further 10 as a reservist battalion before being stood down. As a result, one can assume that there are five-times as many reserve than active battalions. This holds under the assumption that a reserve battalion does not suffer an attrition of personnel to a point of being rendered operationally ineffective. Table 2 provides an estimate of active and reserve battalions that are the best prepared in the SAF. The table precludes reserve NS battalions cobbled together from NSmen who rendered active duty in units for which there are no reserve equivalents (e.g., training schools). The key point is that conscription allows the SAF to assemble a mobilised combat force of *at least* 12 infantry brigades, four guards brigades, six armoured (mechanised) brigades, and the equivalent of four commando and six tank battalions. The manoeuvre brigades possess their own organic combat support elements (i.e., signals, artillery, and engineer) and at higher echelons are further supported by at least six artillery and six engineer brigades. The deterrence factor presented by this quantitative snapshot of the SAF's ORBAT is certainly impossible without conscription.

The army might be the most reliant on conscripts but NSFs and NSmen are also important in maintaining the structure of the air force and navy. The Republic of Singapore Air Force (RSAF) is arguably the most technologically advanced outfit in Southeast Asia. A snapshot of the ORBAT after the 2009 reorganisation includes five operational commands — Air Defence and Operations (all peacetime operations), Air Combat (fighter and transport assets), Participation (rotary-wing assets supporting the army and navy), Air Power Generation (airbases), and Unmanned Aerial Vehicle (battlefield intelligence) — and the Air Force Training Command. NSFs may not be pilots and usually hold junior billets elsewhere but they, together with NSmen, a segment of whom are ex-regulars, certainly populate units (albeit in differing proportions) across the RSAF. One estimate of their contribution is gauged by the existence of 57 squadrons — a majority but not all of the entire air force — represented at the 2016

Table 2. Estimate of active and reserve combat and combat support battalions

Unit Type	Active Battalions	Reserve Battalions (×5)	Total No. Battalions	Equivalent No. Brigades (÷3)
Infantry (light and motorised)	6 [1, 2, 3, 4, 5, 6 SIR]	30	36	12
Infantry (light and POI)	1 [9 SIR]	5	6	2
Infantry (POI)	1 [8 SIR]	5	6	2
Guards (light)	2 [1, 3 Guards]	10	12	4
Commando (airborne)	1 [1 CDO Bn]	3 (service limits)	4	N/A (possibly independent or incorporated into brigades, divisions, and army HQ)
Armour (mechanised)	3 [40, 41, 42 SAR]	15	18	6
Armour (tank)	1 [48 SAR]	5 (or fewer due to equipment limitation)	6 (or fewer due to equipment limitation)	N/A (possibly independent or incorporated into armoured brigades)
Signals	≥5 [1 Signals, 10 C4I Bn (ex-8 Signals and 2 Signals), 11 C4I Bn (ex-1 MI Bn), 12 C4I Bn, 17 C4I Bn (ex-3 Signals)]	Unknown (likely adequate for one C4I Bn per brigade and higher echelon HQs)		N/A (possibly independent or incorporated into brigades, divisions, army, and joint levels)

Artillery (fires)	3 [20, 21, 23 SA]	15	18	6 to 9 (two- and three-battalion brigades incorporated into divisions, and army HQ)
Artillery (radar)	1 [24 SA]	5	6	N/A (possibly independent or incorporated into artillery brigades)
Engineer (field & bridging)	2 [30, 35 SCE]	10	12	6 (two-battalion brigades incorporated into divisions, and army HQ)
Engineer (EOD & CBRE)	2 [36, 39 SCE]	10	12	N/A (active components in CBRE Group; other components possibly in reserve Groups or incorporated into brigades, divisions, and army HQ)
Engineer (armoured)	1 [38 SCE]	5	6	N/A (incorporated into armoured brigades)

Table 3.   RSAF command challenges 2016[43]

Challenge	Number of Squadrons Involved	Specialisation
Top Guardian	9	Command, Control, and Communications
Air Warrior	5	Rotary-wing
Big Shot	4	Transport
Eagle	23	Air Power Generation
Flaming Arrow	7	Ground-based Air Defence
Hotshot	4	Fighter
Top Notch	5	Unmanned Aerial Vehicle

RSAF Command Challenges (see Table 3). Such numbers are once again certainly impossible without conscription.

National Servicemen also play an essential role in the Republic of Singapore Navy (RSN) as they augment regular naval personnel. NSFs fill billets in varying proportions across the service with the only exceptions being the submarines of 171 Squadron, and elements of the Naval Diving Unit (NDU) that form part of the SOTF. The Base Defence Squadrons protecting the naval bases at Changi and Tuas, the navy's contribution to the inter-agency Accompanying Sea Security Teams of 180 Squadron, and naval logistics all rely heavily on conscripts to fill their respective ORBATs.[44] They are also an integral part of the crews manning support vessels of 191, 192, and 193 Squadrons under the Third Flotilla.[45] A specially selected breed is posted to NDU where they undergo arguably the most physically demanding vocation for NSFs as naval combat divers. The navy also initiated the Expertise Conversion Scheme to harness the professional civilian expertise of NSmen, such as those from the shipping

---

[43] Christopher Tan and Marcus Teng, "RSAF Command Challenges", *Air Force News* 138 (2016), 12–20.

[44] "Recognising NSmen's Contributions to Total Defence", *Navy News* 5 (2006), 11.

[45] "National Service Appreciation Dinner 06", *Navy News* 5 (2006), 11; S. V. Samy, "A Family Day of Sun & Sea for 192/193 SQN", *Navy News* 1 (2007), 18; Jesse Leow, "A Ship Captain's Newfound Calling", *Navy News* 6 (2010), 22; "Minister of State (Defence) Visit to 192/3 Sqn", *Navy News* 3 (2013), 5; "191 Squadron NSMen Engagement", *Navy News* 1 (2015), 8.

industry.[46] The experiences of ex-regulars are tapped and together with their NSF counterparts entrusted with great responsibilities. For example, NS teams from the missile corvettes RSS Vigilance and RSS Vengeance won the Best Naval National Service Unit awards in 2015 and 2016, respectively.[47] Another example is the frequent inclusion of NSmen and NSFs on expeditions to aid the reconstruction of Iraq (Persian Gulf) and on anti-piracy missions (Arabian Sea). The RSN has woven national servicemen in the fabric of the navy family and in return has benefitted greatly from their contributions to the navy's capabilities and readiness, both ashore and afloat.

Conclusion

NS was not a foregone conclusion when Singapore became independent on 9 August 1965. The geo-political and socio-economic milieu presented a myriad of obligations and challenges for which conscription was the optimal solution. The manpower harnessed has allowed the SAF to anchor a national defence strategy designed to deter potential aggressors in peace, and provide the means to fight and win in war. The longevity of NS bears testament to the perseverance and societal support that has seen more than a million men conscripted since the pioneers reported for duty five decades ago in August 1967. Without NS, the SAF would not have and will never be able to field a technologically-advanced field force of operationally-ready brigades and divisions, of expeditionary-capable flotillas to protect sea lanes both near and abroad, and protect the skies overhead with an integrated umbrella of squadrons. Conscription will persist as long as there is political will to ensure high standards within the SAF, and most importantly, for conscripts to see that it is worthwhile to sacrifice a portion of their youth for the greater good that is Singapore.

---

[46] "Senior Military Expert Appointment Ceremony", *Navy News* 4 (2015), 6.
[47] S. Mitra and Jonathan Ryan, "Top of the Class", *Navy News* 3 (2015), 15.

Chapter 6

National Service and Nation-Building: Successes and Limitations of the Singaporean Experiences

Kai Ostwald

The 1967 implementation of National Service (NS) in Singapore was motivated by two ends. The first was to rapidly and inexpensively increase defence capacities, made necessary by Singapore's precarious relationship with its far larger neighbours. The second, and the focus of this chapter, was to contribute to the nation-building process by bringing together the country's diverse population and inculcating in it loyalty to the nascent nation. There should be little surprise that NS was among the chosen approaches to addressing this goal: military (and quasi-military) institutions have a long history that stretches back to the Ancient Greeks of being seen as a "school for the nation" capable of bringing about comprehensive social transformation.[1] The purpose of this chapter is to examine how effective NS in Singapore has been in contributing towards the nation-building process.

On one level, NS has contributed substantially to building the Singaporean nation. A vague notion of being Malayan was the closest that the ethnically, linguistically, and religiously diverse population of Singapore had to an overarching collective identity in the years preceding

---

[1] Maury Feld, *The Structure of Violence: Armed Forces as Social Systems* (Beverly Hills: Sage Press, 1977).

independence.[2] When separation from the Malaysian Federation happened suddenly in 1965, there were preciously few collective experiences or institutions upon which to build a new national identity that was simultaneously inclusive enough to incorporate all of the island's diverse population, yet exclusive enough to meaningfully differentiate it from Malaysia.

In the intervening 50 years, NS has become a defining feature of Singapore: together with Singlish (a colloquial local variant of English) and public housing known as HDBs, few things are seen as more quintessentially Singaporean. NS has become a rite of passage for male citizens and has inspired documentaries, books, theatre, movies, and countless personal stories.[3] It is referenced in key speeches and takes centre stage at the annual National Day Parade, which celebrates the country's independence. It is one of the rare shared experiences that all Singaporeans have an intimate personal connection to, whether direct, or indirect through brothers, sons, or fathers. By becoming deeply engrained in the collective Singaporean psyche as a symbol for the nation, it has had significant success as a nation-building vehicle.

If creating an abstract pillar of Singaporean identity constituted the entirety of that mandate, the chapter could end here. But it does not. The nation-building mandate has a more ambitious dimension as well: NS is meant to *transform* those that pass through it by altering their attitudes and behaviours in particular ways, to *socialize* them into becoming ideal citizens. By providing "an opportunity for all races to come to know one another," it aspires to reduce prejudice against ethnic, religious, or class difference.[4] By seeking to instil love for the nation, it aspires to increase

---

[2] Singapore maintains a model of "multiracialism" that essentialises ethnic difference and identifies three main ethnic groups: Chinese, Malay, and Indian, in addition to an "Other" category. Since independence, Chinese have comprised roughly 75% of the population; Malays 13–15%; and Indians 7–9%. See: *Singapore Census of Population 2010*, published by Department of Statistics Singapore, January 2011.

[3] For documentaries, see the *Every Singaporean Son* series; for books, see Koh Buck Song and Umej Bhatia eds., *From Boys to Men: A Literary Anthology of National Service in Singapore* (Landmark Books, 2002); for theatre, see *Botak Boys* by Julian Wong; for movies, see *Army Daze* or the *Ah Boys to Men* series.

[4] Ministry of Interior and Defence (MID), *National Service and You* (Singapore: Government Printing Office, 1967), 5.

the affinity towards fellow Singaporeans. It aspires, in other words, to change the very way that National Servicemen (or "NSmen") view and live in the society around them, thereby reducing the degree of social division in Singapore. It is far less clear whether NS has been effective on this dimension as well.

Contemporary research from other countries suggests healthy scepticism, as it is clear that achieving long-term attitudinal or behavioural changes capable of bridging the divide between military and civilian life is difficult. Singapore is, however, unique in ways that theoretically should facilitate these kinds of changes. Many anecdotes suggest that NS has had a positive transformative effect for some, but these limited accounts do not provide an adequate basis for broader generalisations. There are a small number of empirical studies that attempt to produce systematic insights, but none are definitive. In lieu of conclusive evidence, this chapter turns to theory. Specifically, I make the argument that, when successful, NS shapes the attitudes and behaviours of conscripts through the two mechanisms of *socialisation* and *contact*.[5] Where those are more pronounced, the transformative potential of NS is greater; where they are constrained, it is smaller. This framework allows a systematic assessment of how the transformative potential of NS has evolved over the 50 years of its existence, and how a range of other factors — including unit, vocation, rank, and even the ethnicity of NSmen — impacts its potential for change.

The Inchoate Nation: Singapore in 1965

Singapore was vulnerable on multiple fronts when it became independent in 1965. With constrained access to its economic *hinterlands* on the Malay Peninsula, the previous economic model required substantial modification. The absence of natural resources on the island, including an adequate water supply, forced an uncertain reliance upon the peninsula. While remnant British forces and a close defence partnership with Malaysia provided temporary security against external aggression, Singapore's own forces were woefully insufficient to act as a guarantee of independence in their absence.

---

[5] Ronald Krebs, "A School for the Nation? How Military Service Does Not Build Nations, and How It Might", *International Security* 28 (2004), 85–124.

Indeed, the defence partnership with Malaysia would break down by March 1966. Only a few months later, the United Kingdom (UK) announced plans for a military withdrawal from Singapore by 1969–1970.[6]

An equally significant challenge presented itself on the domestic front, where separation from Malaysia created an urgent need to articulate a new Singaporean identity and a *raison-d'etre* for the independent nation. After nearly two decades of pronouncements that Singapore's natural place was within a Malaysian federation, there existed no basis for a "national myth" around which to construct an independent identity.[7] However relevant, the abstract questions of identity were of secondary importance relative to the immediate need of bridging Singapore's substantial social divisions. While less pronounced than in Malaysia, the colonial administration's practice of geographically segregating ethnic groups, as well as coupling ethnicity and economic activity, created a plural society in which communal groups led largely self-contained existences.[8] The "Malayanisation" of the civil service and the growth of autonomous businesses that preceded merger with Malaysia led to significant disparities in opportunity, as both favoured the minority English-speaking community. Resentment rose among those who were left marginalised.

These social and economic divisions manifested themselves in episodes of civil unrest during the 1950s and 1960s. While the ethnic violence between Chinese and Malays — in particular the Prophet Muhammad birthday riots of 1964 — still receives significant attention in public discussions about Singapore's past inter-ethnic strife,[9] class-based unrest was

---

[6] Singapore's defence cooperation with those traditional allies became more formalised again in 1971 with the Five Power Defence Arrangements (FPDA) that includes Malaysia, the UK, Australia, and New Zealand. Simultaneously, Singapore began closer military cooperation with the US, following the latter's build-up in the region during the Vietnam conflict (1961–1975). See: Tim Huxley, *Defending the Lion City: The Singapore Armed Forces* (St. Leonards: Allen and Unwin, 2000).

[7] Michael Hill and Lian Kwen Fee, *The Politics of Nation Building and Citizenship in Singapore* (Routledge, 1995), 41–62.

[8] J. S. Furnivall, *Colonial Policy and Practice* (Cambridge University Press, 1948), 304–312.

[9] Richard Clutterbuck, *Conflict and Violence in Singapore and Malaysia: 1945–1983* (Boulder: Westview Press, 1984).

actually more frequent in the day.[10] Whether or not either had the potential to fundamentally destabilise Singapore is open to debate, but even if they did not pose an existential threat, they clearly had deleterious consequences. On the economic front, a substantial body of literature has demonstrated that salient ethnic divisions hamper economic growth.[11] Even minor instability also harmed efforts to attract the foreign investment necessary for Singapore's export-oriented industrialisation strategy.[12] Further research has shown a similar negative effect of ethnic division on other areas critical to development, including governance and the provision of public goods like education and infrastructure.[13] As rapid improvements in these areas were needed to ensure the viability of an independent Singapore, bridging social divisions through the consolidation and strengthening of a unifying identity was imperative.

Nation-Building through NS

The nation-building aspirations of the NS initiative were made clear from the moment of its launch. Shortly after the February 1967 parliamentary tabling of the amended National Service Ordinance,[14] the Ministry of Interior and Defense (MID) — which oversaw the Singapore Armed

---

[10] This includes the 1954 National Service riots, the 1955 Hock Lee bus riots, and the 1956 Chinese middle school riots.

[11] William Easterly and Ross Levine, "Africa's Growth Tragedy: Policies and Ethnic Divisions", *Quarterly Journal of Economics* 112 (1997), 1203–1250.

[12] Garry Rodan, "Singapore: Globalization, the State, and Politics", in *The Political Economy of South-East Asia: Markets, Power and Contestation*, eds. Garry Rodan, Kevin Hewison and Richard Robison (Victoria: Oxford University Press, 2006).

[13] For governance, see: Rafael La Porta, Florencio Lopez-de-Silanes, Andrei Shleifer and Robert Vishny. "The Quality of Government", *Journal of Law, Economics, and Organization* 15 (1999), 222–279. For public goods provision, see: Alberto Alesina, Reza Baqir and William Easterly, "Public Goods and Ethnic Divisions", *Quarterly Journal of Economics* 114 (1999), 1243–1284.

[14] The British colonial government passed the initial National Service Ordinance in late 1953. This specified that all males between the ages of 18 and 20 residing in Singapore were to register for part-time NS. The proposal was met with significant resistance, predominantly from the Chinese-educated population. Following several violent confrontations with the police, the initiative lost momentum and conscription was ended in 1956.

Forces (SAF) — released a booklet that provided a full justification and explanation of NS.[15] It begins with the aforementioned defence needs, stating that "[a]s an island Republic, Singapore is of tremendous strategic importance in this part of the world, [thus] it is essential that we should never allow ourselves to be caught unprepared ... We cannot afford to have a large standing army, and, therefore, the next best thing to do is to train our people for short periods and teach them the use of arms ...".[16] It continues by articulating, in explicit fashion, the nation-building aim of the initiative:

> The community in Singapore ... is not a closely knit one. National Service will provide an opportunity for all races to come to know one another better in an environment in which they will be taught to love their Nation, to understand social obligations and develop civic minded-ness and strength of character. The aim of National Service is not only to train our youths to be efficient fighting men skilled in the arts of war, but to be good citizens imbued with the values and principles of any free, democratic and self-respecting Nation. Above all, National Service is the supreme test by which the Nation will know those who have in them true and unswerving loyalty to our people, the concern for their well-being and an abiding faith in our nationhood.[17]

The Enlistment Act of 1970 expanded conscription to all male citizens and permanent residents (PRs). It also stipulated a full-time National Service period (or NSF) of between two and 2.5 years, together with yearly reservist liabilities that now extend to the age of 40 years for non-commissioned officers and 50 years for commissioned officers.[18] In 1975, the NSF scheme was expanded to include the Singapore Police Force (SPF). It was further expanded to include the (now) Singapore Civil Defence Force (SCDF) in 1981.[19] The SAF continues to take on the vast majority of

---

[15] MID, *National Service in Singapore*.

[16] MID, *National Service in Singapore*, 5.

[17] MID, *National Service in Singapore*, 5–6.

[18] In 2004, the shortest period of service was reduced down to 22 months for those that met especially high physical fitness criteria.

[19] The SPF and SCDF are often collectively referred to as the "Home Team".

conscripts from the available pool of eligible males each year. While the SAF is itself divided into the Army, the Air Force (RSAF), and the Navy (RSN), most conscripts are assigned to the Army, as the RSAF and RSN are smaller in size and rely more heavily on professional personnel because of the highly technical tasks involved.

The decision to turn towards a conscription and military-based NS was a natural one. Dr Goh Keng Swee, Minister of the then MID in 1967 and chief architect of NS, found guidance in a range of classics from Sun Tzu's *Art of War* to Thucydides' *Peloponnesian War* and Aristotle's *Politics*.[20] A central theme common to these works is that military institutions — in particular an armed citizenry — contribute to a civilised and well functioning polity.[21] That these ideas influenced Dr Goh is evident from a 1967 parliamentary speech, in which he notes that "[n]othing creates loyalty and national consciousness more speedily and thoroughly than participation in defence and membership of the armed forces."[22]

The belief in the ability of military service to act as a "school for the nation" capable of transforming a citizenry *en mass* became especially pronounced in late 19th century.[23] Historian Eugen Weber argues that France's conscription-based military service of that era created, together with the spread of public schooling, a nation of Frenchmen where there had previously been only a disparate population of peasants with local loyalties.[24] This same transformation marked not only other European countries,[25] but also rapidly modernising societies like Meiji Japan.[26] The power of this apparent transformation inspired new theoretical assessments of the

---

[20] Ooi Kee Beng, *In Lieu of Ideology: An Intellectual Biography of Goh Keng Swee* (Singapore, ISEAS Publishing, 2010), 132.

[21] Barton Hacker, "Military Institutions and Social Order: Transformations of Western Thought since the Enlightenment", *War and Society*, 11 (1993), 1–23.

[22] Singapore, *Legislative Assembly Debates*, 1967.

[23] Krebs, "A School for the Nation?".

[24] Eugen Weber, *Peasants into Frenchmen: The Modernization of Rural France, 1870–1914*, (Stanford: Stanford University Press, 1976).

[25] Geoffrey Best, "The Militarization of European Society, 1870–1914", in *The Militarization of the Western World*, ed. John R. Gillis (New Brunswick: Rutgers University Press, 1989).

[26] Harold Hakwon Sunoo, *Japanese Militarism: Past and Present* (Chicago: Nelson-Hall, 1975).

military's role in structuring society. Max Weber saw military institutions as providing the social discipline necessary for "shifting the basis of social action from charisma to bureaucracy, from ephemeral enthusiasm to stable routine, from passion to reason."[27] In other words, social discipline modernises, and the roots of that discipline lie in military institutions. With this intellectual foundation, not to mention the ubiquity of NS in the post-World War II years, it is little surprise that Dr Goh, Lee Kuan Yew, and others at the heart of the governing People's Action Party (PAP) placed great faith in the ability of NS to rapidly forge a nation of loyal Singaporeans.[28]

The broader academic sentiments around the transformative potential of national service have cooled substantially during the past half-century. Some of this work challenges the core theoretical assumptions that underpin the belief in military service as an effective nation-building tool, arguing that it is ultimately ill-suited to bringing about long-lasting and general (as opposed to narrow, context-dependent) identity changes, particularly at the collective level.[29] The very mixed empirical evidence from contemporary studies supports this cautious reading. While some studies on US veterans of the Second World War and the Korean War suggest that interethnic contact had positive effects on attitudes towards social integration, similar studies on Vietnam War veterans showed either no meaningful effect or an *increase* in racial consciousness.[30] Considerable

---

[27] Max Weber, *Economy and Society* (Tuebingen: JCB Mohr, 1922). Quote from Hacker, "Military Institutions and Social Order", 9.

[28] There is an additional but seldom articulated possible motivation for the implementation of NS: Antonis Adam argues that countries with instable democratic institutions frequently opt for conscription as a means to exercise greater control over the military and reduce the probability of a coup. While the risks of a traditional coup were presumably small in immediate post-independence Singapore, there were concerns about the loyalty of military personnel, given the mismatch in ethnic makeup between the military and the broader population. Warranted or not, conscription was the fastest manner of dramatically altering the ethnic composition of the military. Antonis Adam, "Military Conscription as a Means of Stabilizing Democratic Regimes", *Public Choice* 150 (2012), 715–730.

[29] Krebs, "A School for the Nation?".

[30] For the Second World War see: Samuel Stouffer, *The American Soldier* (Princeton: Princeton University Press, 1949). For the Korean War see: Leo Bogart ed., *Social Research and the Desegregation of the US Army* (Chicago: Markham, 1969). For the Vietnam War see: Charles Moskos, "The America Dilemma in Uniform", *Annals of the American*

evidence from the Israeli Defence Force, which likewise has cultivated close proximity amongst its troops via a conscription model, similarly does not suggest that deeper social integration or stronger attitudes on nationhood have been forged because of it.[31]

Fewer studies have attempted to capture the transformative effect of military service outside of conflict environments. A study of France's conscription-based national service (which was replaced by an all-volunteer force in 2002) finds very little support for the positive expectations of earlier theorists.[32] The paper, which leverages a natural experiment to mitigate concerns around selection bias, found that those who had completed national service did not meaningfully differ from their non-serving counterparts in terms of organisational involvement and civic attitudes; against expectations, in fact, they seemed *less* likely to engage with their communities. Another study that leverages a natural experiment examines the effect of integrating military units in post-civil war Burundi on the inter-ethnic attitudes of servicemen, finding a general decrease in prejudicial behaviours.[33] The empirical evidence for the efficacy of national service in shaping attitudes and behaviours towards integration is clearly mixed and strongly suggests that details matter: the particular institution arrangements of a given national service programme, together with the broader context in which that programme operates, play an instrumental role in determining its effects.

Is Singapore Exceptional?

There are two main reasons for the generally limited long-term effects of military service. The first involves the typical duration of service. For

---

Academy of Political and Social Sciences (1973); and Alvin Schexnider, "The Development of Racial Solidarity in the Armed Forces", *Journal of Black Studies* 5 (1975): 415–435.

[31] See Micha Popper, "The Israeli Defense Forces as a Socialization Agent", in *Security Concerns: Insights from the Israeli Experience*, eds. Daniel Bar-Tal, Dan Jacobson and Ahron Klieman (Stamford: JAI, 1998).

[32] Ryan Garcia, "National Service and Civic Engagement: A Natural Experiment", *Political Behavior* 37 (2015), 845–864.

[33] Cyrus Samii, "Perils of Ethnic Integration? Evidence from a Hard Case in Burundi", *American Political Science Review* 107 (2013), 558–573.

many servicemen and servicewomen around the world (particularly in non-combat and conscription environments), the military is but a temporary deviation from their life trajectories: it is completed and then rapidly left behind. The duration of service is simply insufficient to induce meaningful long-term changes, especially in the absence of regular reinforcement. The second reason involves the context-dependent nature of most behavioural and attitudinal changes: while military service may well induce changes *within the context of military institutions*, those changes do not transfer into civilian contexts.

It can plausibly be argued that Singapore's NS is atypical on both fronts. This begins with the extensive obligations that follow full-time NS. After the roughly two years of full-time NS, servicemen become Operationally-Ready NSmen (NSmen) for a period of ten years, during which they are liable for up to 40 days of in-camp training (ICT) per year.[34] ICT comprises training exercises, assessments, operational deployments, or some combination thereof, and is generally completed within the unit where servicemen served their full-time obligations. While NSmen are not typically called in for the full 40 days each year, at least seven years must include what is known as High-Key Training (defined as ICT of at least one week in length). Following this, servicemen enter the Ministry of Defence (MINDEF) reserves until the age of 50 years for commissioned officers and 40 years for non-commissioned officers and other ranks.

This system has several implications for the ability of NS to *durably* shape attitudes and behaviours. While the aggregate time of service added through the NSmen obligations is short relative to the two-year full-time period, the ICT sessions act as a refresher for the earlier effects of full-time NS, thereby reinforcing them and slowing their decay. In addition, since ICT is typically completed within the former full-time NS unit, the friendships and linkages forged during full-time NS can be regularly reinvigorated and sustained. This provides ready channels for maintaining long-term social linkages across ethnicity and class. Singapore's physical size is an additional contributing factor: whereas former US Army soldiers, for example, disperse across the vast area of the US following completion of

---

[34] "Operationally ready" NSmen are the functional equivalent of reservists in many other countries.

their military service and are thus typically separated by hundreds if not thousands of kilometres, most NSmen, reservists, and ex-NS live in relative proximity to one another. Anecdotal evidence suggests that this network can and often does play a significant role in people's lives.[35] Ultimately, there is almost certainly some decline in the effect of NS on attitudes and behaviours over time, but the extensive reservist obligations, in tandem with Singapore's size, mitigate this in a way that has no equivalent in most other post-military contexts.

The second reason for the typically limited long-term effects of military service is the difficulty of bridging the natural gap between military and civilian contexts. Simply put, the attitudinal and behavioural changes that occur in military contexts do not carry over into civilian settings for most former servicemen and servicewomen. Singapore's unique approach to security may also facilitate this transfer. The vulnerability narrative that emerged at the time of Singapore's independence stressed the need for a comprehensive approach to security that not only extended beyond military capacity, but that also brought elements of military defence into the civilian context. This led to the articulation of the Total Defence (TD) doctrine established in 1984, which calls on every citizen to play a role in building "a strong, secure and cohesive nation that is prepared and able to deal with any crisis.[36]

TD is comprised of five pillars: military defence, civil defence, economic defence, social defence, and psychological defence. Collectively, they call for comprehensive vigilance against a wide range of threats. That message is integrated into the national school curriculum and is regularly reinforced through the media and other public channels. Actual large-scale mobilisations, such as the one that occurred in reaction to the 1991 Malaysian paratrooper exercises just kilometres from Singapore's northern border (codenamed *Pukul Habis* or "total wipe out" in the Malay language),

---

[35] To provide a personal example, I once shared an HDB unit with a man in his late 40s who had a physical disability which left him reliant on occasional assistance from others. Next to his family, his NS mates from over 25 years earlier provided the most regular support.

[36] See the MINDEF website on Total Defence. For detailed discussions, see also Huxley, *Defending the Lion City*; or Ho Shu Huang and Samuel Chan, *Singapore Chronicles: Defence* (Singapore: Institute of Policy Studies and Straits Times Press, 2015).

further reinforce the need for preparedness against military contingencies by Singapore's authorities. While it stops short of militarising Singaporean society, TD does infuse elements of the military ethos and military defence into the minds of the country's civilians. This makes is easier for some of the personal changes that occur during NS to transfer into civilian contexts.

Empirical Evidence from Singapore

There is no shortage of anecdotal accounts that provide rich and vivid descriptions of individual NS experiences. Unsurprisingly, those that find their way into official coffee table books on NS are overwhelmingly positive and often recount deep personal transformations. The many that can be found in online discussions are decidedly more mixed. Regardless of where the balance falls, most comprehensive narratives of the NS experience reflect a blend of positive and negative sentiments that evolves over time.[37]

While the anecdotal accounts are invaluable as case studies, there are many issues with simply aggregating them up for the purpose of making broader conclusions on NS's efficacy in shaping attitudes and behaviours towards the purposeful end of minimising social divisions. Robust conclusions about NS require a more systematic approach to sampling and measurement. There have been several internal initiatives that meet this requirement, most notably the 2013 Committee to Strengthen National Service (CSNS), which engaged more than 40,000 Singaporeans.[38] The CSNS provided numerous insights into NS and engendered further professionalisation of NS. But even it should be approached with some caution, given the inevitably issues with social desirability bias that arise when an organisation asks those subordinate to it to assess its efficacy: we would expect at least some participants to provide the response they perceive as being *socially correct*, rather than the one that reflects their true sentiments.

---

[37] Many conversations I have had share a common theme: during the full-time period, NS frequently felt like a poor usage of time and resources. Reflecting back on the experience after several years, however, brought far more positive assessments.

[38] See the Committee to Strengthen National Service (CSNS) report, available online at www.mindef.gov.sg

As part of the CSNS initiative, the Institute of Policy Studies (IPS) conducted 1,200 interviews to generate a better understanding of how Singaporeans feel about NS.[39] Most of the questions address the role of NS in society. As alluded to earlier, there is overwhelmingly positive support for the notion that NS is an important pillar of the Singaporean identity. Interestingly, several questions also indirectly assess the impact of NS on individuals. Those responses are equally positive and strongly supportive of the notion that NS instils discipline and values in the young; that it promotes understanding between people of different backgrounds; that it teaches important life values and makes recruits more resilient; and that it increases a sense of rootedness in Singapore.

There is relatively little external systematic research that directly addresses NS in Singapore.[40] One exception is the work of Elizabeth Nair, a former Senior Lecturer in Psychology at the National University of Singapore, who conducted two relevant studies during the mid-1990s.[41] While both rely on a small sample size, they do find support for the existence of individual-level changes from full-time NS. A number of interesting studies from SAF scholars are likewise insightful, but also do not providing conclusive evidence.

The paucity of targeted studies — not just on Singapore's NS, but on others as well — are partly a result of the fundamental research design challenges that confront research in this area. The selection issue is the single biggest obstacle to making causal statements about the effects of NS on attitudes and behaviours. In the context of volunteer armies, for example, it is hard to conclude whether observable differences between veterans and non-veterans are caused by their military experience, or by the underlying personality characteristics that compelled some individuals

---

[39] See: "Singaporean's Attitudes to National Service" from the Institute of Policy Studies, 2013.

[40] Many list NS as among Singapore's "successful" nation-building initiatives, but stop short of explicitly examining its individual-level effects.

[41] Elizabeth Nair, "Nation Building through Conscript Service in Singapore", in *The Military in the Service of Society and Democracy: The Challenge of the Dual-Role Military*, ed. Daniella Ashkenazy (London: Greenwood Press, 1994); Elizabeth Nair, "Conscription and Nation-Building in Singapore: A Psychological Analysis", *Journal of Human Values* 1 (1995), 93–102.

to join the military in the first place with others choosing to eschew it. Singapore's universal conscription brings about a similar issue. Since all males are conscripted, there is no suitable control group against which to make comparisons. It is not possible, for example, to simply compare the attitudes and behaviours of new NSmen to female Singaporeans of the same age, since males and females differ in more ways than just the experience of NS. It is likewise problematic to rely on a pre- and post-NS measurement of attitudes and behaviours: even if there are differences, we do not know whether they are the result of the NS experience, or just the natural maturation that a male typically undergoes between the formative years of between 18 and 20.

Other research takes a different methodological approach to this problem.[42] Specifically, I try to isolate the effects of NS by leveraging variation in its intensity. At a very general level, the NS units can be broken into two categories: the first are "stay-in" units, where servicemen live on base for the vast majority of their two-year full-time obligations. The second are "stay-out" units, where servicemen complete the equivalent of "boot camp" known as Basic Military Training (or BMT), which is a stay-in arrangement, but then serve the balance of their full-time period in roles that resemble a normal full-time job: they work a set number of hours per day before clocking off to return to their residential homes rather than to utilise the accommodation that their camps can provide. It can be assumed that NSmen from stay-in units have, on average, a more immersive and intense NS experience, given that they are in camp for a significantly longer period of time than their stay-out counterparts.

Assignment into stay-in or stay-out units is based in large part on the medical screening that precedes NS. SAF conscripts that are deemed combat-fit (defined by a Physical Examination Status of A, B, or BP) typically proceed to a BMT geared towards combat skills, after which most are assigned to combat units that are overwhelmingly stay-in. Conscripts that are deemed non-combat-fit (PES C and E) proceed to a BMT that is geared towards combat-support or service skills, following which most are assigned to non-combat vocations that are typically stay-out. Since the

---

[42] Kai Ostwald, "Using Policy to Engineer Identity: Singapore's National Service and the Salience of Ethnic Diversity" (working paper, University of British Columbia, 2015).

basis for assignment into stay-in or stay-out units (health) is presumably independent of the outcome of interest (identity), this approach approximates a natural experiment that can isolate the causal effects of NS.

A preliminary application of this research design from 2013, based on a relatively small sample size of 165 respondents,[43] suggests several statistically significant differences in attitudes and behaviours between former NSmen from stay-in units and those from stay-out units. Specifically, NSmen from stay-in units were relatively less likely to endorse strong *intra*-ethnic cohesion in politics or in response to important public issues. In addition, they showed stronger positive sentiments towards fellow Singaporeans from different ethnic groups than did their counterparts from stay-out units. Unfortunately, the small sample size requires an aggregate analysis, rather than a controlled comparison within individual areas of NS, for example a comparison limited to stay-in and stay-out servicemen from the infantry. As the latter would be necessary to have full confidence that the selection issue is being adequately addressed, these results should also not be treated as conclusive. A follow-up project using more comprehensive data is underway, but the findings are not yet available. Ultimately, the current empirical evidence on NS in Singapore is suggestive of a transformational effect, but falls short of being conclusive.

Theory: Socialisation and Contact

In lieu of conclusive empirical evidence, turning to theory can provide additional insights on the efficacy of NS. From a theoretical perspective, the impact of NS on identity occurs primarily through the two mechanisms of *socialisation* and *contact*.[44] Socialisation is the transmission and shaping of norms and values, which occurs in a wide range of settings throughout the private and public spheres. It is a central and necessary component of military training, given that the primary purpose of this training is to

---

[43] I thank the Singapore Identity research team, especially Ahmad Zaki, Kai Heng, Hazel Tan, and Su Yin Tay, for its insights and support throughout the 2013 project. I would also like to thank Yun Han Yap, Bryan Lim, and Hema Nadarajah for their comments on this chapter.

[44] See Krebs, "A School for the Nation?".

transform civilians whose norms generally promote autonomous decision making, into disciplined soldiers that follow a command hierarchy and are willing to exercise violence on the battlefield and risk their own lives on behalf of the state.[45] The closely related contact mechanism derives from the influential *contact hypothesis*, which posits that — under conducive conditions — bringing people from dissimilar backgrounds together in such a way that facilitates communication and mutual understanding can reduce inter-group prejudice.[46]

Research from social psychology provides insights into how these mechanisms can alter the attitudes and behaviours of servicemen. The *social identity theory* posits that humans have a natural tendency to divide their social surroundings into "in-groups" and "out-groups" comprised respectively of the "us" and the "them".[47] This division can occur at levels as high as the nation ("We Singaporeans" versus "Those Malaysians") or as low and trivial as a sports team ("Our Tampines Rovers" versus "Those Choa Chu Kang Warriors") or a university faculty ("We from the Arts" versus "Those socially awkward geeks from Engineering"). The process of categorising others is largely subconscious, as well as fluid and context dependent. Regardless of the basis for the division, humans have a natural tendency to confer a positive bias onto those that comprise the in-group (the "us") and a negative bias against those from the out-group (the "them").[48]

---

[45] John Lovell and Judith Hicks Stiehm, "Military Service and Political Socialization" in *Political Learning in Adulthood: A Sourcebook of Theory and Research*, ed. Roberta Sigel (Chicago: University of Chicago Press, 1985).

[46] See Thomas Pettigrew and Linda Tropp, "A Meta-Analytic Test of Intergroup Contact Theory", *Journal of Personality and Social Psychology* 90/5: 751–783.

[47] Henri Tajfel and John Turner, "An Integrative Theory of Intergroup Conflict", *The Social Psychology of Intergroup Relations* 33 (1979), 33–47.

[48] This tendency is thought to derive from a subconscious drive to enhance self-image: if the out-group ("them") are lazy, dirty, and incompetent (or some milder version thereof), then by contrast "we" are more hardworking, more beautiful, and more able. An interesting experiment, often repeated in university psychology courses, demonstrates how innate the tendency is: Students are randomly separated into two groups upon entering the lecture hall. Representatives of each group are then asked to complete some task, which the remaining group members evaluate. A large proportion of students subconsciously inflate the evaluation of their (in-group) members while judging those from the other group (the out-group) more harshly, despite the basis of in-group/out-group division being entirely random.

Precisely because ethnicity is so visible (not just in terms of outward appearance, but also through its linguistic and cultural manifestations), it forms a natural and frequent basis for this division. This is especially the case when other (in particular socio-economic) divisions fall along ethnic lines, or where there is a history of inter-group conflict.[49]

Nation-building efforts, through the socialisation and contact mechanisms, implicitly or explicitly seek to change how citizens categorise the individuals around them. Strengthening the attachment to the Singaporean identity, for example, may lead some citizens to classify those from different ethnic backgrounds as in-group members ("we Singaporeans") rather than as out-group members on the basis of ethnic division.[50] Alternatively, a stronger affiliation with a particular institution ("we members of Orion company"), might likewise reduce classifications along ethnic lines. Stated differently, the intention is to have unifying and less socially divisive identities supplant ethnicity as the basis for inevitable social classifications, thereby mitigating the risks of instability and the many other inimical effects that frequently activated ethnic divisions bring about.[51]

While the socialisation and contact mechanisms are active in numerous settings — including in the home, in communities, in schools, and in the workplace — their effects are particularly pronounced in military and quasi-military institutions. This is because the camp/barracks environment of the military is an example of what Erving Goffman calls "total institutions", in which nearly all aspects of life are carefully and instrumentally controlled by a single authority in an environment that is

---

[49] See: Stephan Van Evera, "Primordialism Lives!", *APSA-CP: Newsletter of the Organized Section in Comparative Politics of the American Political Science Association* 12 (2001), 20–22.

[50] For an interesting study that captures this shift from ethnic to national levels of classification, see: John Transue, "Identity Salience, Identity Acceptance, and Racial Policy Attitudes: American National Identity as a Unifying Force", *American Journal of Political Science* 51 (2007), 78–91. See also, Samuel Gaertner, Mary Rust, John Dovidio, Betty Bachman and Phyllis Anastasio, "The Contact Hypothesis: The Role of Common Ingroup Identity on Reducing Intergroup Bias", *Small Group Research* 25 (1994), 224–249.

[51] There is little evidence that it is possible — nor that it would even be desirable — to completely eliminate the tendency to make social classifications along ethnic lines. The aim, instead, is to decrease the frequency with which this occurs in public settings where bias along ethnic lines is socially harmful.

physically separated from the outside world.[52] Within this environment, the typical barriers between the private and public spheres break down, leading to total immersion and a greater vulnerability to attitudinal and behavioural changes.

NS in Singapore encompasses a wide range of institutions and experiences. This extends far beyond the simple distinction between the SAF, the SPF, or the SCDF. Within the SAF, a basic distinction can be made between three NS experiences: those channelled into a leadership stream (most notably, Officer Cadet School); those selected to train in highly-prestigious and specialised units (including the Commando formation in the SAF Army and the Naval Diving Unit under the Republic of Singapore Navy); and those of the remaining standard units. Even at this disaggregated level, there is substantial variation depending on the particular vocational assignment within a given organisation. While the diversity of Singapore's NS experiences complicates generalisations, a great majority of NSmen experience at least some immersion in a military or quasi-military total institution. For the bulk of conscripts that enter the SAF, this begins with nine-week BMT undertaken at an island off the northeast coast of Singapore that is used exclusively for SAF training called Pulau Tekong.[53] Many of these NSmen are assigned to stay-in units that remain in-camp for the balance of their NSF obligations, which extends the length of their immersion in the total institution. The BMT programmes of the SPF and SCDF Home Team — the 13-week Basic Police Training (BPT) and the seven-week Basic Rescue Training (BRT) — also have many characteristics of a total institution, even if they are known to be typically less regimented than their SAF counterparts. Like those from the SAF, many Home Team NSmen complete the balance of their NSF obligations in units that comprise immersive elements. While the following discussion will focus on the SAF Army's BMT programme to illustrate the socialisation process, many of its points are transferable to the SPF and SCDF as well.[54]

---

[52] Erving Goffman, "On the Characteristics of Total Institutions", *Symposium on Preventive and Social Psychology* (1961).

[53] The duration of BMT is longer for conscripts with a high Body Mass Index or poor physical fitness.

[54] It is important to note that the SPF and SCDF typically select from Army BMT conscripts for their NS officer stream. As a consequence, NS officers in SPF and SCDF have an *Army*

BMT uses the immersive environment of the military barracks to maximise its socialisation efforts on the attitudes and behaviours of NSmen. With access to the outside world essentially cut off, each hour of the 24-hour day and each human interaction — whether with a superior or fellow conscript — can be structured towards some purposeful end. Entry into BMT is designed to achieve a clean separation from the civilian existence of conscripts.[55] The transition is rich in symbolism. It begins with the Oath of Allegiance, in which conscripts swear to obey the orders of their commanders and make the pledge that they will "protect the honour and independence of the Republic of Singapore with [their lives]."[56] It continues with the surrender of the civilian National Registration Identity Card (NRIC) and the assignment of a four-digit ("4D") identification number, by which recruits are sometimes called in place of their actual names. All recruits are given standard issue buzz cuts that remove another important marker of individuality. Fatigues and standardized workout attire extend the uniformed environment and reduce external differences between recruits to their natural limits. An often-repeated mantra speaks to the intended result: "in the Army, we are all green."

There is an immediate emphasis on establishing identification with the military institution, its history, and its mandate. Conscripts engage in ritualistic drills, parades, and ceremonies, many of which are designed to foster the embrace of the SAF's eight Core Values consisting of "Loyalty to Country", "Leadership", "Discipline", "Professionalism", "Fighting Spirit", "Ethics", "Care for Soldiers", and "Safety".[57] While there is no

---

BMT background. This naturally influences how they structure their training and command, as well as facilitates the transfer of military norms and values into the SPF and SCDF.

[55] Efforts have been made in recent years to smooth this transition, including through such measures as expanding the reception programme into camp and allowing for more extensive camp tours with conscripts' families. These measures reflect a shift in the SAF during the 1990s away from the philosophy of "breaking down the civilian to rebuild a soldier". Facilities on Pulau Tekong are now far more comfortable and modern than the wooden barracks used by the first generation of NS servicemen.

[56] MINDEF's *SAF Recruit's Handbook*, available online at http://www.mindev.gov.sg

[57] https://www.mindef.gov.sg/imindef/mindef_websites/atozlistings/saftimi/units/cld/keyideas/corevalues.html

explicit equivalent of the US military hierarchy of priorities (my nation, my service, my unit, my family, and myself), the subsuming of the individual by the broader collective is implied and continuously reinforced, including through the first song learned in BMT called "Training to be Soldiers". The importance of command hierarchy is emphasised and failure to comply with it is met with punishment. The stated purpose of this is not to instil blind obedience, but rather recognition that operating effectively as a unit requires clear coordination that must often take a structured and top-down form. Effective leadership, it is emphasised, also requires the ability to follow instruction. From a nation-building perspective, the hierarchy of ranks can have an additional and valuable effect: recruits from different backgrounds — including ethnic, religious, and socio-economic — are forced not only to work as equals, but often to take orders from superiors that have a dissimilar background. For some NSmen, it represents the first time that their social advantages (or disadvantages) are not only meaningfully challenged, but potentially even inverted.

Discipline and precision are emphasised in all aspects of military training. There is, for example, one (and only one) correct way to assemble and disassemble the standard issue SAR 21 automatic rifle that NSmen are trained to use. There is one correct way to knock on the door of a superior officer; one correct way to answer a phone call; one correct way to pack the field pack; and one acceptable standard for civilian clothes worn during "book-in" and "book-out" of camp. The totality of the institution even extends to the correct way of folding the "Admin Tee" — the standardised olive-green t-shirt embossed with the SAF Army crest that is used as garrison wear.

The standardisation of day-to-day life is designed in part to foster a desired group identity: when every recruit is subject to the same imposing regulations, then ostensibly every recruit also experiences each day in a similar way, creating a vast bank of shared experiences. The difficulty of the physical drills, exacerbated by overbearing drill sergeants, has a similar purpose: the institution and the superior officers that represent it take on the role, even if only momentarily, of a common enemy that unites the unit and strengthens the horizontal ties between its members. Other aspects of BMT are designed around this same end. Drills are structured to build trust between unit members and instil a sense of responsibility for their wellbeing.[58] From a narrow perspective, conscripts are paired in what is known as a "buddy system". Paired recruits are tasked with looking out for each other and are held accountable to one another. More broadly, punishments are often doled out not to the responsible individual alone, but to the whole section. The intention behind these practices is to underscore the principle that an individual's mistake can carry dire consequences for the rest of the group, especially in actual field operations. Once live firing exercises begin, the weight of this responsibility is palpably impressed upon all soldiers since mistakes can have fatal consequences.

The demands of BMT are intense and intentionally difficult to meet. BMT is structured, however, to bring those demands within the reach of most servicemen following completion of the programme. When they are finally met, especially as a group, the sense of achievement can be substantial and can lend credibility to the process. More importantly, given that the achievement is a collective one, it serves to deepen group identification. The capstone manifestations of this "rite of passage" — such as the infantry route march of a distance of 24 kilometres that all recruits must complete together before graduating from BMT — have an especially powerful symbolic effect.

In their entirety, the total institution characteristics of barracks, the purposefully constructed drills, and the general rituals of the military environment all serve to deepen the horizontal ties between servicemen that can shift the in-group/out-group distinction away from ethnic or class lines. Ceremonies involving the state and military flags and other symbols of the nation, together with the emphasis on the SAF's Core Values, implicitly seek to strengthen the loyalty to the imagined community of Singapore. In these ways, Singapore's approach to basic training is similar to that used by the US and other Western countries. Singapore diverges from those cases, however, with the inclusion of a formal National Education (NE) component, which is intended to instil deeper sense of

---

[58] A poster released by the SAF to celebrate the 45th anniversary of NS captures this well. It shows three recruits — identified by name to make clear that one is Malay, the other Chinese, and the third Indian. This is accompanied by the following caption: "Our backgrounds don't matter; we serve a higher purpose." The poster proceeds by stating that: "NS bonds us with a sense of camaraderie. It taught us that when you're a team, united for a common purpose, differences don't matter. The brotherhood we share is lifelong."

national loyalty and bolster the willingness of citizens to defend it.[59] The "vulnerability narrative" — again focusing on external threats posed by hostile neighbours and internal threats that can arise through social division — structures the content, which includes components on the World War II-era Japanese occupation, the race riots of the 1950s and 1960s, and the separation from Malaysia.[60]

Independent of the explicit socialisation efforts of BMT, NSmen are also exposed to a second powerful mechanism that also has the potential to shape attitudes and behaviours in a significant way. This is the closely related contact mechanism. It derives from the "contact hypothesis" originally articulated by Gordon Allport in 1954, which posits that close contact between individuals of dissimilar backgrounds can reduce negative sentiments towards the "other", provided that four conditions are met.[61] The first is that group members are given equal status. The second requires that members work towards common goals, while the third specifies that attaining those goals should be possible only through cooperation among members. The final condition requires that the institution within which the members operate openly endorses integration.

Much evidence has been accumulated in support of the contact hypothesis in the years since it was first formulated.[62] Through its emphasis on rank-based (rather than social) hierarchies, collective action, and group identification, military environments tend to fulfill the above conditions more comprehensively than most others. The SAF is no exception, at least when viewed broadly.[63] Moreover, the total institution characteristics of barrack life intensify the nature of the contact, as NSmen spend 24 hours a day in an environment where there is nearly no semblance of any privacy. They sleep shoulder to shoulder, they share a daily schedule and

<hr>

[59] Aaron Koh, "Imagining the Singapore 'Nation' and 'Identity': The Role of the Media and National Education", *Asia Pacific Journal of Education* 25/1 (2005), 75–91.

[60] Heng Yee-Kuan, "A Global City in an Age of Global Risks: Singapore's Evolving Discourse on Vulnerability", *Contemporary Southeast Asia: A Journal of International and Strategic Affairs* 35/3 (2003), 423–446.

[61] Gordon Allport, *The Nature of Prejudice* (New York: Addison-Wesley, 1954).

[62] Thomas Pettigrew, "Intergroup Contact Theory", *Annual Review of Psychology* 49 (1998), 65–85.

[63] Objections can certainly be raised, as the next section of the chapter does.

most meals, and they are constantly asked to complete tasks that require cooperation. The intensity of this cohabitation is greater than what is possible in most other contexts, which increases its theoretical potential to shape attitudes and behaviours.

A Spectrum of NS Experiences

The earlier discussion of BMT makes substantial generalisations and reflects an idealised version of the institution. Reality is more complex. The actual experience of many NSmen deviates from the idealised model in ways that have deep implications for the efficacy of the socialisation and contact mechanisms. Assessing some of the major factors that account for this variation provides insights into where and when the NS experience had the greatest potential to shape attitudes and behaviours towards the intended ends, and where and when it was more poorly positioned.

One important factor behind the variation concerns selection and sorting: in short, while NS generally has and continues to favour ethnically integrated and otherwise diverse units, many servicemen have found themselves in units that do not reflect the overall ethnic composition of Singapore, whether in terms of ethnicity, religion, or socio-economic status. The selection and sorting issue has several dimensions. The most widely discussed, including by another chapter in this volume, concerns the role of Malays in the SAF. While the Enlistment Act of 1970 stipulated that all Singaporean citizens and permanent residents are liable for conscription into NS, virtually no Malays were conscripted until 1973. Those that were found themselves largely relegated to nonessential support roles.[64] The reasons for this are rooted in the ethnic composition of Singapore's security forces at the time of independence, which are estimated to have been between 50% and 80% Malay for the military and around 85% Malay for the police.[65] Concerns over the possibility of divided loyalties among Malay personnel in the event of armed conflict

---

[64] See: Huxley, *Defending the Lion City*; Alon Peled, *A Question of Loyalty: Military Manpower Policy in Multiethnic States* (Ithaca and London: Cornell University Press, 1998); Sean Walsh, "The Roar of the Lion City: Ethnicity, Gender, and Culture in the Singapore Armed Forces", *Armed Forces & Society* 33 (2007), 265–285.
[65] Peled, *A Question of Loyalty*.

against (majority Muslim) Malaysia or Indonesia left the PAP determined to rebalance the SAF's ethnic composition.[66] Limiting intake of Malay Singaporeans while encouraging the Chinese community to embrace NS obligations was to bring that about.

Full conscription of Malays was finally reached in the mid-1980s. Concerns about divided loyalties had not, however, fully subsided. As a consequence, Malays continued to be underrepresented, if not completely absent, in certain vocations of the SAF deemed to be sensitive, including signals, armour, reconnaissance, and intelligence. Malays were likewise underrepresented from the prestigious SAF Overseas Scholarship (SAFOS) and SAF Merit scholarships, both of which typically lead to a rapid rise through the ranks. The senior ranks of the officer corps were nearly devoid of Malays for much of the SAF's history.[67] In recognition of the discord between its mantra of meritocratic promotion and the lack of opportunity for Malays, the SAF has sought to increase inclusivity more recently. While still relatively underrepresented, there is today a greater Malay presence in the Commando and Armour formations within the SAF Army, the RSN, and the Republic of Singapore Air Force, including in a range of roles that are deemed sensitive and mission critical.

The historical marginalisation of Malays in the SAF implied a second-class citizenship and without question led to the alienation of many from the community. For the Malays that were conscripted, it reduced the effectiveness of the NS socialisation efforts, as the credibility of the SAF suffered when it called for loyalty from them while simultaneously signalling a lack of faith in that loyalty. The consequences of the marginalisation, however, extended to non-Malays as well, given that many were denied the opportunity to experience the deep coming together with their Malay fellow citizens that NS has the capacity to provide.

NS has occasionally fallen short in its mandate to bring together Singapore's diverse population on other dimensions as well. Some of this

---

[66] A comprehensive discussion of whether these concerns constituted legitimate security vulnerabilities is beyond the scope of this chapter. It is clear, however, that the concerns were driven by several particular events. See: Peled, *A Question of Loyalty*.

[67] In 1975, Mandarin was made the operational language for senior commanders; an oral Mandarin exam was required for all promotions above the rank of captain (see Peled, *A Question of Loyalty*). It has since reverted back to English.

was unavoidable. The generally limited command of English as a common language in the 1960s and early 1970s, for example, compelled the SAF to create a small number of linguistically homogenous units like the early *Hokkien* platoons (i.e., those Chinese Singaporean conscripts who spoke the Hokkien dialect, being descendants of Chinese immigrants who originally hailed from the province of Fujian). These were not only ethnically homogenous, but were typically also comprised of conscripts from similar socio-economic backgrounds. Benefits from the contact mechanism, in these cases, were virtually absent. In other cases, policy decisions around sorting of conscripts into different NS areas had the unintended side effects of reducing unit-level diversity. The SAF has long used educational attainment as a criterion for placement and advancement within the organisation, including during full-time NS. Notwithstanding whether this is operationally justifiable, it has reduced diversity within the officer corps and elite units, if not in terms of ethnic background, then certainly in terms of socio-economic status. The sorting of conscripts even extends to their body weight: conscripts with a Body Mass Index (BMI) of greater than 26 currently see their BMT obligations extended to either 15 weeks or 26 weeks, most of which is completed together with others of similar stature. While this again can be operationally justifiable in that it allows fitter servicemen — who do not need the additional physical training to reach operational readiness — to reduce their total length of service, it carries consequences for contact between different segments of society.

Ultimately, a large majority of the more than 900,000 men that have completed NS in Singapore found themselves in units that reflected, at least to some extent, the substantial diversity of their nation. For many, this exposure to others from different backgrounds broadened their understanding of their own country and altered their reflective and reflexive responses to social difference.[68] Nonetheless, the SAF's selection and sorting policies have served to constrain the breadth of exposure in minor ways for some servicemen and in significant ways for others. Especially for those on the latter end of the spectrum, this has negative implications for the transformative potential of NS.

---

[68] Interestingly, the level of contact with all dimensions of society may be greatest among servicemen in the SPF or SCDF, given their mandates to directly serve the public. This is especially true for vocations like SCDF emergency responders.

There has been clear variation in the potential efficacy of the socialisation mechanism as well. Describing BMT and subsequent ICTs as having the characteristics of a total institution where "every hour is structured towards some purposeful end" assumes a highly professionalised and efficient organisation. Few would contest that the SAF now meets this ideal, but it was not always so. The SAF came into existence with few resources and without an existing foundation of military expertise. The first years of NS reflected this. Former Prime Minister Lee Kuan Yew describes its launch in the following terms: "[NS] was a crash program with everybody on crash courses. There was much confusion. Arrangements were never 100 percent prepared and crisis management was the order of the day, but it was an urgent and crucial task that had to be accomplished in the shortest possible time. We had to achieve it with men of little experience and unexceptional ability. But the esprit de corps was excellent and they made progress."[69]

The growing pains of NS's first decade are reflected in the experiences of many who served during that period. Despite Singapore's precarious position as a newly independent state, the lack of professionalisation and frequent inefficiencies of NS led many to question its purpose and view it as a waste of time. Not before additional initiatives to professionalise and promote NS during the 1980s, in fact, there was a significant shift in the attitudes of most servicemen.[70] While less substantial, the SPF and the SCDF NS also experienced similar teething problems following their launch in 1975 and 1981, respectively.

The efficacy of NS socialisation efforts hinges on more than just the programme's evolving level of professionalism. There has been — and remains to this day — a general divide between conscripts who are given significant responsibilities, whether through entrance into the officer corps or through selection into elite units, and those that serve in lower-level roles. This results from a challenge inherent to all socialisation efforts: concerted attempts to induce particular behavioural or attitudinal changes are not always received as intended. They may well, under unfavourable

---

[69] Lee Kuan Yew, *From Third World to First* (New York: Harper Collins, 2000), 20.

[70] Huxley (*Defending the Lion City*, 94) cites Goh Chok Tong's discussion of a 1983 survey that found 40% of respondents felt that NS was a "waste of time". Huxley further notes a 1990 statement by the SAF that most servicemen were finally entering NS with a generally positive attitude.

circumstances, come across as unwanted indoctrination. Simply stated, from the ground-level view, the line between socialisation and propaganda can be thin. When it is perceived as moving too far towards the latter, it is naturally met with scepticism, if not outright resistance.

Many factors affect how socialisation efforts are received. All else equal, relative position within the SAF plays a strong role. Conscripts that are given greater responsibility and made to feel that their efforts constitute a meaningful contribution to the security and well being of Singapore are likely to be more receptive to the SAF's messages. This is particularly the case for conscripts in elite units, given the prestige that surrounds them. Those in key positions may also be granted access to classified information, which renders the threats to Singapore far less abstract and underscores the importance of their — and more generally, the SAF's — contributions to the nation. By contrast, those who feel they are interchangeable cogs that are kept occupied with no real purpose are less likely to find the socialisation efforts of NS convincing. Rank certainly does not have a deterministic effect on how a conscript experiences NS, but it does provide some traction in explaining why the experience is more transformative for some than for others.

Other Dimensions

It is not possible to conclude a chapter on NS's contributions to nation-building in Singapore without briefly discussing two additional issues. The first is the fact that NS is and has, since 1967, been limited to males. While females are eligible to join the SAF, SPF, and the SCDF as regular personnel, they have not been subject to conscription and do not play a central role in NS. The implications of this for the nation-building mandate of NS are clear: roughly half of Singapore's population is not directly exposed to the potentially transformative effects of NS in the SAF, SPF, or SCDF. Singapore is not atypical in limiting conscription to males, but that fact does not mitigate the implications.[71]

---

[71] Most countries that have maintained a conscription-based national service limit it to males. Israel is an exception in officially making all females liable for service, though up to one-third are granted exemptions on religious grounds. Females are liable for conscription in a number of other countries, including Norway and China, but only a portion of each cohort is called into service.

The issue of gender and conscription has many dimensions; a short section at the end of this chapter cannot possibly do justice to them. From a practical perspective, however, a few things must be mentioned. It is unlikely that there will be an extension of conscription to females, since the SAF has little demand for increasing personnel numbers following its shift in priorities towards acquisition of new technologies and skills that can act as force multipliers. Overall public sentiments are also mixed. The aforementioned IPS survey of 2013 found that fewer than half of respondents felt NS should be extended to females, though there is broad support for increasing the channels through which they are able to volunteer. Nonetheless, the regular appearance of this issue in the media and in other public discussions underscores the great significance it holds for many.

The second issue concerns the prevalence of ex-military personnel in the ranks of Singapore's political elite. While this is somewhat tangential to the previous discussions, it has implications for nation-building. Nearly all males in the current generation of political leadership have been through NS. It is noteworthy, nonetheless, that a significant portion of Singapore's political elite held high ranking positions in the military, and thus had full-fledged military careers preceding their arrival at the apex of politics. The current Prime Minister Lee Hsien Loong, for example, is a former brigadier general in the SAF. Deputy Prime Minister Teo Chee Hean is a former Chief of the Navy. Chan Chun Sing, another senior minister, is also a former Chief of the Army. In total, roughly one-third of the current slate of ministers in the Cabinet are former senior military personnel.[72] Previous cabinets have had similar compositions.

The strong military presence in Singapore's political elite is not necessarily surprising, given the country's small size and the general transferability of leadership ability from the military to political contexts. It is not unreasonable to expect, however, that this past experience influences policy preferences, including around nation-building. As Krebs writes, "[i]f nation building is the product of political competition, the winners of such contests are particularly well positioned to set the boundaries of nationality. Through

---

[72] It is noteworthy that this and previous cabinets have fairly few female ministers. While this may have nothing to do with the relatively high number of former military elites, a potential connection should not be dismissed.

the passage of legislation, the creation and alteration of institutions, political agitation, and rhetorical appeals, these elites can shape the social categories through which the populace apprehends their national world." Thus, it is reasonable to expect that the substance of policies in a wide range of areas becomes infused with the norms and ideals of the military ethos. The TD doctrine, the NE programmes, and the vulnerability narrative more generally, can all be seen as reflections of this. Even the maintenance and celebration of NS — whose implementation 50 years ago facilitated the entrance of today's political leadership into the military environment — carries this forward in a clear example of values reproduction.

Conclusion

Though its creation followed Singapore's independence by two years, NS has played an important role in the evolution of Singapore's national identity. For many, NS has become a symbol of the nation, which — together with a small number of other institutions — gives substance to the "imagined community" of Singapore. It is one of the few experiences shared by nearly all citizens, whether directly, or indirectly through brothers, sons, and fathers. As its place in the collective psyche of Singapore has become entrenched, it has fulfilled at least some part of its mandate to contribute towards the building of a Singaporean nation.

Beyond this symbolic role, its nation-building mandate calls upon NS to *transform* those who pass through it in ways that reduce the depth and intensity of Singapore's ethnic, religious, and class-based social divisions. There is no conclusive answer for how successful it has been towards this end. NS itself has evolved in remarkable ways since its launch in 1967, from an impromptu programme intended to quickly instill some military competence in a fledgling citizen army, to a professionalised institution that encapsulates a wide breadth of organisations and roles. For some, the particular circumstances of their service brought about deep and largely positive personal change. For others, circumstances were less favourable, making their NS experience, on balance, a lost opportunity. In this respect, reflecting upon the strengths and shortcomings of NS as a nation-building institution should be an ongoing effort, especially as Singapore's nation-building needs evolve along with the ever-changing nature of nationhood itself.

Chapter 7

Re-imagining National Service in the Era of Hyperculturalism

Leong Chan-Hoong

Introduction

As Singapore becomes ever more globalised and cosmopolitan, a growing number of immigrants and transient labour will call the city-state home. National Service (NS) liability may be a potential fault-line between citizens and non-citizens in the years to come. At the same time, the burgeoning number of foreign spouses, and Singaporeans working and living abroad will redefine the ethnocultural texture of Singapore and may have a possible impact to the city-state's operational readiness of the Singapore Armed Forces (SAF), including perceptions on national defence and NS. This chapter will explore the changing social fabric of the nation and how it may shape the future of NS. It will first describe the guiding principles of NS, and how the role of the institution has evolved over the years arising from the shifting political values in the city-state. The chapter will also present findings from a recent survey on attitudes to NS commissioned by the Committee to Strengthen NS (CSNS). The implications of these results in the context of an evolving demographic landscape, particularly, how the cosmopolitan contour and having a non-distinctive Singaporean identity can affect opinions to Singapore's enlistment policy, will be discussed.

Principles of National Service

In 1967, the National Service (Amendment) Act introduced full-time conscription in Singapore. Three years later, the Enlistment Act of 1970 codified NS into its present form. The Act mandates all medically-fit Singapore citizens and permanent residents (PRs) who reach the age of 18 will be liable to enlist for NS.[1] At the end of this statutory period, the servicemen may be recalled for further service for a maximum of 40 days a year, and up to the age of 40 or 50 depending on his rank or appointment in the unit.[2]

The conception and implementation of national service are founded on three fundamental principles.[3] First, NS must serve a critical defence need and it should not be used for other purposes beyond those that contribute directly to Singapore's security and survival. This is a crucial consideration as conscription imposes significant sacrifices and cost to National Servicemen (NSmen) and their family members. Second, enlistment must be universal. NS-liable men who reach 18 years of age and who are medically fit will be drafted for NS. Deferment or exemption from NS will be granted only in exceptional cases. The legitimacy of the institution will be undermined if there are too many exceptions. Third, the servicemen will be deployed according to operational requirements, and all soldiers will be treated the same way regardless of their background. This principle ensures that the system is equitable and therefore fair.

The three principles form the pillars of Singapore's NS policy and collectively underscore the social compact between Singaporeans and the state. Enlistment is not taken lightly because of the great sacrifices and danger shouldered by the servicemen and their family members. Occasional accidents and training misconducts have resulted in severe injuries and

---

[1] Women and first generation PRs are administratively exempted from NS. The duration of full-time NS has been revised on several occasions, most recently in 2004. The exact duration depends on factors such as physical fitness and rank attained (which is partially determined by educational attainment).

[2] Currently known as Operationally Ready National Service, or Operationally Ready NSmen.

[3] Ministry of Defence (2006), "Ministerial Statement on National Service Defaulters by Minister for Defence Teo Chee Hean". https://www.mindef.gov.sg/imindef/press_room/official_releases/sp/2006/16jan06_speech.html (accessed 5 January 2017).

even death. How NS is implemented on the ground is thus paramount to the perceived justice and acceptance of the policy. Deviation from these principles risks the erosion of public confidence and support.

NS is now deeply entrenched in the national psyche of Singaporeans. The two years of mandatory service is not only a call to defend the nation, but it is commonly conceived as a rite of passage to adulthood among male Singaporeans, and a ubiquitous element of the Singapore identity. This is a view that is shared by Singaporeans of both genders, and more so among the older generations.[4]

Identity and Contestations

National Service has served the needs of the nation well for half a century, both as a form of military deterrence and in nurturing a sense of collective ownership and rootedness in Singapore. For a small city-state that has neither hinterland nor natural resources, citizen soldiers are an effective way to raise and sustain a military in Singapore, with all things considered.

In recent years however, some Singaporeans, including online bloggers, have questioned the role of this institution amidst changing socio-economic and cultural contours.[5] For instance, there are questions on whether foreigners should serve NS, why there is a need for a large defence budget, whether conscription can be replaced with a professional army, and whether the defence imperatives justify the opportunity cost of two years of full-time NS. As Singapore becomes more affluent and globalised, more citizens are travelling abroad to work, live, and study, whilst many more foreign-born nationals have taken residency in the Republic. Singapore's status as a transnational hub and global city is a regional magnet to both transient and permanent migrants.

Table 1 shows the changing demographic trend in Singapore from 1970 to 2015. Notably, the city-state's population grew rapidly between 1990 and 2010, aided by both short- and long-term migration.

---

[4] Institute of Policy Studies, "IPS Report on Singaporeans' Attitudes to National Service (2013)". http://lkyspp.nus.edu.sg/ips/wp-content/uploads/sites/2/2013/10/NS-study-8-Oct-2013_web.pdf (accessed 5 January 2017).

[5] Hao Shuo, Andrew Wan and David Tang, "Generation Why: So What?", *POINTER*, 35 (2009).

Table 1.   **Demographic background of Singapore's population**

	1970	1980	1990	2000	2010	2015
Total Population ('000)	2,074.5	2,413.9	3,047.1	4,027.9	5,076.7	5,535.0
Citizens ('000)	1,874.8	2,194.3	2,623.7	2,985.9	3,230.7	3,375.0
PRs ('000)	138.8	87.8	112.1	287.5	541.0	527.7
Non-residents ('000)	60.9	131.8	311.3	754.5	1,305.0	1,632.3
Total Fertility Rate	3.07	1.82	1.83	1.60	1.15	1.25

Source: Department of Statistics.

Short-term migrants are mostly transient workers employed in low wage jobs that Singaporeans shun; there is also a small but sizeable number of white-collar expatriates that work in Singapore on employment passes. Long-term migrants on the other hand refer to PRs and naturalised citizens.

More crucially, the population of PRs and non-residents, including transient labour, professionals, and their dependents, has doubled every 10 years. In 1980, the proportion of citizens-to-population was 90.9%; by 2010, the ratio of citizens had fallen to 63.6%. The sharp decline was a product of a low fertility rate, ageing baby boomers, an economy that is heavily reliant on foreign professionals to fill jobs in globalised knowledge-based emerging industries as well as foreign unskilled or semi-skilled labour to take up jobs that Singaporeans shun. Immigrants — both short and long term — are needed to supplement economic growth as baby boomers retire, provide essential services such as healthcare and transportation, and make up for the manpower shortfall in almost every working sector.

How has the seismic shift in the ethno-cultural landscape affected attitudes to NS? Some Singaporeans perceive enlistment as inherently unfair to the native born and bred citizens as the first generation permanent residents (PRs) are administratively exempted for NS. The travel restrictions and obligations imposed on operationally ready NSmen are said to have adversely influenced employers' opinion on the former.[6]

---

[6] Leong Chan-Hoong, Yang Wai Wai and Jerrold Hong, "National Service: The Holy Grail in the Management of Social Diversity", in *Managing Diversity in Singapore: Policies and*

There has also been criticism among some Singaporeans that immigrants, particularly PRs, received all the residential benefits but without the need to shoulder any of the city-state's defence obligations.[7] The first generation PRs are administratively exempted in lieu of their economic contribution.[8] The second generation PRs however are mandated to serve NS. In-spite of this obligation, a significant number of second generation PRs have renounced their residential status to avoid serving NS.[9] In 2011, in a written reply to a Parliamentary Question, Minister for Defence Ng Eng Hen revealed that one-third of all NS-liable, second generation PRs renounced their residency prior to conscription in the preceding five years. This interval also coincided with the large influx of permanent and transient residents (2006–2012).[10] The disquiet was palpable in the social media although there was a lack of objective quantifiable data on the prevailing sentiment of Singapore residents, including both citizens and PRs.

Beyond social tension linked to migration, opponents of conscription also view NS as a repressive state apparatus that is at odds with the contemporary social terrain. Table 2 shows some of the developed countries that maintain a universal conscription programme; anecdotally, many of them have a seemingly more flexible regime of service than Singapore. For instance, enlistees may have more lenient options for deferment and get to choose their preferred vocation of service.

Prospects, eds., Mathew Mathews and Chiang Wai Fong (Singapore: Imperial College Press, 2016), 299–328.

[7] Leong Chan-Hoong, "Bridge the foreign-local divide with NS", *The Straits Times*, 10 May 2012.

[8] Ministry of Defence (2006), "Round Up Reply by Minister for Defence Teo Chee Hean in Parliament". https://www.mindef.gov.sg/imindef/press_room/official_releases/sp/2006/16jan06_speech2.html (accessed 5 January 2017).

[9] Ministry of Defence (2011) "Written Reply by Minister for Defence Dr Ng Eng Hen to Parliamentary Question on Permanent Residents in National Service". https://www.mindef.gov.sg/imindef/press_room/official_releases/ps/2011/22nov11_ps.html (accessed 5 January 2017).

[10] Yap Mui Teng, "Immigration in Singapore: An Overview", in *Immigration in Singapore*, eds., Norman Vasu, Yeap Su Yin and Chan Wen Ling, 25–36 (Amsterdam: Amsterdam University Press, 2014).

Table 2. Countries with conscription policy

Country	Duration of Conscription
Finland	6–12 months
Israel	21–48 months (Depending on gender and rank)
Norway	12 months
South Korea	21–24 months
Switzerland	260 days

Source: CIA World Factbook (https://www.cia.gov/library/publications/the-world-factbook/fields/2024.html).

Committee to Strengthen National Service (CSNS)

In 2013, the Committee to Strengthen National Service (CSNS) was formed to study how the then 46-year-old institution could be enhanced to keep up with the changing demographical landscape, and engage a more mature and educated populace. As part of the review, the Institute of Policy Studies (IPS) was commissioned to conduct an independent survey on how Singaporeans feel about NS. The research questions included what the respondents thought were the intended purposes and outcomes of NS, questions on the fairness, legitimacy, and acceptance of enlistment, quality of custodianship such as training safety and medical care, character building and recognition of servicemen, and issues on the broader, non-defence missions such as social integration and citizenship.

The survey comprised a list of statements where each respondent rated how much they agreed or disagreed with each on a scale of 1 (Strongly disagree/definitely no) to 6 (Strongly agree/definitely yes). Results demonstrated that nearly all Singaporeans interviewed supported the enlistment policy, and believed that NS provided the critical foundation for economic prosperity, peace, and stability. Interestingly, female respondents expressed a positive opinion on NS as much as their male counterparts, including the perceived benefits and impact of enlistment. 42% of men and 36% of women indicated they would like to see women serve NS. Both genders were also equally supportive of women volunteering for national defence. More crucially, most Singaporeans viewed the institution and its implementation as independent, unbiased, and professional. The silent majority had spoken and reaffirmed the role of NS in Singapore's defence architecture.[11]

The study also revealed that NS was not perceived as a policy designed solely for the purpose of national defence but encompasses other broader social objectives that are not necessarily aligned with the principles of enlistment. In particular, NS was considered a personal milestone for all male Singapore citizens and a quintessential marker of the Singaporean identity. Furthermore, it was considered as much a vehicle to instil discipline and inculcate the right values in younger Singaporeans as an instrument for national defence. It was also perceived as, but to a lesser extent, a means to promote understanding between people from different backgrounds.[12]Although the social construction of enlistment is unsurprising in light of its historical legacy in Singapore, these outcomes do not fulfil a critical survival need, at least not directly.

What about the attitudes of PRs to NS? The results were mixed but there was more convergence than divergence in the responses of citizens and PRs. Both groups agreed that NS was indispensable for Singapore, and that sufficient attention has been devoted on the ground to the welfare and safety of NSmen. More importantly, both PRs and citizens were just as confident in how enlistment was administered. All servicemen were believed to be treated fairly and equally regardless of their background (see Table 3).

However, while both groups recognised the importance of NS to securing Singapore's future, forging national resilience, and in the creation of a shared identity, the PRs' perspectives differed from the citizens' on exemption from NS and whether it should be a criterion for citizenship application (see Table 4). Additionally, the PR respondents believed that those with special talents should be allowed to postpone their mandatory service. The citizen sample on the other hand felt that the two years of statutory obligation should be considered a prerequisite for citizenship,

---

[11] Institute of Policy Studies, "IPS Report on Singaporeans' Attitudes to National Service (2013)".

[12] Institute of Policy Studies, "IPS Report on Singaporeans' Attitudes to National Service (2013)".

Table 3. Attitudes to National Service: Items without significant differences between Citizens and Permanent Residents

	Mean (Std dev)	
	Singapore Citizen	**Singapore PR**
Singapore's Future		
NS provides the security needed for Singapore to develop and prosper	5.22 (0.75)	5.20 (0.60)
NS is essential/necessary for Singapore's survival	5.12 (0.85)	5.06 (0.68)
Custodianship		
Servicemen's needs are considered during NS	4.85 (0.88)	4.90 (0.76)
Servicemen are cared for during NS	4.86 (0.82)	4.94 (0.67)
There are feedback channels to suggest improvements to NS	4.77 (0.94)	4.77 (0.67)
Feedback on NS is taken seriously	4.75 (1.00)	4.81 (0.83)
Recognition		
Servicemen's contributions during NS are valued	4.89 (0.89)	4.93 (0.75)
Universality		
Servicemen from different family backgrounds are treated equally during NS	4.87 (0.95)	4.87 (0.69)
NS policies are applied consistently (i.e., in the same way) to everyone in similar situations	4.87 (0.87)	4.87 (0.63)
Safety and Medical Attention		
NS training is conducted safely	4.82 (0.85)	4.84 (0.67)
I have confidence in the medical support that servicemen receive during NS	4.82 (0.88)	4.86 (0.65)
Character Building		
NS makes a person more resilient (able to recover from failures or cope with difficulties)	5.00 (0.74)	5.05 (0.63)
NS teaches many important life values	5.03 (0.77)	5.00 (0.69)
NS provides opportunities to learn something useful	4.97 (0.85)	4.92 (0.67)

Table 4. Attitudes to National Service: Items with significant differences between Citizens and Permanent Residents

	Mean (Std dev)	
	Singapore Citizen	**Singapore PR**
Significant Differences but Small Effect Sizes		
Singapore's Future		
NS will continue to be important for Singapore in the future*	5.16 (0.80)	5.06 (0.70)
Recognition		
If servicemen do their best during NS, their efforts will be recognised*	4.88 (0.89)	4.99 (0.58)
Character Building		
NS is a rite of passage for the Singaporean man***	5.01 (0.78)	4.78 (0.80)
NS develops leadership skills***	5.00 (0.77)	4.83 (0.68)
NS for Defence Purpose		
NS is necessary for the defence of Singapore*	5.30 (0.75)	5.19 (0.70)
NS for Social Purpose		
NS helps Singaporeans understand people from different backgrounds***	4.94 (0.78)	4.75 (0.74)
NS increases the sense of rootedness to Singapore*	5.00 (0.84)	4.88 (0.71)
Significant Differences and Large Effect Sizes		
NS Implementation[a]		
Should foreigners who want to become Singapore citizens serve 2-year full-time NS?***	5.12 (1.00)	4.59 (1.22)
Should those with special talents be allowed to defer NS (i.e., serve NS at a later time)?***	2.86 (1.33)	3.28 (1.43)
Today, those who are already working when they take up PR are administratively exempted from serving NS. Should this group be allowed to contribute to defence as a volunteer?***	4.40 (1.31)	3.98 (1.23)

Note:

[a] Respondents rate on a scale of 1 (Definitely no) to 6 (Definitely yes).

$*p < 0.05$, $**p < 0.01$, $***p < 0.001$

and first generation PRs who are administratively exempted from NS should be allowed to defend Singapore as a volunteer.

What is more significant is not how the two groups differ but the substantive overlap in attitudes. In particular, there was strong support for NS and a high degree of trust and perceived confidence in the legitimacy of the institution. More crucially, in-spite of the cosmopolitan texture of Singapore society, there was a broad consensus that NS should remain a ubiquitous facet of the city-state's character.

The findings from the IPS survey have lent support to several high-level initiatives on national security and defence programmes. Among the key changes include having a new platform for PRs, and women to partake in national defence and greater recognition for the servicemen's contributions. Recruitment for the SAF Volunteer Corps (SAFVC) began in October 2014 to enable residents between 18 and 45 years old who are not eligible for NS, such as women and first generation PRs, to contribute to national defence. An SAFVC volunteer may contribute in areas such as information-media management, naval and security operations, maritime training, medical trainers, legal officers, military psychologist, engineering and in the 4C's (i.e., command, control, communication, and computers). It is crucial to emphasise that SAFVC is not an alternate vehicle to NS. NS-liable Singaporeans and permanent residents are still obliged to serve their duties in accordance to the requirements stipulated under the Enlistment Act. Another notable suggestion adopted includes effort to match the interests of pre-enlistees with NS vocations. They may now indicate the NS vocations that they are interested in prior to their enlistment. While their preferences will be considered, it is not the sole factor for making deployment decisions.

The most valuable dividend from the CSNS review, however, was neither the policy changes nor the new initiatives, but how the exercise had morphed into a public discourse on the future of NS and its role in contemporary Singapore. There is now renewed awareness on the city-state's geopolitical vulnerabilities that has re-energised a sense of collective ownership for Singapore's survival and success. There is also greater appreciation of how citizen-soldiers can serve both military and non-military imperatives. The CSNS review revealed that NS is neither obstinate nor parochial. It also raised the PRs' awareness of their NS obligations and the gravity of the offence should they default.[13]

Beyond NS50: Headwinds and Opportunities

The recommendations from the CSNS have been implemented progressively since 2014. The strong public endorsement ensures that NS remains as a cornerstone for Singapore's defence and security. Notwithstanding the public support and enthusiasm, emerging changes in Singapore's social fabric point to a number of fault-lines that may undermine the role and status of NS in the next 50 years.

First, the influx of long-term immigrants and transient labour will become a permanent feature of Singapore's economic strategy and social fabric. Similar to other global developed economies, the city-state faces the twin challenge of a low fertility rate and rapid ageing society. This hints to a shrinking proportion of citizens in the years to come. In 2016, close to 40% of the current labour force was made up of non-residents. This citizen-population ratio is set to fall as the proportion of transient labour expands to meet economic and social imperatives, such as the provision of eldercare services, to supplement the domestic workforce, and fill in jobs that the locals shun.[14] Indeed, according to the 2012 Population White Paper, by 2030, Singapore's population is projected to be between 6.5 and 6.9 million, with citizens forming between 52.1% to 58% of it.[15]

The impending shift in the demographic terrain, a situation where the native-born find themselves forming the minority in their own backyard, will understandably result in a strong psychological impetus to "push back", to essentialise a Singaporean core built on the basis of birthrights,

---

[13] Ministry of Defence (2014), "Reply by Minister for Defence Dr Ng Eng Hen to Parliamentary Question on Children of Permanent Residents Serving National Service". https://www.mindef.gov.sg/imindef/press_room/official_releases/ps/2014/07jul14_ps.html (accessed 5 January 2017).

[14] Ministry of Manpower (2015), "Labour Force in Singapore 2015". http://stats.mom.gov.sg/Pages/Labour-Force-In-Singapore-2015.aspx (accessed 5 January 2017).

[15] National Population and Talent Division (2013), "Population White Paper 2013". http://www.nptd.gov.sg/portals/0/news/population-white-paper.pdf (accessed 5 January 2017).

and to erect more cultural barriers in achieving full citizenship and inclusion. This point was supported by a study by Leong Chan-Hoong who found that local-born Singaporeans who perceived increased threats from immigrants imposed a more stringent benchmark for naturalisation; they expect immigrants to do more in terms of how they should behave, the values they should embrace, and in the enforcement of social norms. The impetus for an inward focused sentiment is not just socially corrosive but is also tempting for the political office bearers to exploit the divisive lines for political gains like what has been observed in Europe or the US.[16]

The CSNS survey in 2013 offers a glimpse to the PRs' perspectives on NS. Although the majority of PRs share similar opinions on the role of NS as the native born and bred citizens, the question on using NS as a criterion of citizenship will remain a bugbear, and is unlikely to vanish with the downward slide in citizen ratio. Both PRs and citizens agree that NS is indispensable for Singapore and it is administered professionally by the state. However, few PRs agree that citizenship should be tied to participation in NS. In other words, NS should not be a criterion in citizenship application.

Second, the city-state has a large number of transnational marriages and this figure has steadily increased. In 2005, there were 8,406 unions between a Singapore citizen and a foreign spouse, i.e., non-citizen. In 2015, this figure has increased to 8,562, representing 36% of all newly married couples registered in the year (see Fig. 1).[17] This elevated quotient of transnational marriages is one of the highest in the world but ostensibly not unexpected in view of the close interactions between citizens, PRs, and non-residents in Singapore owning to its position as a global business hub.

There are several implications from having a large number of transnational marriages. The foreign spouses for instance, need to be acquainted with the conscription ethos; they have to appreciate and accept Singapore's

---

[16] Leong Chan-Hoong, "Social Markers of Acculturation: A New Research Framework on International Adaptation", *International Journal of Intercultural Relations* 38 (2014), 120–132.

[17] National Population and Talent Division (2016), "Population in Brief 2016". http://www.nptd.gov.sg/Portals/0/Homepage/Highlights/population-in-brief-2016.pdf (accessed 5 January 2017).

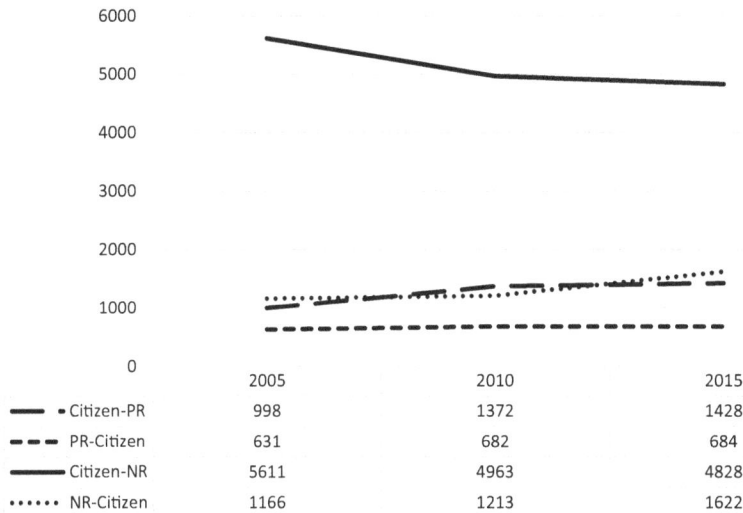

	2005	2010	2015
━ ▪ Citizen-PR	998	1372	1428
━ ━ PR-Citizen	631	682	684
━━ Citizen-NR	5611	4963	4828
•••••• NR-Citizen	1166	1213	1622

Figure 1. Number of marriages by residency status of grooms and brides (Groom-Bride)
Note: PR = Permanent Resident, NR = Non-Resident.
Source: Population in Brief 2016.

defence imperatives and other statutory requirements that underscore the enlistment policy should they decide to sink their roots in the city-state. The children of transnational couples have the option to hold dual-citizenship until the age of 21; for the male offspring, they need to fulfil their NS obligations even if the child intends to renounce his Singapore citizenship.

On the whole, it is unclear how transnational spouses may influence their partners on attitudes to NS and security. It is also simplistic to assume that all foreign spouses can assimilate at the same rate, or will embrace communal values that support conscription like their Singaporean partners. Among all transnational marriages, the majority Singaporean grooms have foreign brides from the region, whilst the local brides have married grooms from more varied cultural backgrounds. How gender and power dynamics are reproduced within transnational families and how that consequently determines opinions to NS remains an unknown and it warrants further investigation.

Finally, more Singaporeans will work and live abroad as the economy becomes more interconnected with others. Presently, about 213,400

Singaporeans are living overseas.[18] The figure represents more than 6% of the city-state's population, one of the highest in the world (see Fig. 2). The population of overseas Singaporeans today has markedly increased by 35% compared to 2004. Anecdotally, those who chose to work and live abroad are mostly younger, highly qualified, and therefore globally mobile individuals whose aspirations for themselves and their families include this overseas experience. The number of overseas Singaporean is set to rise with improved global economic growth, and as more multi-national companies recruit talent from Singapore, a city-state that is known for quality education, English (or multi-lingual) proficiency, and a disciplined workforce.

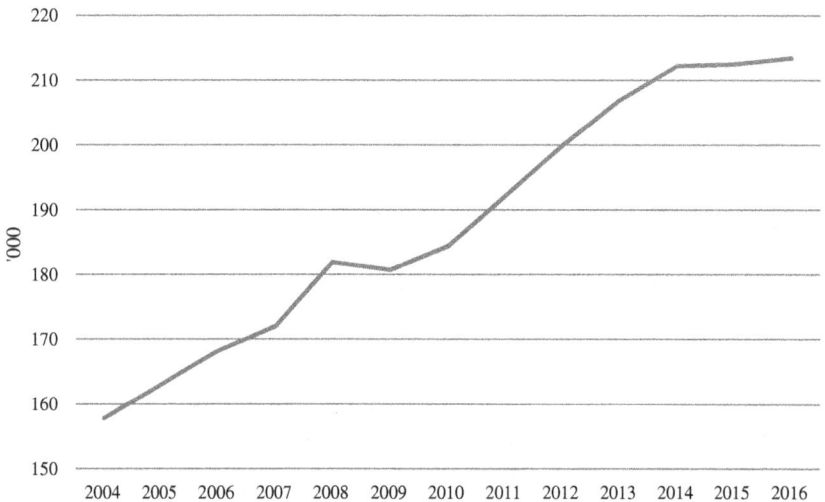

Number of Overseas Singaporeans ('000)												
2004	2005	2006	2007	2008	2009	2010	2011	2012	2013	2014	2015	2016
157.8	163.0	168.2	172.0	181.9	180.7	184.4	192.2	200.0	207.0	212.2	212.5	213.4

Figure 2.   Number of overseas Singaporeans ('000)

Source: Population in Brief 2016.

---

[18] National Population and Talent Division (2016), "Population in Brief 2016". http://www.nptd.gov.sg/Portals/0/Homepage/Highlights/population-in-brief-2016.pdf (accessed 5 January 2017).

The burgeoning population of overseas Singaporeans will have significant ramifications not just to the social fabric of the nation, but also on operational ready National Service (ORNS) duties, colloquially known as "reservist". Presently full-time NSmen often continue their reservist duties in the same ORNS unit. This arrangement enables the servicemen to work with their peers in the same cohort serving their ORNS duty. The increase in turnover of NSmen from deferment and emigration will be a major disruption to the planning of In-Camp-Trainings (ICT) and deployment of soldiers as unfilled vocations will need to be replaced by other appropriately trained NSmen.

More crucially, will the prolonged absence from Singapore of such NSmen diminish the sense of commitment to defend the city-state? And will those who do not go overseas resent those who defer their ORNS duties by working and living abroad? Will the increase in the number of overseas NSmen erode the principle of equity for NS? How effectively and rapidly can the authorities mobilise NSmen who reside overseas should there be a security crisis? In essence, the nascent divide in socioeconomic class may have a collateral impact on commitment to NS. These are some emerging issues that policy makers will have to grapple with in reconciling NS, a domestic policy, with an increasingly international Singapore.

National Service in the Era of Hyperculturalism

What can we then expect from NS in the years ahead? What can we do to ensure it remains a strong foundation of Singapore's defence architecture? To envision the future of this policy, we first need to visualise the social contours of Singapore 50 years from now. The previous section has identified various demographic forces that will reshape NS and defence attitudes. The growing number of non-citizens living in the country, the sizeable pool of overseas Singaporeans, and the complex but deep relationships intertwined in transnational marital unions make the city-state a hyperculture nation.

A hyperculture state is a dynamic, fluid, and complex society where spatial parameters are becoming irrelevant due to technological advancement and cross-cultural interactions.[19] The accelerated rate of change in connectivity, human interactions, and the transformation of values and norms bring forth an environment with unlimited possibilities but one that is motivated by materialistic or self-centred goals (i.e., "what do I get out of it?"). This proposition is neither new nor surprising for a globally integrated city-state like Singapore where the role and influence of the state on the personal lives of the populace has diminished over the years.

At the individual level, the range of opportunities for employment, education, and leisure, will expand exponentially for the majority population, with many options available beyond the island's shores. For the young, talented, and mobile individuals, Singapore may just be another revolving door depending on their life stage and priorities. At the national level however, Singapore's future — and indeed, its survival and existence — will be influenced by mega international forces. For the nation to thrive and to maintain a high quality of life, it will have no choice but to blend in with the ebbs and flows of global trends. Transnational migration, intercultural engagement, desire for personal autonomy, and the swift adoption of emerging technology and social norms will dictate the socio-demographic texture of the global-city. These variables, and the country's geo-political landscape, have made Singapore an epitome of a hyperculture.

The transition to a hyperculture points to the potential for a diverse and polarised populace that share similar opinions in some aspects of being Singaporean, but embrace an antagonistic view in other areas. According to the CSNS survey, most Singaporeans — including citizens and PRs — have shown strong faith in the legitimacy, fairness, and virtue of NS. This concurrence of view augurs well for NS as a social edifice. But how will their points of divergence impact NS? The objective of NS has evolved in the minds of the people since the turbulent era of the 1960s and 1970s. Enlistment is not solely regarded as a vehicle to defend national sovereignty. Beyond the regimental discipline and physical training, NS is also a criterion of citizenship from the native-born perspective. It is a critical

---

[19] For a fuller examination of hyperculture, see: Stephen Bertman, *Hyperculture: The Human Cost of Speed* (Westport: Praeger, 1998).

marker of social identity and a tool to define equitable relations. This differing view on the objective of NS will be a key contestation between Singaporeans who are NS liable and those who are not. In this new environment, cost-benefit analysis will be the critical benchmark in measuring fairness, and personal sacrifices will be amplified in a rapidly changing competitive job environment.

Hyperculture is also a by-product of an advanced, integrated global economy, and significant prestige is associated with the cosmopolitan experience. Singaporeans who travel far and beyond, have an extensive network in other global cities and may adopt values which are ostensibly more outward looking. They may appear to enjoy a superior social status in contrast to those without such experience, i.e., Singaporeans who do not have the means or interest to work, live, or study abroad. The distinction between these two groups of Singaporeans could be conflated with a socio-economic class divide, and commitment to NS becomes collateral damage. NSmen residing in Singapore may feel disadvantaged as their overseas-based counterparts are exempted from military recalls and ICTs.

However, the clash of perspectives between "citizen and non-citizen" or "local and overseas Singaporeans" is not inevitable. Rather than focus on the schism, the emphasis can be centred around their shared memories of NS, and NS as a personal developmental milestone. In particular, the benefits of NS in shaping personal resilience and character development, NS as the embodiment of Singaporean values such as equality, justice and vision. In the CSNS survey, these features are equally and strongly embraced by both the citizen and PR samples; the characteristics exemplify developmental milestones that all parents would like their children to have, and a source of pride for being associated with this unique institution. In essence, the NS institution could be reconstructed as a personal developmental milestone as opposed to a narrative that revolves around national obligations or sacrifices to the servicemen and their families.

At a broader level, could the enlistment policy be curated as a hallmark of Singapore cultural identity? The SAFVC was created two years to provide a platform for first generation PRs, and women to partake in national defence, albeit in a limited form. The scheme was a step in the right direction and the response to the SAFVC has so far been encouraging.[20] By expanding the scope of their defence contribution, for instance, having a longer period of service in a wider range of vocations, a stronger global imprint of the Singapore identity and citizenship can be forged amidst forces of globalisation. In essence, the common space for all groups could be expanded considerably if the NS narrative tilts towards individual growth and the formation of a distinct social identity. This will enable citizens, PRs, foreign spouses, and overseas Singaporeans to become a part this platform.

This perspective of using NS as cultural marker is akin to demographer Lily Kong's argument to re-imagine "Singaporeanness" as a non-territory bound national identity that exists no matter where the Singaporean is, as certain distinguishing features (e.g., slang, accent, shared experiences) will differentiate them from the rest.[21] According to Kong, this salient sense of identity will spill over into a stronger sense of rootedness to and ownership of Singapore. While this view is seemingly inconsistent with the first principle of NS, i.e., to serve a critical defence need, in the long run it is a step towards serving a more fundamental larger mission, the development of a Singapore identity and a deeper sense of home. Having both are key to any commitment to defend Singapore.

Indeed, to re-imagine what NS is like decades from now, policy makers will need to keep track of the evolving social terrain and the changing socio-emotional tempo of Singaporeans. To continually preserve and strengthen the ethos and shared memories of NS at the personal and national levels requires an alignment of all social indicators. NS has been a critical pillar to the success story of Singapore; but this story will be best transmitted in the format that most if not all people are familiar with.

---

[20] Chan Luo Er, "First cohort of SAFVC volunteers mark end of basic training", *Channel News Asia*, 22 August 2015.

[21] Lily Kong, "Globalisation and Singaporean Transmigration: Re-imagining and Negotiating National Identity", *Political Geography* 18 (1999), 563–589.

Part 3
Debates

Chapter 8

Dual Citizenship and National Service in Singapore

Terri-Anne Teo and Priscilla Cabuyao

In Singapore, discussions about dual citizenship often occur in tandem with the issue of mandatory National Service (NS). While debates about dual citizenship include a range of issues,[1] this chapter focuses on how it affects loyalty and identity rather than the security arguments surrounding dual citizenship and NS. Drawing from empirical examples, this chapter evaluates the tenability of one of the often held key arguments against dual citizenship: dual citizenship is antithetical to NS' goal of nation-building.

We recognise the various interpretations of citizenship that include legal and normatively substantive definitions, where the latter places moral judgment on what citizenship should entail and how a "good" or "bad" citizen looks. For the purposes of this chapter, we refer to citizenship in a legal sense, where it indicates an individual's formal status of membership to a nation-state.[2] Dual citizenship, therefore, refers to the

---

[1] For elaboration on concerns over voting rights, ethnonational identity and societal decline, see: T. Alexander Aleinikoff and Douglas Klusmeyer, "Plural Nationality: Facing the Future in a Migratory World", in *Citizenship Today: Global Perspectives and Practices*, eds. T. Alexander Aleinikoff and Douglas Klusmeyer (Washington, D.C.: Brookings Institution Press, 2001), 63–88; Peter J. Spiro, *At Home in Two Countries* (New York: New York University Press, 2016); Thomas Faist and Peter Kivisto, eds., *Dual Citizenship in Global Perspective: From Unitary to Multiple Citizenship* (Basingstoke and New York: Palgrave Macmillan, 2007).

[2] See: Audrey Macklin, "The Securitisation of Dual Citizenship", in *Dual Citizenship in Global Perspective: From Unitary to Multiple Citizenship*, eds. Peter Kivisto and Thomas

occurrence where individuals are citizens of more than one country as a result of birthright based on *jus soli* (born in the territory), *jus sanguinis* (right of blood, that is, by descent), a combination of both or by naturalisation without the renunciation of previous citizenships. The trajectories leading to dual citizenship and the conditions and exclusions guarding it vary across national legislation.[3] Our discussion also includes the recognition that citizenship(s) holds different meanings and functions among individuals. For some, it evokes feelings of loyalty and identity, while for others, it represents a "prosaically instrumental good" that provides privileges, resources and political and social capital.[4]

This chapter argues that NS may be compatible with a dual citizenship policy in Singapore when the arguments over identity and loyalty are weighed up. We begin by introducing the context of Singapore and the main contentions surrounding dual citizenship in relation to NS and national security. Then, we contest the view that NS and dual citizenship policies are incompatible in Singapore. First, we evaluate the widespread view that dual citizenship dilutes national identity and loyalty. This section argues that there is scarce evidence showing how dual citizenship policies negatively affect one's sense of belonging or loyalty to a nation-state. Loyalties are situational and complex, finding commonality across dual nationalities and multiple identities. Second, it is unlikely for dual citizenship to affect social cohesion and an individual's loyalty to the nation-state. Arguments in support of single citizenship, which are based on the belief that dual citizenship will diminish NS' ability to construct the nation, are increasingly untenable. Our arguments demonstrate how the significance placed on NS in Singapore will still prevail should a dual citizenship policy, along with its complementary benefits, be introduced.

Faist (New York: Palgrave Macmillan, 2012), 53.

[3] Conditions for dual citizenship include age, refugee or ex-refugee statuses, certain country restrictions and so on. For a more extensive spectrum of conditions, see: Tanja B. Sejersen, "'I Vow to Thee My Countries' — The Expansion of Dual Citizenship in the 21st Century", *International Migration Review* 42/3 (2008), 523–549.

[4] Gary P. Freeman and Nedim Ögelman, "Homeland Citizenship Policies and the Status of Third Country Nationals in the European Union", *Journal of Ethnic and Migration Studies* 24/4 (1998), 770.

Situating Singapore

Singapore maintains a single citizenship policy alongside mandated conscription through NS. Where these policies are not necessarily interdependent, they are closely intertwined in the context of Singapore. This section first outlines the legal requirements binding citizenship to NS in Singapore. Second, prominent cases where male dual citizens sought to renounce their Singaporean citizenship or failed to report for NS illustrate the emotional and contentious nature of the subject in Singapore. Third, state responses to debates and rationale for policy demonstrate its strong stance against dual citizenship and its established relationship with Singapore's conscription policy.

Singapore Citizenship Laws and NS

Singapore's Constitution declares that Singapore citizens who acquire citizenship with another country will be deprived of Singapore citizenship and those who hold dual citizenship are required to renounce their other citizenship if they wish to retain their Singapore citizenship beyond the age of 21.[5] However, permission to renounce could be withheld if a male Singaporean citizen has not fulfilled his NS liabilities under the Enlistment Act.[6]

Upon fulfilling their conscription duties, male Singaporean dual citizens are required to renounce one of their citizenships upon reaching the age of 21 as per Singapore law. Able-bodied male Singaporean citizens and second generation Permanent Residents (PRs) typically serve

---

[5] Singapore Statutes Online, "Part X: Citizenship, Art. 128, 134", *Constitution of the Republic of Singapore*, accessed 20 December 2016, downloaded from http://statutes.agc. gov.sg/aol/download/0/0/pdf/binaryFile/pdfFile.pdf?CompId:62847936-2328-4409-aa97-2ff69536bc2a; Ministry of Foreign Affairs, "Renunciation of Singapore Citizenship", *Embassy of the Republic of Singapore, Washington D.C.*, accessed 18 October 2016, https://www.mfa.gov.sg/content/mfa/overseasmission/washington/consular_services/wstcon_renouncesc.html

[6] Singapore Statutes Online, "Part X: Citizenship, Art. 128"; "Enlistment Act", accessed 20 December 2016, downloaded from http://statutes.agc.gov.sg/aol/download/0/0/pdf/binaryFile/pdfFile.pdf?CompId:b442670e-ca1a-49af-bd54-1aaf3a7710d6

full-time NS for two years at 18 and are liable for annual obligations until the age of 40.[7] Similarly, male Singaporeans holding dual citizenship serve for two years at age 18 unless they are granted an exit permit, which allows postponement of NS. Singaporean male dual citizens are "expected to fulfil NS obligations" and non-compliance leads to imprisonment, a fine, or both.[8]

Controversies

This issue of Singaporean citizens defaulting from serving NS often receives public attention. Such cases are complicated when citizens hold another citizenship, as a result of immigrating abroad at a young age while still holding Singaporean citizenship that was upon birth in Singapore to Singaporean parents. For instance, the recent sentencing of a Singaporean-Canadian dual citizen Jonathan Tan to a four-month jail term for evading conscription for a decade was widely reported in the local media.[9] The increasing ubiquity of these cases may be attributed in part to Singaporean emigration (i.e., renunciation of Singaporean

---

[7] Officers are liable to serve until the age of 50. See Enlistment Act; Contact Singapore, "National Service", accessed 20 December 2016, https://www.contactsingapore.sg/en/investors-business-owners/visa-passes/residency-and-citizenship/national-service

[8] Enlistment Act; Parliament of Singapore, "Ministerial Statement: National Service Defaulters (Statement by the Minister for Defence, Sitting Date: 16 January 2006)", accessed 23 November 2016, http://sprs.parl.gov.sg/search/topic.jsp?currentTopicID=00071202-ZZ&currentPubID=00075183-ZZ&topicKey=00075183-ZZ.00071202-ZZ_1%2B%2B; Singapore Statutes Online, 'Singapore Armed Forces Act', accessed 17 October 2016, http://statutes.agc.gov.sg/aol/search/display/view.w3p;page=0;query=DocId%3A%22f7446be9-daef-4a09-bb63-8e8da8b61f4c%22%20Status%3Apublished%20Depth%3A0;rec=0

[9] Shaffiq Idris Alkhatib, "Man admits evading NS for a decade", *The Straits Times*, 14 January 2017, http://www.straitstimes.com/singapore/courts-crime/man-admits-evading-ns-for-a-decade-0; Valerie Koh, "Son of senior lawyer hauled to court for evading NS", *Today Online*, 13 January 2017, http://www.todayonline.com/singapore/son-senior-lawyer-hauled-court-evading-ns; Justin Ong, "Man who dodged NS for 10 years sentenced to 4 months' jail", 2 February 2017, http://www.channelnewsasia.com/news/singapore/man-who-dodged-ns-for-10-years-sentenced-to-4-months-jail/3486142.html; Vanessa Paige Chelvan, "Man pleads guilty to defaulting on NS obligations for a decade", *CNA*, 13 January 2017, http://www.channelnewsasia.com/news/singapore/man-pleads-guilty-to-defaulting-on-ns-obligations-for-a-decade/3436532.html

citizenship for that of the host country), increasing number of Singaporeans living overseas,[10] rise in transnational marriages and a corresponding increase in children who hold dual citizenship. From 2005 to 2015, at least one-third of marriages involving Singaporeans were transnational.[11]

Controversy over dual citizenship often occurs when male dual citizens default from NS and do not fulfil the conditions for renunciation. The state repeatedly places emphasis on the fulfilment of NS as a matter of obligation and national identity. In a 2006 ministerial statement on NS defaulters, then Minister for Defence Teo Chee Hean stated that "only those who have emigrated at a young age and have not enjoyed substantial socioeconomic benefits are allowed to renounce their citizenship without serving National Service."[12] Beyond anecdotal evidence and commentary on online fora,[13] there is no official documentation that explicates what "substantial socioeconomic benefits" indicate or when "a young age" expires,

---

[10] See: National Population and Talent Division, Strategy Group, Prime Minister's Office, Singapore Department of Statistics, Ministry of Home Affairs, Immigration & Checkpoints Authority, *Population in Brief* (2016). From 2004 to 2008, there had been a noticeable growth in the population size of overseas Singaporeans. In 2009, there was a slight dip in the total number of Singaporeans overseas before a continuous increase from 2010 to 2016.

[11] National Population and Talent Division, *Population in Brief* (2016). The dramatic increase in transnational marriages is not unique to Singapore, evident across the region and on a global scale. See: Gavin Jones and Hsiu-hua Shen, "International Marriage in East and Southeast Asia: Trends and Research Emphases", *Citizenship Studies* 12/1 (2008), 9–25; Katharine Charsley, ed., *Transnational Marriage: New Perspectives from Europe and Beyond* (New York and Abingdon: Routledge, 2012).

[12] Parliament of Singapore, "Ministerial Statement: National Service Defaulters (Statement by the Minister for Defence, Sitting Date: 16 January 2006)".

[13] Anecdotal evidence and online fora suggest that legal exemptions for male Singaporean citizens only apply if they (a) hold another citizenship before the age of 11; (b) inform the Ministry of Defence of their intention to renounce Singaporean citizenship and apply for an exit permit from the age of 13 and obtain deferment at age 18; (c) do not use or benefit from Singaporean citizenship after age 11 (i.e., does not reside in Singapore upon turning 11); and (d) renounce Singaporean citizenship at age 21. See: Singapore Expats, "Guide to NS Issues", 25 June 2009, http://www.singaporeexpats.com/resources-in-singapore/articles/guide-to-ns. htm; The Law Commission, "Enlistment Act", 93 § (2015), http://statutes.agc.gov.sg/aol/ download/0/0/pdf/binaryFile/pdfFile.pdf?CompId:b442670e-ca1a-49af-bd54-1aaf3a7710d6

which may explain the diverse contestations that emerge during such controversies.[14]

In 2008, three Norwegian-Singaporean male dual citizens sought to renounce their Singapore citizenship and were not permitted to do so due to unfulfilled NS obligations.[15] Born in Singapore to a Norwegian father and Singaporean mother, the Bugge brothers left for Norway at age five, three, and two respectively and returned to Singapore after 10 years. All three chose to renounce their Singapore citizenship, but renunciation attempts were rejected as "only persons who have emigrated at a very young age together with their families, and who have not enjoyed the privileges of Singapore citizenship, will be allowed to renounce their Singapore citizenships without serving national service," according to a representative from the Ministry of Defence.[16]

Online discussions on the case of the Bugge brothers comprise disparate views on NS and citizenship. Notably, these comments about NS revolve around issues of bureaucracy and the meaning of citizenship, rather than national security issues concerning the loyalty of dual citizens. They include views similar to that of the state, that the brothers should serve NS as they have benefitted from Singapore citizenship. Others question why female citizens are not required to serve NS if the reasoning is the enjoyment of the privileges of Singapore citizenship; display confusion towards the age limit when one can be deemed to have not benefitted from the citizenship; blame the parents for not renouncing their sons' Singaporean citizenships at birth; note that infants cannot decide for themselves, and thus decision on citizenship choice should indeed be done at a

---

[14]According to the Singapore government's eCitizen website, the privileges and rights of Singapore citizenship include suffrage, ease of travel, tax reliefs/rebates, property ownership, healthcare subsidies, and affordable education. Singapore Government, "Singapore Citizenship: Your Privileges and Rights", *eCitizen*. https://www.ecitizen.gov.sg/Topics/Pages/Singapore-citizenship-Your-privileges-and-rights.aspx (accessed 22 December 2016). There is also a lack of clarity and contestation involving the penalties of defaulters. See: Jermyn Chow, "Punishing NS dodgers: What's fair, What's not?", *The Straits Times*, 25 February 2016, http://www.straitstimes.com/opinion/punishing-ns-dodgers-whats-fair-whats-not

[15]Amelia Tan, "Give up citizenship? Brothers must do NS first", *The Straits Times*, 25 August 2008, 27.

[16]Tan, "Give up citizenship? Brothers must do NS first", 27.

later age; accuse the Singapore government of being "childish" and "unforgiving"; and label the Bugge brothers as "victims of procedural requirements."[17] Others posted comments and questions about their own cases as Singaporeans holding dual citizenship, foreigners married to Singaporeans and vice versa.[18]

Another publicised case linking NS to dual citizenship emerged in 2016. Brandon Smith, born to a New Zealander father and Singaporean mother, reportedly applied for NS deferment until the age 21 (the legal age at which he is permitted to renounce Singapore citizenship).[19] However, Smith's NS deferment application was rejected and his obligation to enlist was stressed by the authorities.[20] Smith's failure to fulfil NS obligations resulted in a jail term and fine. In a press release, the Ministry of Foreign Affairs reiterated the underlying tenets of Singapore's conscription policy, which include the "fundamental principles of universality

[17] ClubSNAP, "Thread: Norwegian Brothers". http://www.clubsnap.com/forums/showthread.php?t=408649, http://www.clubsnap.com/forums/showthread.php?t=408649&page=2, http://www.clubsnap.com/forums/showthread.php?t=408649&page=3 (accessed 18 October 2016); nofearSingapore, "National Service — Letter from Father of Bugge Brothers". http://nofearsingapore.blogspot.sg/2008/09/national-service-letter-from-father-of.html (accessed 18 October 2016); takchek (读书), "Give Up Citizenship? Brothers Must Do NS First". https://takchek.wordpress.com/2008/08/25/give-up-citizenship-brothers-must-do-ns-first/ (accessed 18 October 2016). See also: Chua Chin Leng aka redbean, "Bugging Singapore", *My Singapore News*. http://mysingaporenews.blogspot.sg/2008/08/bugging-singapore.html (accessed 18 October 2016); soc.culture.singapore, "Cannot Renounce Singapore Citizenship", *Google Groups*. https://groups.google.com/forum/#!searchin/soc.culture.singapore/cannot$20renounce$20singapore$20citizenship%7Csort:relevance/soc.culture.singapore/67WNdBe-_LU/9xLkjd0OZuIJ (accessed 18 October 2016).
[18] Simply Jean, "Of Dual Citizenship, National Service, Exemptions and Your CPF Money". http://blog.simplyjean.com/2008/08/26/of-dual-citizenship-national-service-exemptions-and-your-cpf-money/ (accessed 18 October 2016).
[19] Erin Speedy and Cate Broughton, "Kiwi Teenager Forced to Do Singaporean National Service or Risk Jail Time and Fines". http://www.stuff.co.nz/national/76183007/Kiwi-teenager-forced-to-do-Singaporean-national-service-or-risk-jail-time-and-fines (accessed 18 October 2016).
[20] Lee Min Kok, "Singapore-born New Zealand teenager faces fine, jail as he seeks to avoid National Service call-up", *The Straits Times*, 24 January 2016, http://www.straitstimes.com/asia/australianz/singapore-born-new-zealand-teenager-faces-fine-jail-as-he-seeks-to-avoid-national (accessed 18 October 2016).

and equity for NS. All Singaporeans are expected to fulfil our NS obligations as citizens. It would not be fair to allow citizens to avoid NS just
because they reside overseas."[21]

Smith's case prompted commentaries and online debates echoing those
that surfaced during the Bugge controversy.[22] While a considerable number of comments acknowledge NS as a duty that needs to be fulfilled by
male Singapore citizens, others argue that requiring (with some using the
term "forcing") dual citizens who intend to renounce Singapore citizenship at 21 to still serve NS is a waste of state resources.[23]

Significantly, views in favour of dual citizenship were rearticulated
in the aftermath of Smith's case. Commentators highlighted that PRs
are more likely to apply for Singaporean citizenship if they are not
forced to relinquish the citizenship of their home country due to

---

[21] MFA, "Written Answer to Question 32 of Notice Paper 37 of 2016", *Press Room*, 29 February
2016, https://www.mfa.gov.sg/content/mfa/media_centre/press_room/pr/2016/201602/press_
201602291.html

[22] Chirag Agarwal, "Commentary: Dual citizenship: Little to fear, much to gain", *TODAY*, 8
March 2016, http://www.todayonline.com/commentary/dual-citizenship-little-fear-much-gain
(accessed 17 November 2016); Neo, "Voices: Dual citizenship compromises a person's loyalty
to Singapore"; Grace Wang Shi Jia, "Voices: Dual citizenship may strengthen immigrants'
loyalty", *TODAY*, 28 March 2016, http://www.todayonline.com/voices/dual-citizenship-may-
strengthen-immigrants-loyalty (accessed 10 October 2016); Terry Xu, "New Zealand teenager
to serve National Service in Singapore or face jail-time and fines (Comments)", *The Online
Citizen*, 25 January 2016, http://www.theonlinecitizen.com/2016/01/25/new-zealand-teenager-
to-serve-national-service-in-singapore-or-face-jail-time-and-fines/ (accessed 16 November
2016); The Straits Times Facebook Page, "'All Singaporeans Are Expected to Fulfil Our NS
Obligations as Citizens,' said the Foreign Affairs Ministry. 'It Would Not Be Fair to Allow
Citizens to Avoid NS Just Because They Reside Overseas'", https://m.facebook.com/
TheStraitsTimes/posts/10153313180397115?comment_tracking=%7B%22tn%22%3A%22O
%22%7D (accessed 16 November 2016); Yawning Bread, "Pay Back Our Love". https://yawn-
ingbread.wordpress.com/2016/01/26/pay-back-our-love/ (accessed 2 September 2016); Aisyah
Lyana, "No Escaping from National Service", *Youth.sg*. https://www.youth.sg/Our-Voice/Your-
Take/2016/3/No-escaping-from-national-service (accessed 19 October 2016).

[23] Xu, "New Zealand teenager to serve National Service in Singapore or face jail-time and
fines (Comments)"; The Straits Times Facebook Page, "'All Singaporeans Are Expected
to Fulfil Our NS Obligations as Citizens,' said the Foreign Affairs Ministry. 'It Would Not
Be Fair to Allow Citizens to Avoid NS Just Because They Reside Overseas'"; Yawning
Bread, "Pay Back Our Love"; Lyana, "No Escaping from National Service".

sentimental reasons. Dual citizenship may also address concerns about a brain drain, due to the number of highly-skilled economic migrants who renounce Singaporean citizenship in favour of their host countries. Given the option, they may instead choose dual citizenship, which may encourage links between the Singaporean diaspora and home country.[24]

In relation to conscription, commentators propose that Singapore should make NS optional for dual citizens.[25] While acknowledging the possibility that Singaporeans living overseas may lose their attachment or belonging to Singapore, they suggest looking at dual citizens' individual willingness to serve NS based on their ties to their host nation and Singapore as their birthplace. Such views demonstrate cognisance that loyalty and identity are not experienced in an exact, rigid, and uniform way.[26]

Recent Changes to Policy

New benchmarks for NS defaulters have increased the severity of punishments. This change has greatest impact on those who default for longer periods as it affects their fitness for service and the length of time they can serve as reservists. This ruling particularly affected Singapore's longest NS defaulter, Ang Lee Thye, who defaulted for more than 23 years. Ang's jail term was increased from 24 to 33 months.[27]

In 2016, two Singaporean brothers were convicted for failing to report for NS for more for more than three years while remaining in India

---

[24] Agarwal, "Commentary: Dual citizenship: Little to fear, much to gain".

[25] Agarwal, "Commentary: Dual citizenship: Little to fear, much to gain"; Neo, "Voices: Dual citizenship compromises a person's loyalty to Singapore"; Terence Lim, "Voices: A mistake to equate citizenship with loyalty", *TODAY*, 29 March 2016, http://www.todayonline.com/voices/mistake-equate-citizenship-loyalty (accessed 16 November 2016); Wang, "Voices: Dual citizenship may strengthen immigrants' loyalty".

[26] Lyana, "No Escaping from National Service" (see comments); The Straits Times Facebook Page, "'All Singaporeans Are Expected to Fulfil Our NS Obligations as Citizens,' said the Foreign Affairs Ministry. 'It Would Not Be Fair to Allow Citizens to Avoid NS Just Because They Reside Overseas'"; Agarwal, "Commentary: Dual citizenship: Little to fear, much to gain" (see comments section).

[27] Chelvan, "Man pleads guilty to defaulting on NS obligations for a decade".

without a valid exit permit for more than five years. They were convicted despite serving NS upon their return and doing so exceptionally well, with one being selected for Officer Cadet School and the other winning a Soldier of the Month award.[28] Sakthikanesh Chidambaram was jailed for three weeks, as he failed to report for NS for more than five years while he pursued his university education at the National Institute of Technology in Kurukshetra, India. His younger brother Vandana Kumar Chidambaram was fined $6,000 for not reporting to NS for more than three years.

The new benchmarks affected the Chidambaran brothers' sentencing, which increased in July 2017. The panel of judges argued that exceptional NS performance should not justify reduced sentences as "it is the obligation of every male Singaporean to do his best in his NS ... It seems to us wrong for a defaulter who does no more than that ... should be rewarded in this way."[29] Consequently, Sakthikanesh Chidambaram now faces ten weeks in jail instead of three and Vandana Kumar Chidambaram has also been sentenced to jail for seven weeks.[30]

State Responses

Responding to debates around these controversies, the Singapore Government emphasises the importance of single citizenship and NS in relation to national identity and social cohesion. While NS and dual citizenship are two separate matters in legal terms, justifications for their existence overlap. Both policies are variously rationalised through the crucial role they play in fostering a strong national identity and loyalty.

Government officials state that Singapore (and by extension Singaporeans) is not yet ready for dual citizenship, arguing that single

---

[28] Amir Hussain, "Brothers sentenced to jail and fine for not returning for NS duties in time", *The Straits Times*, 19 October 2016, http://www.straitstimes.com/singapore/courts-crime/brothers-sentenced-to-jail-and-fine-for-not-returning-for-ns-duties-in-time

[29] Selina Lum, "Court sets out punishment guidelines for NS dodgers", *The Straits Times*, 26 July 2017, http://www.straitstimes.com/singapore/court-sets-out-punishment-guidelines-for-ns-dodgers

[30] Ibid.

citizenship fortifies the Singaporean identity and dual citizenship would dilute it.[31] It was argued in Parliament that Singapore, as a young nation, is not ready for the issues that may emerge with the introduction of dual citizenship and there is no certainty that one "would still retain his identity and loyalty to Singapore as his homeland wherever he goes."[32]

In 2013, Deputy Prime Minister Teo Chee Hean responded to queries with the familiar refrain that "allowing Singaporeans to retain or acquire a second citizenship is unlikely to enhance identity but could dilute it."[33] There appears to be an assumption that national ties, belonging, identification or loyalty to Singapore, whether through parentage, birth or long-term domicile, are automatically removed when one acquires another citizenship.

In addition, the renunciation of former citizenship has been declared in parliamentary debates as an insurance of long-term commitment to Singapore.[34] The same rhetoric reappears in the Immigration and

---

[31] Derrick A Paulo, "Time not ripe for dual citizenship", *TODAY*, 24 August 2006, 3; Loh Chee Kong, "Citizenship not a 'free gift'", *TODAY*, 28 May 2008, 3; Lee U-Wen, "No dual citizenship for now: DPM Teo", *The Business Times*, 8 March 2013, 2.

[32] Parliament of Singapore, "Oral Answers to Questions: Singapore Citizens Taking Up Dual Citizenship (Sitting Date: 8 March 1999)", accessed 21 December 2016, https://sprs. parl.gov.sg/search/topic.jsp?currentTopicID=00066722-ZZ&currentPubID=00069821-ZZ&topicKey=00069821-ZZ.00066722-ZZ_1%2Bid003_19990308_S0005_T00061-oral-answer%2B; Parliament of Singapore, "Written Answers to Questions: Dual Citizenship (Sitting Date: 6 March 2000)", accessed 21 December 2016, https://sprs.parl. gov.sg/search/topic.jsp?currentTopicID=00067342-ZZ&currentPubID=00069850-ZZ&topicKey=00069850-ZZ.00067342-ZZ_1%2Bid015_20000306_S0008_T00151-written-answer%2B

[33] Cited in Nasir and Turner, *The Future of Singapore: Population, Society and The Nature of the State*, 60.

[34] Parliament of Singapore, "Oral Answers to Questions: Singapore Citizens Taking Up Dual Citizenship (Sitting Date: 8 March 1999)"; "Written Answers to Questions: Dual Citizenship (Sitting Date: 6 March 2000)"; "Oral Answers to Questions: Dual Citizenship (Sitting Date: 7 March 2013)", accessed 21 December 2016, https://sprs.parl.gov.sg/search/topic. jsp?currentTopicID=00079072-WA&currentPubID=00079066-WA&topicKey=00079066-WA.00079072-WA_2%2Bid-e4e59212-0323-4e21-a2a7-5c2528971927%2B; "Written Answers to Questions for Oral Answer Not Answered by 3.00 pm: Singaporeans Who Previously Held Foreign Citizenship (Sitting Date: 21 January 2014)", accessed 21 December 2016, https://sprs. parl.gov.sg/search/topic.jsp?currentTopicID=00008111-WA&currentPubID=00005488-WA&topicKey=00005488-WA.00008111-WA_2%2BhansardContent43a675dd-5000-

Checkpoint Authority's responses to published concerns about lack of access to dual citizenship.[35] This discourse about dual citizenship demonstrates an overarching state narrative that dual citizenship will have a negative effect on national identity, unity and commitment to Singapore.

Similar to their stance on citizenship, the state maintains an unwavering position on NS. While acknowledging the removal of military conscription in other countries, the state emphasises that NS is a priority for Singapore for two reasons: (a) the need for critical manpower mass to have a security force capable of competently defending the state and (b) the role of NS in nation-building. While the debate regarding the former remains open,[36] this section addresses the arguments for the latter through the role NS has in the formation of the citizen-soldier identity and social cohesion.

42da-9fd5-40978d79310f%2B; "Written Answers to Questions for Oral Answer Not Answered by End of Question Time: Possibility of Dual Citizenship for Singaporeans (Sitting Date: 7 November 2016)", accessed 21 December 2016, https://sprs.parl.gov.sg/search/topic.jsp?currentTopicID=00010222-WA&currentPubID=00010243-WA&topicKey=00010243-WA.00010222-WA_5%2BhansardContent43a675dd-5000-42da-9fd5-40978d79310f%2B#

[35] Immigration & Checkpoints Authority, "Response to 'Close Escape Route' of PR Spouses", 'Dilemma of a Foreign Bride with No Long-Term Pass' & 'Allow Dual Citizenship for S'porean Kids with Foreign Parent' (The Straits Times, 12 Feb 2013)", accessed 15 November 2016, https://www.ica.gov.sg/news_details.aspx?nid=12847

[36] For expert opinions on the subject, see: Joachim K Blatter, Stefanie Erdmann, and Katja Schwanke, "Acceptance of Dual Citizenship: Empirical Data and Political Contexts" (Lucerne: Institute of Political Science, University of Lucerne, 2009); Triadafilos Triadafilopoulos, "Dual Citizenship and Security Norms in Historical Perspective", in *Dual Citizenship in Global Perspective: From Unitary to Multiple Citizenship*, eds. Thomas Faist and Peter Kivisto (Basingstoke and New York: Palgrave Macmillan, 2007), 27–41; Marjan Malesic, *Conscription vs. All-Volunteer Forces in Europe* (Baden-Baden: Nomos Verlagsgesellschaft, 2003); Rafael Ajangiz, "The European Farewell to Conscription?", in *The Comparative Study of Conscription in the Armed Forces*, eds. Lars Mjøset and Stephan van Holde (Amsterdam: Elsevier Science, 2002), 307–333; Sejersen, "'I Vow to Thee My Countries' — The Expansion of Dual Citizenship in the 21st Century"; Charles C. Moskos, John Allen Williams and David R. Segal, *The Postmodern Military: Armed Forces after the Cold War* (New York: Oxford University Press, 2000); Nasir and Turner, *The Future of Singapore: Population, Society and The Nature of the State*, 53.

NS represents the identity of the Singaporean citizen, symbolising loyalty, rite of passage and national values. The completion of NS is constructed as a mark of success and an achievement of the citizen-soldier, a view that is embedded within the Singaporean psyche.[37] A key aspect of the citizen-soldier identity is loyalty, as emphasised by Singapore's first defence minister Dr Goh Keng Swee, who asserted that "nothing creates loyalty and national consciousness more speedily and more thoroughly than participation in defence and membership of the armed forces."[38]

The ability of NS to fulfil affective purposes is bolstered by narratives of shared experience and that it represents a pivotal stage in a citizen's life. Framed as a national institution and "way of life", NS (re)constructs national values of universality (all fit men are required to serve) and equity (where every conscript is treated the same way "regardless of background or status") of its diverse citizenry.[39] Through gendered themes of manhood, family, and generational achievements, NS is described within state and military discourse as a "rite of passage" to becoming a fully-fledged active and serving Singapore citizen, and from adolescence to manhood.[40]

This sense of social cohesion extends beyond male National Servicemen. While only male citizens are mandated to enlist, the image of NS as a collective and universal experience for Singaporeans is presented through an acknowledgment of the role, support, and contributions of family

---

[37] Leong Chan-Hoong, Yang Wai Wai and Jerrold Hong, "National Service: The Holy Grail in the Management of Social Diversity", in *Managing Diversity in Singapore: Policies and Prospects*, eds. Mathew Mathews and Chiang Wai Fong (London: Imperial College Press, 2016), 304.

[38] Alon Peled, *A Question of Loyalty: Military Manpower Policy in Multiethnic States* (Ithaca and London: Cornell University Press, 1998), 97–98.

[39] Chan, "The Citizen-Soldier in Modern Democracies: The Case for Conscription in Singapore", 48. Parliament of Singapore, "Ministerial Statement: National Service Defaulters (Statement by the Minister for Defence, Sitting Date: 16 January 2006)"; Ministry of Defence (MINDEF), "Committee to Strengthen National Service Report", accessed 7 November 2016, downloaded from https://www.mindef.gov.sg/strengthenNS/ csns-recommendations.html#.V9utavl96M8. See also: https://www.mindef.gov.sg/ strengthenNS/assets/pdf/CSNS_Full_Report.pdf

[40] Nasir and Turner, *The Future of Singapore: Population, Society and The Nature of the State*.

members, spouses, employers, and female volunteers to the operation of NS.[41] Leong *et al.* write[42]:

> Singapore cannot be defended with the SAF alone, and National Service cannot achieve its mission without the support of family members, colleagues and employers of servicemen. These include parents who risk having their sons injured in military exercises; spouses who take up the slack in parenting duties; workplace colleagues who shoulder the extra workload from colleagues attending in-camp training; and business sectors that need to make alternate arrangements to ensure continuity when NS men are called up for duty.

NS also maintains state-sponsored constructions of Singapore's multi-racial national identity. The 1971 Singapore Yearbook articulates this relationship where it states that "apart from fulfilling military requirements, NS has the wider object of integrating a multi-racial, multi-lingual, and multi-religious community committed to Singapore and the well-being of its citizens."[43] In these ways, Singapore's policy of NS is justified as the protector and driver of national security and national identity.

Despite the state's robust defence of its policies, there are calls for dual citizenship and the eradication of military conscription[44] alongside polar-

---

[41] National Archives of Singapore, "Speech By Mr Lee Hsien Loong, Prime Minister, at '40 Years Of National Service Commemoration Dinner', 27 September 2007, 7.30 PM at Pasir Laba Camp", accessed 30 October, http://www.nas.gov.sg/archivesonline/speeches/view-html?filename=20070927975.htm; Leong *et al.*, "National Service: The Holy Grail in the Management of Social Diversity"; MINDEF, "Committee to Strengthen National Service Report"; MINDEF, "NS is…", accessed 24 October 2016, downloaded from https://www.mindef.gov.sg/dam/publications/eBooks/Featured/NSis.pdf

[42] Leong *et al.*, "National Service: The Holy Grail in the Management of Social Diversity", 304.

[43] Peled, *A Question of Loyalty: Military Manpower Policy in Multiethnic States*, 99.

[44] Bryan Cheang, "Conscription: Necessary Or Outdated?", *The Online Citizen: A Community of Singaporeans*, 20 June 2012, https://www.theonlinecitizen.com/2012/06/20/conscription-necessary-or-outdated/; Ajax Copperwater, "Conscription — An Illusion of Security", *The Online Citizen: A Community of Singaporeans*, 20 December 2010, https://www.theonline-citizen.com/2010/12/20/conscription-an-illusion-of-security/; Guanyinmiao, "A Case against National Service", Weblog, 20 June 2014, https://guanyinmiao.wordpress.com/2014/06/20/a-case-against-national-service/; Facebook, "Anti-Conscription Singapore",

ising debates about whether there should be penalties for dual citizens who default from their military service obligations and if dual citizenship should be allowed.[45] These contentions are likely to remain salient issues with demographic trends indicating a rise in transnational marriages, migration and concurrent rise in dual citizenship.

Public Responses

The increasing visibility of these issues calls for an updated state response and adjustments to existing policies that better address demographic needs and voices in the public domain.

For more than a decade, many have argued that dual citizenship would ease Singapore's "brain drain", which has prevailed since the 1980s.[46]

Facebook group, accessed 24 April 2017, https://www.facebook.com/groups/7893452702/; Singapore Policies Straight Talk, "Why National Service Must Be Abolished or Made Voluntary", Weblog, 10 November 2012, http://singaporepolicies.blogspot.sg/2012/11/why-national-service-ns-must-be.html; Redwire Singapore, "National Service Must Be Abolished for Singapore to Progress. Here's Why.", *Redwire Times*, 2 January 2015, http://redwire-times.com/cow-beh-cow-bu/sg50-national-service-abolish/; Justin Ong, "Singapore Blogger Calls NS 'Slavery', Draws Passionate Response", *Yahoo News*, 7 October 2013, https://sg.news.yahoo.com/blogs/what-is-buzzing/singapore-blogger-calls-ns-slavery-draws-passionate-response-094212412.html; Alvin Lim, "On Alex Liang, a Singaporean Who Gave up His Singapore Citizenship", Weblog, (4 October 2013), https://alvinology.com/2013/10/04/on-alex-liang-a-singaporean-who-gave-up-his-singapore-citizenship/

[45] J, "It's All to Do with Dual Citizenship"; Agarwal, "Dual Citizenship: Little to Fear, Much to Gain"; Desker, "Say yes to dual citizenship, minimum wage and treating foreign workers with respect"; Ishikawa, "Dual citizenship way to retain talent?"; The New Paper, "Why not allow dual citizenship?"; Wee Shi Neo, "Dual citizenship compromises a person's loyalty to Singapore", *Today Online*, 21 March 2016, http://www.todayonline.com/voices/dual-citizenship-compromises-persons-loyalty-singapore; Terence Lim, "A mistake to equate citizenship with loyalty", *Today Online*, 29 March 2016, http://www.todayonline.com/voices/mistake-equate-citizenship-loyalty; Robert William Straughan, "Pain of dual citizenship holders", *Today*, 25 May 2005, sec. ISay, Microfilm NL26323.

[46] Catherine Gomes, *Transient Mobility and Middle Class Identity: Media and Migration in Australia and Singapore* (Singapore: Palgrave Macmillan, 2017), 234; Ashley Chia, "4 in 10 S'poreans married foreigners in 2012", *Today*, 30 January 2013, http://www.todayonline.com/photos/gallery-4-10-sporeans-married-foreigners-2012; Ishikawa, "Dual citizenship way to retain talent?", *The Straits Times*, 28 October 2008, sec. Opinions, http://news.asiaone.com/News/AsiaOne+News/Asian+Opinions/Story/A1Story

Such a policy would further mitigate Singapore's ageing population by encouraging PRs to apply for citizenship and discouraging existing citizens to relinquish theirs.[47] Awarding dual citizenship to immigrants is seen as a means of encouraging and aiding the naturalisation of legally resident foreigners and integrating following generations who may be better regarded — and better regard themselves, as equal members of society if they are accorded citizenship.[48] As we later explain, immigrants are likely to apply for citizenship if they are not forced to give up their original citizenship. For example, the Swedish government encouraged naturalisation and integration through political participation by promoting voting rights among its foreign resident population and their descendants.[49] The state also encouraged children of binational parents who are dual citizens by birth to develop specific competencies related to a transnational background through language fluencies and tools of intercultural communication.[50]

In the EU context, economic advantages tied to dual citizenship allow for greater mobility, contributing to a higher probability of socioeconomic integration.[51] As integration functions as a two-way street, dual citizenship can also help cultivate a more multicultural society where citizens-by-descent, or those who self-identify as "natives", are better able to recognise immigrants as equal members, as hyphenated identities become more ubiquitous.

A dual citizenship policy also allows the increasing numbers of Singaporeans abroad to retain links here, encouraging a sense of

---

20081028-96732.html; The New Paper, "Why not allow dual citizenship?", *The New Paper*, 10 October 2002, National Library Board, Microfilm Reel NL24803.

[47] Gomes, *Transient Mobility and Middle Class Identity: Media and Migration in Australia and Singapore*, 234; Chia, "4 in 10 S'poreans married foreigners in 2012"; Ishikawa, "Dual citizenship way to retain talent?"; The New Paper, "Why not allow dual citizenship?"; Desker, "Say yes to dual citizenship, minimum wage and treating foreign workers with respect".

[48] Triadafilopoulos, "Dual Citizenship and Security Norms in Historical Perspective", 35.

[49] Sejersen, "'I Vow to Thee My Countries' — The Expansion of Dual Citizenship in the 21st Century", 535.

[50] Thomas Faist and Jürgen Gerdes, "Dual Citizenship in an Age of Mobility" (Washington, D.C.: Migration Policy Institute, 2008), 10.

[51] Ibid., 11.

belonging as citizens.[52] Retaining citizenship in one's home country while abroad encourages cultural ties to places-of-origin while strengthening diasporic ties through cross-border networks that facilitate transnational modes of integration.[53] While affective bonds of citizenship may prevail among single citizenship-holders, they are denied civic duties usually ascribed to citizens. The simultaneous participation in two polities has been found to be mutually reinforcing and "those who participate more in the country of origin are also those who feel more attached".[54] The significance of dual citizenship lies in its extension of formal rights to dual citizens, creating political belonging established through a shared relationship between the state and its citizens, and buttressing existing affective bonds to the nation.

Economically, maintaining links to emigrants through dual citizenship also enhances transnational participation in the labour market, educational institutions and privileges such as inheritances and property rights. While previously resistant, immigrant-sending countries such as the Philippines, Turkey and Mexico now permit dual citizenship with the objective of fortifying membership ties with overseas nationals and encouraging an open channel of foreign exchange, investment, markets, entrepreneurial initiatives and political representation abroad.[55]

Contesting the Incompatibility of Dual Citizenship and NS

Contrary to state rhetoric, we argue that NS and dual citizenship policies are not mutually exclusive.

---

[52] Desker, "Say yes to dual citizenship, minimum wage and treating foreign workers with respect".

[53] Faist and Gerdes, "Dual Citizenship in an Age of Mobility", 10; Irene Bloemraad, "Who Claims Dual Citizenship? The Limits of Postnationalism, The Possibilities of Transnationalism, and the Persistence of Traditional Citizenship", *International Migration Review* 38/2 (2004), 389–426.

[54] Andrea Schlenker, Joachim Blatter and Ieva Birka, "Practising Transnational Citizenship: Dual Nationality and Simultaneous Political Involvement Among Emigrants", *Journal of Ethnic and Migration Studies*, 2016, 433.

[55] Peter J. Spiro, "Mandated Membership, Diluted Identity: Citizenship, Globalization, and International Law", in *People Out of Place: Globalization, Human Rights, and the Citizenship Gap*, eds. Alison Brysk and Gershon Safir (New York: Routledge, 2004), 97.

Off the back of public discourse, we discuss dual citizenship in relation to national identity. Drawing on scholarship on transnationalism and case studies that permit and prohibit dual citizenship, we show how identities and loyalties cannot be solely and narrowly defined by the legal and territorial bounds of the nation-state. Second, we discuss the question of divided loyalties and examine safeguards that can be put in place to mitigate the concerns highlighted.

Identity as Indivisible

Detractors of dual citizenship in Singapore argue that changing the current single citizenship policy is detrimental to loyalty to Singapore and tantamount to having an exit strategy should conflict arise.[56] The implication is that dual citizens would not stay to defend the nation at times of crisis as they have another country to relocate to. Underlying this stance is the perspective that identities and loyalties are indivisible and immutable. The traditional view that national identification and loyalty can only be absolute and bound to one state at a time is problematic in an era where globalisation and movement of peoples have transformed the concept of national membership.[57] This sub-section shows the prevalence of dual citizens who articulate multiple loyalties and national identities, and express as much civic duty to their host nations as those who hold single citizenship. The studies cited demonstrate how the construction of identities is contingent on situational factors rather than formal citizenship status alone, debunking the view that a policy of dual citizenship dilutes national

---

[56] Sunny Goh, "Mixed reactions to dual citizenship idea", *The Straits Times*, 2 February 1990, 2; Elaine Quek, "Second link: Is Singapore ready for dual citizenship?" *TODAY*, 21 January 2002, 1; Neo, "Voices: Dual citizenship compromises a person's loyalty to Singapore".

[57] Yasemin Nuhoğlu Soysal, *Limits of Citizenship: Migrants and Postnational Membership in Europe* (Chicago: The University of Chicago Press, 1994); "Postnational Citizenship: Rights and Obligations of Individuality". https://heimatkunde.boell.de/2011/05/18/postnational-citizenship-rights-and-obligations-individuality (accessed 24 October 2016); Saskia Sassen, "Towards Post-National and Denationalized Citizenship", in *Handbook of Citizenship Studies*, eds. Engin F. Isin and Bryan S. Turner (London: SAGE Publications Ltd, 2002); Saskia Sassen, "The Repositioning of Citizenship: Emergent Subjects and Spaces for Politics", *Berkeley Journal of Sociology* 46 (2002), 4–25.

identity and loyalty. Scholarship on transnationalism, and case studies on permitting and prohibiting dual citizenship, show how identities and loyalties cannot be solely and narrowly be defined by the legal and territorial bounds of the nation-state. Single citizenship policies may instead inhibit emotional ties to the nation-state.

Situational factors such as living environment, personal necessities, and day-to-day contact contribute to the fluidity of national identities and sentimental attachments to a nation, which are largely subject to individual experiences and the state of relations between both countries.[58] To the latter observation, individuals are less likely to bear strong identification and loyalty with two nation-states if the two are in a "highly antagonistic international relationship".[59]

Various sociological studies also demonstrate the co-existence of identities and loyalties among dual citizens of different ethnoreligious groups, socio-economic classes and migration trajectories. For example, Robert Conway *et al.*'s qualitative study on highly educated professional Trinidadians with dual citizenship concluded, "transnationalism does not appear to supplant nationalism irrevocably, but rather to accompany it for some, to strengthen it for others, and to constitute a favourable experience for most."[60] Jussi K. Ronkainen's study of Finnish youths also affirmed the plausibility and ubiquity of multiple identities amongst dual citizens who are described as holding "strong and meaningful ties in multiple dimensions to both of their 'home-countries'."[61]

If offering dual citizenship does not have a negative impact upon emotional bonds, enabling Singaporean citizens to retain dual

[58]Terence Chong, "Rethink S'pore nationalism", *The Brunei Times*, 17 March 2008, http://www.bt.com.bn/analysis/2008/03/17/rethink_spore_nationalism (accessed 1 November 2016).
[59]Andrea Schlenker, "Divided Loyalty? Identification and Political Participation of Dual Citizens in Switzerland", *European Political Science Review* 8/4 (2016), 536; Takeyuki Tsuda, "Whatever Happened to Simultaneity? Transnational Migration Theory and Dual Engagement in Sending and Receiving Countries", *Journal of Ethnic and Migration Studies* 38 (2012), 643.
[60]Robert Conway, Robert B. Potter and Godfrey St Bernard, "Dual Citizenship or Dual Identity? Does 'Transnationalism' Supplant 'Nationalism' among Returning Trinidadians?" *Global Networks* 8/4 (2008), 393.
[61]Jussi K. Ronkainen, "Mononationals, Hyphenationals, and Shadownationals: Multiple Citizenship as Practice", *Citizenship Studies* 15/2 (2011), 256.

citizenship may encourage them to maintain ties with Singapore instead of severing them. For example, with these ambitions, Italy altered their legislation in 2002 to permit dual citizenship. Italian embassies also made extensive efforts to inform émigrés of their right to vote in Italian elections, which improved political participation and expanded its overseas constituency.[62] Other examples include France and Spain that introduced dual citizenship in effort to "re-ethnicise" their national identities,[63] as well as Ghana and Senegal that established dual citizenship at times of liberation to reconnect with those who fled during periods of dictatorship.[64] In the context of Singapore, Leong *et al.* observe that there are individuals who are willing to fulfil the criteria of NS for Singaporean citizenship but are deterred by the requirement that they terminate their citizenship of origin.[65]

Beyond emotional bonds, studies also show that dual citizenship does not necessarily compromise civic duty. Andrea Schlenker's analysis on Swiss dual citizens with different migratory experiences demonstrated that they are as attached and politically active as citizens holding single citizenship. Schlenker concluded that "fears about divided loyalty are not backed by our data."[66] One can be a member of multiple national communities while concurrently identifying with and participating in political activities in the country of domicile.

A dual citizenship policy therefore allows the increasing numbers of Singaporeans abroad to retain links here by encouraging a sense of belonging as citizens.[67] Civic duties usually ascribed to Singaporean citi-

---

[62] Sejersen, "'I Vow to Thee My Countries' — The Expansion of Dual Citizenship in the 21st Century", 535.

[63] Christian Joppke, *Citizenship between De- and Re-Ethnicization* (New York: Russell Sage Foundation, 2003).

[64] Beth Elise Whitaker, "The Politics of Home: Dual Citizenship and the African Diaspora", *International Migration Review* 45/4 (2011), 755–783.

[65] Leong Chan-Hoong, Yang Wai Wai and Jerrold Hong, "Management of Social Diversity", in *Managing Diversity in Singapore: Policies and Prospects*, eds. Mathew Mathews and Wai Fong Chiang (London: Imperial College Press, 2016), 322.

[66] Schlenker, "Divided Loyalty? Identification and Political Participation of Dual Citizens in Switzerland", 536.

[67] Desker, "Say yes to dual citizenship, minimum wage and treating foreign workers with respect".

zens are denied to Singaporean émigrés who hold citizenship of their host countries. According Singaporean émigrés with dual citizenship and the civic duties that come with it may enhance their sense of belonging to Singapore. The simultaneous participation in two polities has been found to be mutually reinforcing and "those who participate more in the country of origin are also those who feel more attached."[68] The significance of dual citizenship lies in its extension of formal rights to dual citizens, creating political belonging established through a shared relationship between the state and its citizens, and buttressing existing affective bonds to the nation.

The policy of single citizenship itself may negatively affect the strength and resilience of national identity and loyalty. Zeynep Yanasmayan's study of Turkish migrants in Spain, the Netherlands, and the UK showed how the mandate of single citizenship could cause individuals to set aside these sentimental attachments for practical needs.[69] In the case of the Netherlands, which bans dual citizenship, Turkish immigrants tended to approach citizenship in practical terms as they were affected by the "self-bargaining" (intense negotiation before naturalisation) that took place upon renouncing their original citizenship. Turkish citizenship, which used to have an "identity-conferring role", was abandoned and replaced by one that they saw as economically pragmatic. In comparison, where dual citizenship is allowed, such as in the UK, individuals are given an opportunity to maintain multiple allegiances, engendering "thick citizenship" or the emotional bond and positive sentiments to the legal citizenship status.[70]

These studies offer two observations. First, the argument that dual citizenship threatens national loyalty and identity is too simplistic. Membership to one group does not necessarily prevent mutual affiliation with another as loyalty is not a zero-sum game. Singaporeans with "hyphenated" identities may have the ability to understand and accept the duties that come

---

[68] Andrea Schlenker, Joachim Blatter and Ieva Birka, "Practising Transnational Citizenship: Dual Nationality and Simultaneous Political Involvement among Emigrants", *Journal of Ethnic and Migration Studies*, 2016, 433.

[69] Zeynep Yanasmayan, "Citizenship on Paper or at Heart? A Closer Look into the Dual Citizenship Debate in Europe", *Citizenship Studies* 19/6–7 (2015).

[70] While Yasnamayan differentiated emotional bond and sentimental value from national identity and loyalty, she affirmed that the former can be foundations for the latter.

with their dual background such as enlistment and subsequent "reservist" obligations. The possession or acquisition of another citizenship does not necessarily entail the removal of one's commitment and desire to be a dutiful citizen-soldier to Singapore. Second, contrary to the view that dual citizenship dilutes a sense of national identity, our cases demonstrate how single citizenship policies may inadvertently encourage pragmatic attitudes towards citizenship and contravene the affective ties sought. While the results from the aforementioned studies will vary across countries, regions and cultures, they show that there is no clear causal relationship between dual citizenship and the dilution of national identity or loyalties.

Divided Loyalties

Skeptics of dual citizenship policies are still wary of the risk posed by dual citizens in times of crisis, questioning where their loyalties lie.[71] To some extent, a version of these fears is apparent in Singapore with the historical marginalisation of Malays and Muslims within the segments of the national military, premised on fears that their allegiances may lie with Muslim societies and neighbouring Malaysia, further compounded by the view that Singaporean-Malay Muslims are becoming increasingly insular.[72]

These concerns resonate with past norms that opposed dual citizenship on the basis of rigid understandings of identity, which we have already problematised in earlier sections. In addition, we note that public sentiment during controversies, such as that of the Bugge brothers and Brandon Smith, did not include concerns over the security risk of conscripting dual citizens but the converse — many were simply aggrieved that dual citizens did not fulfil their NS requirements.

As it stands, second generation PRs (those granted PR under the sponsorship of their parents) in Singapore are liable to serve under the Enlistment Act, demonstrating an existing openness towards noncitizens.[73] This legislation shows that Singapore's NS system can accom-

---

[71] Nasir and Turner, *The Future of Singapore: Population, Society and The Nature of the State*, 62.

[72] Nasir and Turner, *The Future of Singapore: Population, Society and The Nature of the State*, 59. For an updated analysis on the subject of Malay-Muslims in the Singapore military, see Vasu and Anwar's chapter in this book.

[73] In 2011, the Minister of Defence Dr Ng Eng Hen stated that there were 8,800 second-generation PRs who enlisted and served NS. ICA, "Apply for Permanent Residence",

modate a citizen of another state and there is no inherent belief within the system that non-citizens and by extension dual citizens, pose threats if conscripted. Moreover, the argument that NS can accommodate a citizen of another state gains greater credence from the fact that Singapore now permits first generation PRs to volunteer to join the SAF Volunteer Corps. We add to this suggestion with two further arguments.

International Cases

Policy changes and debates in various countries demonstrate awareness that dual citizenship is not a decisive factor in determining loyalty to a state. The ubiquity of military policies open to dual citizens in this respect reflects evolving understandings of identity as multiple and fluid.

Various states conscript dual citizens including those that continue to be embroiled in conflict, such as Israel. The Israeli Defence Force (IDF) has an open approach to enlistment. Military service is mandatory for Israeli male and female citizens unless they are exempted for medical or religious reasons. It is voluntary for dual citizens who have lived overseas for most of their lives, new citizens and non-citizens through the IDF Mahal programme if they are Jewish-by-descent as described in the Law of Return.[74] There are also different options depending on how long volunteers would like to serve.[75] Some may argue that Israel is an anomaly due to its national identity, and therefore loyalties, defined ethnically, rather than territorially. However, a notable number of other countries without military conscription also permit dual citizens to enlist in national armies, reinforcing the understanding that dual citizens do not pose an intrinsic threat to national security by serving in the military and can be recruited. These countries include Canada, the UK and Germany.

2014, https://www.ica.gov.sg/page.aspx?pageid=151; MINDEF, "Written Reply by Minister for Defence Dr Ng Eng Hen to Parliamentary Question on Permanent Residents in National Service", 22 November 2011, https://www.mindef.gov.sg/imindef/press_room/official_releases/ps/2011/22nov11_ps.html#.UbaZJfmNlBg

[74] The Law of Return accords the right of Israeli citizenship to every individual able to trace his or her ancestry to a Jewish grandparent.

[75] IDF, "Frequently Asked Questions", *Mahal IDF Volunteers*. http://www.mahal-idf-volunteers.org/about/faq.htm#documentationthatyouarejewish (accessed 7 December 2016).

Contrary to the argument that loyalties come into question at times of crisis, it is in those very times that additional manpower is often needed. As such, states such as the US historically adopt more inclusive enlistment and immigration policies to fulfil its manpower needs at wartime.[76] The US military currently does not have a legal bar against the enlistment of dual nationals or non-citizens, with citizenship offered to many in the latter category following their service.[77] Based on the various empirical cases cited, scholars concede that concern over "[m]ilitary service for dual nationals[...] is not even on today's radar screen."[78]

In addition, the number of dual citizens holding high civil service positions in foreign governments exemplifies an understanding of the dynamic relationship between citizenship, identity and national loyalties. In Canada, various members of parliament hold dual citizenship, as well as former Prime Minister John Turner who remains a British and Canadian dual citizen.[79] Serving her second term in the UK, Minister for Internet Safety and Security and Under-Secretary of State Joanna Shields is a dual citizen of both the US and the UK.[80] In 2010–2011, Somalia's prime minister was a US dual citizen. There are also American dual citizens serving in high-ranking positions within the US government and as ministers in foreign governments such as Armenia, Bosnia and Estonia.[81]

The debate surrounding dual citizenship in Sweden further reinforces a shift in perception. Prior to the change in legislation that now permits dual citizenship, critics argued that foreigners may remain

---

[76] Molly McIntosh, Seema Sayala and David Gregory, "Non-citizens in the enlisted U.S. military", *Channel NewsAsia*, 2011, http://citeseerx.ist.psu.edu/viewdoc/download?doi=1 0.1.1.644.3303&rep=rep1&type=pdf

[77] Stephen H. Legomsky, "Dual Nationality and Military Service: Strategy Number Two", in *Rights and Duties of Dual Nationals: Evolution and Prospects*, eds. David A. Martin and Kay Hailbronner (Kluwer Law International, 2003), 141–142.

[78] Aleinikoff and Klusmeyer, "Plural Nationality: Facing the Future in a Migratory World", 79.

[79] Jennifer Wilson, "MPs and dual citizenship", *CBC News*, 8 December 2006, http://www.cbc.ca/news2/background/parliament39/mps-dualcitizenship.html

[80] Joanna Shields, "Biography", *Joanna Shields*, 2016, http://www.joannashields.com/about/

[81] The aforementioned examples are cited in Spiro, *At Home in Two Countries*, 71.

loyal to their former home country and thereby should be excluded from certain military appointments. In response, the 1997 citizenship commission appointed by the Swedish parliament clarified that there was no evidence linking dual citizenship with security threats. The commission stated that while exceptional cases may be deemed unsuitable, "security problems and divided loyalties had more to do with emotional ties than with formal citizenship, and that no crimes against the security of the state were known to have been related to dual citizenship."[82]

Precautionary Measures

Having argued that dual citizenship has positive contributions to national identity and a pragmatic national agenda, we recognise the need for administrative caution. The past consensus that military conscription should not be a barrier to entry for dual citizenship manifested in the 1930 Protocol on Military Obligations in Certain Cases of Double Nationality. This multilateral agreement eased concerns that naturalised dual citizens would face conflicting military duties, one scenario being called to serve in the armies of their countries of origin, rather than in their adopted country. Reaffirming this consensus, the European Convention of 1963 stated that persons with dual citizenship shall be required to fulfil their military obligations in relation to only one of the states, generally understood as the territory they are resident within.[83] In relation to immigrant dual citizens, bilateral and multinational treaties can also be established to prevent the potential for double drafting in fairness to conscripts and to assuage the national security concerns of the state.

Bilateral treaties are common practice among countries that permit dual citizenship. Turkey and Germany have a bilateral agreement ensuring that individuals who have completed their military service in either country

---

[82] Per Gustafson, "Globalisation, Multiculturalism and Individualism: The Swedish Debate on Dual Citizenship", *Journal of Ethnic and Migration Studies* 28/3 (2002), 473. In view of these examples, Spiro concluded that the global landscape is "turning the corner on dual citizenship." See: Spiro, *At Home in Two Countries*, 71.

[83] Thomas Hammar, "Citizenship and Political Integration", *The International Migration Review* 19/3 (1985), 444.

need not serve in the other country.[84] There are discretionary state policies that determine which state a dual national should be either eligible or required to serve in, a decision often contingent on the individual's original place of residence. For example, bilateral treaties between Israel and France, and Spain and Italy, have clauses that require individuals to declare their decision to enlist in one state before the other calls them to enlist.[85] This safeguard against double drafting is usual practice across various countries and reinforced within three multinational conventions prohibiting double conscription of dual citizens.[86]

Countries that allow dual citizens to participate in their military forces also have specific safeguards in place that mitigate perceived risks posed by dual citizens. For instance, while the US has no legal bar on dual nationals serving as officers, there is a practical bar as foreign nationality can affect security clearance, which is required for officer status.[87] Such safeguards can be tailored according to Singapore's geopolitical position and interests in mind. With the recognition that dual citizens do not pose intrinsic threats to national security and with safeguards in place as prudent measures, the inclusion of dual citizens does not contravene the relevance of Singapore's conscription policy.

---

[84] Freeman and Ögelman, "Homeland Citizenship Policies and the Status of Third Country Nationals in the European Union", 783. These bilateral agreements have historical resonance. In the 19th century, various immigrant-sending and -receiving countries signed agreements which recognised naturalised citizens in both countries and removed mandatory military conscription should the individual have served in either country. In the 19th century, the US signed agreements with the Grand Duchy of Badon, Austria-Hungary, Sweden, Switzerland, Czechoslovakia and Latvia that relaxed military conscription for dual citizens and/or their children. See: Spiro, *At Home in Two Countries*, 59–60.

[85] Legomsky, "Dual Nationality and Military Service: Strategy Number Two".

[86] Ibid.

[87] Security clearance will be revoked if individuals exercise benefits of dual citizenship such as possessing a foreign passport without approval and/or if they demonstrate a deep commitment to helping a foreign country or group that shows a preference over the US. See: US Department of Defense, "Eligibility Determinations", *Defense Security Service*, accessed 12 December 2016, http://www.dss.mil/psmo-i/indus_psmo-i_eligibility.html; Center for Development of Security Excellence, "Receive and Maintain Your Security Clearance" (Defense Security Service, 2015), http://www.cdse.edu/documents/cdse/Receive_and_Maint_Sct_Clnc.pdf, 22.

Finally, there are fears that dual citizenship provides existing dual citizens with a way to evade NS.[88] In Singapore, male dual citizens-by-birth (*jus soli* or *jus sanguinis*) are obliged to fulfil their conscription obligations if they have not renounced their citizenship by age 21.

The penalty for not fulfilling their NS obligations is based on the assumption that they are still Singaporean citizens. While arguably harsh, these penalties are not unfair with the premise that all male Singaporean citizens are required to enlist unless exempted for health reasons. Extending this principle to the scenario of dual citizenship, if dual citizens wish to retain their dual citizenship after the age of 18, they should still be required to fulfil their NS. If they fail to do so, they risk losing their dual citizenship status and becoming subject to existing penalties. Upon fulfilment of their NS duties, national servicemen should be able to retain their dual citizenship statuses. This policy offers dual citizens the option of retaining their dual citizenship, as opposed to the current policy of fulfilling their NS obligation and then renouncing Singaporean citizenship. This policy could also encourage return migration at a later stage, benefiting both the individual and nation-state.[89]

Conclusion

We argue that there is little reason to believe the possession of dual citizenship would dramatically affect an important objective of NS — nation-building. By analysing arguments for identity and loyalty in relation to NS (i.e. its role in developing the citizen soldier and its role in constructing the nation), we find that dual citizenship may instead enhance this agenda.

Arguably, there may be security reasons for insisting that dual citizenship is incompatible with Singapore's policy of NS. However, future

---

[88] Brenda Yeoh and Lin Weiqiang, "Rapid Challenges in Singapore's Immigration Population Brings Policy Challenges" (Migration Policy Institute, 2012), http://www.migrationinformation.org/feature/print.cfm?ID=887

[89] In his forthcoming article, David Leblang also explains how dual citizenship has intersecting functions of facilitating remittances and return migration. See: David Leblang, "Harnessing the Diaspora: Dual Citizenship, Migrant Return Remittances", *Comparative Political Studies* 50/1 (2017), 75–101.

arguments made by the government against dual citizenship may want to stay clear from relying on arguments of identity and loyalty owing to their possible untenability.

Apart from political rhetoric, a policy response should also be considered. The relationship between NS and dual citizenship clearly remains a pertinent issue in Singapore and calls for an updated state response. An adjustment in citizenship policy is required as a timely response to the reality of a changing population composition stemming from the rise of transnational marriages and migration. As more Singaporean families experience multiple identities, policies implemented for the last 50 years need to be reviewed to better accommodate Singapore's changing social landscape.[90]

---

[90] Paulin Tay Straughan and Kharina Zainal, "Making Public Policy Relevant for Bicultural Families in Singapore", *Ethos*, Issue 15, June 2016, accessed 21 November 2016, downloaded from https://www.cscollege.gov.sg/Knowledge/Ethos/Lists/issues/Attachments/67/ETHOS15_final.pdf

Chapter 9

The Maligned Malays
and National Service

Norman Vasu and Nur Diyanah Binte Anwar

Perceived systemic discrimination of Malays found within Singapore's system of National Service (NS) remains a perennial bugbear in discussions on the nation's defence. Two questions often arise when Malays and NS are discussed. With NS being the means through which Singapore services the manpower requirements of its military, police and civil defence forces, the first question surrounds whether conscripted Malays are over-represented in the police and civil defence forces while being under-represented in the military. The second question is with regard to whether Malays are unrepresented in elements considered "sensitive" in the military.[1] In response to these queries, the Singapore government maintains that the Singapore Armed Forces (SAF) takes in more Malays than the Singapore Civil Defence Force (SCDF) and the Singapore Police Force (SPF) combined while also emphasising the progress made for the integration of Malays within all elements of the SAF over the years.[2]

This chapter explores the NS experience of Malay Singaporeans in the SAF. The chapter shows that while the military was indeed hollowed out of Malays after Singapore's independence in 1965, attempts have been

---

[1] For example, see: Pritam Singh, Singapore, *Parliamentary Debates Singapore 12*, no. 1, vol. 88, Committee of Supply — Head J (Ministry of Defence), 6 March 2012.
[2] See: Defence Minister's Response, Singapore, *Parliamentary Debates Singapore 12*, no. 1, vol. 88, 6 March 2012.

made in recent years to make all aspects of the armed forces more inclusive. The chapter however argues more can be done through NS in order for greater racial integration be achieved. One practical manner in which greater integration can be achieved would be for the SAF to set racial targets — rather than quotas — for elements of the SAF serviced by conscription to be representative of the racial demographic of Singapore. While it may be too great a demand for every unit or division to be reflective of this demographic, it is possible for the racial demographic to be represented in all three service levels of the SAF. The argument for targets would not be alien for the SAF as targets were set to arrive at a more racially balanced force since its establishment.[3] Also, targets are preferred over quotas as the latter leads to the fixing of outcomes rather than attending to the structural issues leading to undesired outcomes. Instead, targets allow for a process that can focus on attending to structural issues in order to arrive at a desired outcome.

The chapter is divided into four main sections. In the first section, the significant role played by Malays in the military of pre-independent Singapore is highlighted. Stressed here would be their professionalism and dedication to their vocation — a dedication perhaps best displayed by the actions of the 1st Malaya Infantry Brigade in the bloody Battle of Pasir Panjang Ridge and Bukit Chandu during the World War II (WWII), in the Japanese invasion of Singapore in 1942. The second section shows that while Malays were — like every other racial group — deemed to be professional, a combination of two major issues made it difficult for the SAF to accept what amounted to the over-representation of Malays. These two issues are: (1) the perceived existential threat to independent Singapore, and (2) an existential crisis stemming from the new state being the unplanned child of international politics with no clear sense of nationhood or self. The third section then highlights the methods employed to reduce the military's reliance on Malays. In the fourth and final section, it is argued that, while integration of Malays into the military has indeed been occurring, the setting of ethnic targets — one where elements of the SAF serviced via conscription are representative of the racial demographic of

---

[3] Alon Peled, "Singapore: From Inclusion to Exclusion", in *A Question of Loyalty: Military Manpower Policy in Multiethnic States* (New York: Cornell University Press, 1998), 108–109.

Singapore — may have great utility to attain a military fully representative of the multiracial nation it is set up to defend.

Pre-Independence Singapore: Malays in the Military

In pre-independent Singapore, soldiering was the traditional form of employment for Malays, and a manner through which social mobility was attained.[4] The local military (and police force) present in Singapore at the point of independence was almost exclusively Malay, showing how embedded Malays were in the defence of Malaya.[5] Malays made up about "80% and more of the armed forces and the police," and the proportion of Malays employed as soldiers, police or prison guards were about five times the national average.[6] Like the Gurkhas and Sikhs, the British considered Malays a "martial race".[7] Donald Horowitz suggested in his work on ethnic groups in conflict how "the status of 'martialness' was attributed to those groups who could be relied upon to provide a steady stream of

---

[4] Stanley S. Bedlington, *The Singapore Malay Community: The Politics of State Integration* (Ithaca: Cornell University, 1974), 241.

[5] Sean P. Walsh, "The Roar of the Lion City: Ethnicity, Gender, and Culture in the Singapore Armed Forces", *Armed Forces & Society* 33/2 (2007), 275.

[6] The Singapore Census of Population for 1957 measured 18.8% of all employed Malays as soldiers, police or prison guards, compared to 3.8% for the employed population. Bedlington, *The Singapore Malay Community*, 241.

[7] In the early 1900s, the British were initially unsure of the capabilities and the "martial potential" Malays had in defending the lands and picking up arms. Even during wartime, the Malay Regiment's commanding officer, Brigadier J. R. G. Andre stereotyped Malays as follows, "The Malay had for centuries been content to take life as it came, to grow rice and to catch his fish ... The only fighting that had taken place had been small tribal squabbles." However, with the large numbers volunteering for the war effort and establishment of the Malay Regiment — and the eventual formation of the 1st Malay Infantry Brigade — Malay soldiers proved themselves valuable in defending the land. Their sacrifice, "martialness" and value to the military were acknowledged by the British, especially after Malay soldiers' involvement in the Battle of Pasir Panjang and Bukit Chandu. Karl Hack, "Imperialism and Decolonisation in Southeast Asia: Colonial Forces and British World Power", in *Colonial Armies in Southeast Asia*, eds. Karl Hack and Tobias Rettig (Oxon: Routledge, 2006), 255. See also: Alon Peled, "Singapore: From Inclusion to Exclusion", 104.

loyal recruits and withheld from groups who had developed sophisticated forms of military and political organisation in the pre-colonial period."[8]

There is a palpable pride amongst Malays over the devotion to the Malay Regiment — part of the 1st Malaya Infantry Brigade — displayed during WWII.[9] The Malay proverb *"biar putih tulang, jangan putih mata"* (literally translated to "better white bones than white eyes" but better understood as "death before dishonour") is synonymous to the battles, loyalty and bravery shown by the soldiers in the Malay Regiment. Most significant are the Regiment's and the Federated Malay States Volunteer Force's actions in combat during the Battle of Pasir Panjang Ridge and the Battle of Bukit Chandu on 13 and 14 February 1942, during which men such as Lieutenant Adnan Bin Saidi showed great heroism in defending their posts. Until today, Lieutenant Adnan is revered as a post-war national hero for his dogged resistance.[10] Leading a platoon from 'C' Company under the 1st Battalion of the Malay Regiment, he refused to retreat and maintained his "Lewis gun until he was shot down, bayoneted and hung upside down on a tree, reportedly while still alive."[11] The 42 Malay soldiers with Lieutenant Adnan at Bukit Chandu were also killed as they fought with bayonets after exhausting their supply of bullets.[12] Even after the fall of Pasir Panjang and Bukit Chandu, at least eight Malay officers refused to remove their uniforms "out of loyalty to their profession and to King George VI",[13] and were executed near the Pasir Panjang line.[14] Malay soldiers' sacrifices were acknowledged by the British Military

---

[8] Donald L. Horowitz, *Ethnic Groups in Conflict* (Berkeley: University of California, 1985).

[9] Sri Sumirah, "Keberanian Lt. Adnan menjadi kebanggaan", *Berita Harian*, 2 May 1988, 5.

[10] Lieutenant Adnan is reported to have said, "I would not die in vain if the enemy is defeated (*Selepas memusnahkan musuh, saya tidak kesal kalau saya mati)*". Sri Sumirah, "Keberanian Lt. Adnan menjadi kebanggaan".

[11] Hack, "Imperialism and Decolonisation in Southeast Asia", 256.

[12] Sri Sumirah, "Keberanian Lt. Adnan menjadi kebanggaan".

[13] Abu Talib Ahmad. "Resistance, Collaboration and the Malay-Muslims", in *The Malay Muslims, Islam and the Rising Sun: 1941–45*, ed. Abu Talib Ahmad (Selangor: Academe Art & Printing Services, 2003), 88.

[14] Hack, "Imperialism and Decolonisation in Southeast Asia", 257.

commanders General Arthur Percival and Brigadier J. R. G. Andre,[15] and are testimony of Malay "martialness" and loyalty.[16]

This immense loyalty was seen to be typical of Malays to their superiors, or to the cause they were involved in.[17] Malays took pride in defending the land against Japan and its allies, who were "enemies of the motherland".[18] According to Abu Talib Ahmad, "it mattered very little if the motherland was still an intrinsic part of the British Empire" with its political future unclear.[19] Malays were also deeply embedded within all aspects of defence — they held senior ranks in the British colonial military, and were also found in units deemed "sensitive" such as signals.[20] They were greatly present and visible, and contributed their services in the Royal Air Force and the Malayan Naval Forces during WWII — many of whom perished in their line of duty.[21]

This loyalty is matched by the professionalism and self-motivation amongst Malay soldiers — and Malays in the police force as well — as evident in military magazines published pre-independence such as *Majallah Perkawalan* ("Magazine for the Defence Forces"). In a write-up on the Singapore Guard Regiment which was largely made up of Malay

---

[15] Hussin Mutalib. "Roles of Malays and the State", in *Singapore Malays: Being Ethnic Minority and Muslim in a Global City-State*, ed. Hussin Mutalib (Oxon: Routledge, 2012), 142.

[16] Sean Walsh extended on the discourse on "martial races" via a primordialist perspective, suggesting how "Singapore's post-independence policy of conscripting its armed forces has severely undermined their combat effectiveness because the ethnic balance of the forces shifted against the minority Malay community that 'culturally [looked] highly on military service'." Walsh, "The Roar of the Lion City", 283. See also argument presented in Subhashish Ray, "The Nonmartial Origins of the 'Martial Races': Ethnicity and Military Service in Ex-British Colonies", *Armed Forces & Society* 39/3 (2012), 562.

[17] Malays outside of the military also joined Force 136, Wataniah [For the Nation] and Askar Setia Melayu [Loyal Malay Soldier] in their fight to defend their motherland against the Japanese. Wataniah and Askar Setia Melayu were anti-Japanese Malay units formed by Force 136. Ahmad, "Resistance, Collaboration and the Malay-Muslims", 87.

[18] Ahmad, "Resistance, Collaboration and the Malay-Muslims", 87.

[19] Ibid.

[20] For example, it is interesting to note how names of officers present in *Majallah Perkawalan* are largely Malay names save for a few English names of officers commanding the Royal Air Force.

[21] Amin Affandi, "Kesah Lama: Perjuangan Tentera Laut Malaya Dalam Peperangan Dunia Kedua", *Majallah Perkawalan* 14/4 (1954), 573.

soldiers, it was described how they had fought tooth and nail against enemies.[22] Several of the men from the regiment were awarded medals from the Queen of England for the sacrifices they made, and for their long service and good behaviour.[23] In another issue of *Majallah Perkawalan*, it opened with words of encouragement for Malay soldiers in their duties, and a reminder to continually be loyal to their motherland (*"tanah ayer"*).[24] There are repeated calls for the soldiers to "reflect on the responsibilities [they] have on their shoulders", and to be "willing to perish for the country" with dignity, to "protect the country's sovereignty and ... prevent the beloved motherland from being destroyed."[25] There is a strong shared notion of honour as soldiers — "Prove to our motherland, that we value her, and are willing to fight until the last drop of our blood."[26]

Notably, while religion may be seen as a cause for fear and suspicion for Malay loyalty to the country, Islam was used as a rallying call in fulfilling duties as soldiers with courage. For example, articles in *Majallah Perkawalan* included slogans such as "*Allah Peliharakan Ashkar Melayu Diraja* (Allah will protect the Royal Malay Regiment)".[27] The ability to practise religion openly — a practice accommodated by the British as well — was not seen to be in conflict with the ability and willingness to soldier. This can be illustrated in reports showing the opening of a new Royal Air Force Regiment (Malaya) Changi mosque which itself provided the building in which the mosque was set up.[28] This is significant

---

[22] S. M. Shahri Manaf, "Latar Belakang 'Singapore Guard Regiment'", *Majallah Perkawalan* 35/XII (1964), 632.

[23] Shahri Manaf "Latar Belakang 'Singapore Guard Regiment'", 632.

[24] Majallah Perkawalan Bilangan 36 Tahun XIII. "Waspadalah....." June 1964.

[25] Translated from, "... *merenong sejenak, tentang peranan yang dipikolkan diatas bahu kita*"; "*Chabaran tersebut telah dan akan kita sambut dengan meruah dan harga diri kita. Kerana mati hidup atau hanchur musnahnya pertahanan Negara ini ditangan musuh adalah tanggongjawab kita, perajurit2*"; and "*Dan kita jugalah orang2nya yang harus binasa lebih dahulu sebelum Negara yang kita chintai ini musnah atau hanchur*". Ibid.

[26] Translated from, "*Tunjukkanlah kepada ibu pertiwi, bahwa kita ini adalah benar2 menjadi anak kandungnya yang mengenang budi dan sanggup berjuang kerananya hingga titisan darah yang akhir*". Ibid.

[27] Abdul Rashid Muhammad, "Mengenang Jasa2 Ashkar Melayu Diraja", *Majallah Perkawalan* 36/XIII (1964), 34.

[28] Majallah Perkawalan Bilangan 16 Tahun 4, "Berita Masjid Changi (Services)", 1955, 633.

as it showed how personal conviction and loyalty to the country were not hindered by religious faith.[29]

While the Malay soldiers' immense sense of duty was evident through the large role they had played in defence during the war, this trait also manifested during the turbulent early years of Singapore's independence when Malay soldiers were deployed to quell the racial riots in May 1969. Despite the new government's inherent suspicions of Malay loyalties to the state then — for example, Malays were already being removed from combat posts in the army and Malay youth were not being called up for NS — they were vital in subduing the riots.[30] Multiracial military units were sent to "guard the property and lives of Singaporean Malay citizens from the rage of the Chinese street gangs."[31] During the riots, Malays soldiers "reacted against the Malays, and the Chinese against the Chinese, who were causing the trouble."[32] The riot of 1969 showed the Malay soldiers' reliability in executing what was needed to safeguard the integrity of multicultural Singapore society instead of turning against the Chinese.

Existentialist Threat and Existential Crisis

While the Malays had proven themselves both willing and exceedingly able to perform a life of soldiering, it was the geopolitical context in 1965 that arguably led to the decision to make the military less reliant upon them. Broadly, this context was one shaped by two major intertwined issues. Firstly, Singapore was perceived at independence by its leaders as

---

[29] A notable qualitative study on Singaporean Malay experience in the army is Lenore Lyons and Michele Ford's "Defending the Nation: Malay Men's Experience of National Service in Singapore", where it was found that "personal and national loyalty [was] underpinned by religious faith." Interviewees they spoke to also suggested how "... if they [those who fear of Muslim disloyalty] really study the religion, they should know that Islam teaches you to be loyal to your country. So if people who are actually religious, they will be loyal to your country because the religion teaches you to be loyal to your country, defend your country." Lenore Lyons and Michele Ford, "Defending the Nation: Malay Men's Experience of National Service in Singapore", in *Men and Masculinities in Southeast Asia*, eds. Michele Ford and Lenore Lyons (Oxon: Routledge, 2012), 151.

[30] Bedlington, *The Singapore Malay Community*, 242.

[31] Peled, "Singapore: From Inclusion to Exclusion", 111.

[32] Ibid.

facing a serious external existentialist threat — its very existence was thought to be threatened as "a Chinese island surrounded by a Malay sea".[33] Singapore's far from amicable separation from the Federation of Malaysia and its experience of *Konfrontasi* with Indonesia left it feeling exceptionally vulnerable. Secondly, the other major issue at that time was Singapore's own internal existential crisis. Its statehood was unplanned and the conception of it being a nation was largely non-existent — it was effectively experiencing what Soren Kierkegaard refers to as existential despair and anxiety stemming from an unexpected upheaval.[34] This existential crisis contributed to the desire to establish NS as a means to both defend the state and to create a nation. Moreover, related to the absence of a firm sense of self, the nation could not confidently identify the "Us" from the "Other". With racial and religious riots still fresh in the nation's minds — and another major one to come soon after independence — a primordial understanding of communal identity held by Singapore's leaders at the time left them with little confidence in the Malay community's ability to unequivocally defend the state during a crisis.

The Existentialist Threat

As noted by many, Singapore's geopolitical reality informs its sense of vulnerability and threat — especially at the point of independence where it was reliant upon the British for the protection of its sovereignty having little capability for self-defence.[35] Unsurprisingly, the combination of being both geo-strategically valuable — being an important maritime junction between the Pacific and Indian oceans — and its small physical size and the accompanying lack of strategic depth, coupled with an inability to defend itself at the point of independence, worried its leaders.[36]

---

[33] Lee Kuan Yew, *The Singapore Story: Memoirs of Lee Kuan Yew* (Singapore: Times Editions, 1998), 15.

[34] Soren Kierkegaard, *The Sickness unto Death: A Christian Psychological Exposition for Upbuilding and Awakening* (New Jersey: Princeton University Press, 1980), 41.

[35] See for example, Bernard Loo, "Goh Keng Swee and the Emergence of a Modern SAF: The Rearing of a Poisonous Shrimp", in *Goh Keng Swee: A Legacy of Public Service*, eds. Emrys Chew and Kwa Chong Guan (Singapore: World Scientific Publishing & RSIS, 2012), 128.

[36] Tim Huxley, *Defending the Lion City: The Armed Forces of Singapore* (St Leonards, NSW: Allen and Unwin, 2000), 31–33.

Capturing the sense of vulnerability during independence, Dr Goh Keng Swee in a speech to Parliament maintained:

> Our army is to be engaged in the defence of the country and our people against external aggression. This task we are unable to do today by ourselves. It is no use pretending that without the British military presence in Singapore today, the island cannot be easily overrun by any neighbouring country within a radius of a thousand miles ... (Speech to Parliament, 23 December 1965).[37]

If being geo-strategically valuable — combined with the geographic reality of having little strategic depth and being unable to defend itself — was not a worrisome enough mélange, the ambivalence of Singapore–Malaysia relations in 1965 generated significant anxiety. Here, two issues were of particular concern in regard to Singapore's relations with its northern neighbour. Firstly, there was the fear of a "wild card" situation playing out, one where the actions of right-wing Malaysian politicians would want to threaten Singapore's sovereignty. Secondly, Singapore's reliance on Malaysia's water supply left it vulnerable to the taps being turned off during periods of disagreement.

With regard to the first concern, during the course of his recounting of the immediate post-separation period in Singapore-Malaysia relations, former Prime Minister Lee Kuan Yew made numerous references to his worries about Malaysia's threat to Singapore. For example, he noted that immediately after independence, priority placed on building Singapore's defence capabilities stemmed from the fear that Malaysian political elites might commit "rash political acts".[38] Lee believed the Malaysians could put pressure on Singapore through various ways — they could "station troops in Singapore, squat on us and if necessary close the Causeway and cut off our water supply."[39] There was a genuine concern that other

---

[37] Goh Keng Swee, "Speech by Minister of Defence, Mr Goh Keng Swee, in Parliament on The Singapore Army Bill", *National Archives of Singapore*, 23 December 1965, http://www.nas.gov.sg/archivesonline/data/pdfdoc/PressR19651223c.pdf

[38] Lee Kuan Yew, *From Third World to First: The Singapore Story: 1965–2000* (Singapore: Times Media, 2000), 46.

[39] Lee, *The Singapore Story*, 663.

Malaysian leaders less moderate than Tunku Abdul Rahman, the Malaysian Prime Minister, might persuade "Brigadier Alsagoff (the commander of Malaysian forces stationed in Singapore at the time of separation) [that] it was his patriotic duty to reverse separation."[40] Also, another scenario was based on the possibility that

> Malay ultras ... in [Kuala Lumpur, or KL, would] instigate a coup by the Malaysian forces in Singapore and reverse the independence we had acquired. Many Malay leaders in KL believed Singapore should never have been allowed to leave Malaysia, but should have been clobbered into submission. If anything were to happen to Tunku Abdul Rahman, Tun Abdul Razak would become the Prime Minister and he could be made to reverse the Tunku's decision by strong-minded ultra leaders.[41]

Besides these wild card scenarios, the idea of Singapore's dependence on Malaysia for water itself preoccupied Prime Minister Lee. The anxiety over water was understandable as it was informed by the legacy of WWII where the loss of water supplies contributed to the eventual British surrender.[42] The demolition of the Causeway connecting Singapore to the Malayan peninsula during the Malayan Campaign left the British and Allied forces defending Singapore until its eventual defeat — with the loss of the Woodleigh pumping station leading General Percival to conclude that resistance was futile.[43] In his early meetings with former Malaysian Prime Minister Mahathir Mohammed, Singapore's Prime Minister Lee repeated his fears of the prospect of a "random act of madness like cutting off our water supplies, which they had publicly threatened whenever there were differences between us."[44]

At that historical moment, this perception of vulnerability vis-à-vis relations and reliance on Malaysia was further reinforced through many

---

[40] Lee, *From Third World to First*, 31.

[41] Lee, *The Singapore Story*, 22.

[42] See for example, Bernard Loo, "Explaining Changes in Singapore's Military Doctrines: Material and Ideational Perspectives", in *Asia in the New Millenium: APISA First Congress Proceedings 27–30 November 2003*, eds. Amitav Acharya and Lee Lai To (Singapore: Marshall Cavendish International, 2004), 365.

[43] Loo, "Explaining Changes in Singapore's Military Doctrines", 365.

[44] Lee, *From Third World to First*, 276.

actions taken by the Malaysian government at that time. As many Malaysian leaders opposed Singapore's independence, Malaysia took numerous steps to exploit Singapore's nascent military between 1965 and 1969. Malaysian politicians attempted to thwart Singapore's ability to build a strong military capable of threatening Malaysia to the degree that Singapore had to do so without attracting undue attention.[45] Such stealth was illustrated by Singapore's first call-ups for NS being sent by post rather than being announced via television broadcasts in order to avoid the attention of Kuala Lumpur.

Notwithstanding the precarious relationship with Malaysia, it should be noted here that, while relations with Indonesia were not as capricious, Indonesia was the only country to have directly threatened Singapore's security through its initial refusal to recognise the Federation of Malaysia of which Singapore was part of from 1963 to 1965. Then Indonesian President Sukarno also launched a policy of *Konfrontasi* which sought to undermine the international legitimacy and viability of the Malaysian Federation through a low-intensity conflict which saw Singapore a target of Indonesian sabotage and bombing. While relations between Singapore and Indonesia did stabilise by the 1970s, it can be argued that Singapore's policy elites never entirely lost their lingering concerns about the potential threats arising out of Indonesia.[46]

The Existential Crisis

With its survival threatened by the patchy relationship with its northern neighbour and coupled with the experience of aggression from its southern one, the sense of threat and vulnerability felt by Singapore was compounded by an even larger existential crisis. While recognised as a sovereign state, a history of communal violence and the rapid rupture which saw it becoming an independent entity left the feeling that it was a state composed of a fractious disunited people with no unifying sense of a collective self. Undeniably, communal tension within Singapore was

---

[45] Loo, "Goh Keng Swee and the Emergence of a Modern SAF", 132.

[46] Loo, "Explaining Changes in Singapore's Military Doctrines: Material and Ideational Perspectives", 365–366.

held to be "the gravest threat".[47] There had already been two major incidents of communal violence in Singapore prior to independence — the Maria Hertogh riots in 1950 and the 1964 race riots — and another series of race riots post-independence in 1969. As expressed by then Minister of Foreign Affairs, S. Rajaratnam:

> [In] a multi-racial, multilingual and multicultural society like ours, the communal problem ... must be and will always remain one of the major problems which, if we do not resolve intelligently, could break our society, especially of an independent Singapore.[48]

With this existential void, the state believed it needed to create a nation as rapidly as possible — a sense of nationhood among citizens that could act as the veneer over communal differences. NS was held to be, and still continues to be seen to be (as other chapters in this edited volume demonstrate), the experiential ointment to heal the national wound of intercommunal differences by developing commonality through shared experience. As expressed by Singapore's first Defence Minister, Dr Goh, "Nothing creates loyalty and national consciousness more speedily and thoroughly than participation in defense and membership to the armed forces."[49] A corollary of this view was that the numbers of Malays in the military had to be significantly reduced in order to make way for more Chinese and Indian representation as military service had to be experienced by all ethnic groups in order to create a multi-ethnic nation. In effect, what should be appreciated here is that vague racial targets were set for racial representation in the military to better reflect the multiracial racial composition of the state in order to ensure the nation could be created. In the words of Dr Goh:

> When national service began, there was a large preponderance of Malay soldiers in the army because the regulars of the two battalions we

---

[47] Chan Heng Chee and Obaid Ul Haq, eds., *The Prophetic and the Political: Selected Speeches and Writings of S. Rajaratnam* (New York: St. Martin's Press, 1987), 105.

[48] S. Rajaratnam, *Parliamentary Debate on the Findings of the Commission for Minority Rights and Freedoms*, 16 March 1967.

[49] Goh Keng Swee, Singapore, Singapore, *Parliamentary Debates Singapore*, no. 16, vol. 25, col. 1160, 13 March 1967.

inherited from the British were preponderantly Malays. The non-Malays, especially the Chinese, were simply not interested then in joining the army. This was especially true of the regular NCO [or non-commissioned officer] ranks. Because of this, the intake of Malays into national service was limited for some years.[50]

Besides leaving the impression that the state lacked a unified nation and needed to construct one through NS, the racial and religious riots also left the impression on political elites that communal identity is primordial and inter-communal tension would always be present stemming from the differences between these various primordial identities. Regrettably for Malays in the military, this subscription to a primordial understanding of identity by Singapore's political leadership at that time coupled with the existential angst from an unclear sense of self informed a view that Malays as a community could not be trusted if there was a conflict with either Malaysia or Indonesia. Effectively, with no clear sense of "Us" as yet constructed, Malays were viewed as a possible "Other". With such a view, it was believed that if a conflict was to erupt, Malays would, at worst, "naturally" either side with their ethnic and religious brethren in those two countries or they would experience a conflict of interest that would prevent them from performing optimally. This fear, during Singapore's early years, was captured succinctly by then Senior Minister Lee in 2001. He stated that:

> In the early days, many Malay Singaporeans were not called up for NS. When NS started in 1967, race relations were fragile and tenuous, after the riots of 1964 and separation in 1965. The government could not ignore race tensions, simply recruit all young Malays and Chinese and have them do military training side by side.[51]

This view that Malays would experience a conflict of interest in times of war — and that this conflict of interest would only eventually

---

[50] Goh Keng Swee, Singapore, *Parliamentary Debates Singapore*, vol. 36, cols. 398–399, 23 February 1977.

[51] Singapore Government Press Release, Speech by Senior Minister at Dialogue Session with AMP & Majlis Pusat, Ministry of Information and The Arts, 2 March 2001, http://www.nas.gov.sg/archivesonline/speeches/view-html?filename=2001030503.htm

be resolved when a shared national identity was held by all Singaporeans —
ran deep and long in the political pysche. As illustrated by a statement
made by then Second Minister for Defence Lee Hsien Loong in 1987,

> We live in South East Asia. If there is a conflict, if the SAF is called
> upon to defend our homeland, we don't want to put any of our soldiers
> in a difficult position where his emotions for the nation may come in
> conflict with his emotions for his religion, because these are two very
> strong fundamentals, and if they are not compatible, then they will be
> two very strong destructive forces in opposite directions ... And we
> don't want to put anybody in that position where he feels he is not
> fighting a just cause, and perhaps worse, maybe his side is not the right
> side ... It's a reality of life and it is something we cannot dodge, but
> which, gradually, as a national identity develops, will grow to be less
> of a problem.[52]

Moreover, speaking then as a Senior Minister, Lee Kuan Yew, in 1999,
echoed his son's primordial understanding of identity and the conflict of
interest this identity might pose if there was a conflict with Malaysia. He
maintained that, "[i]f, for instance, you put in a Malay officer who's very
religious and who has family ties in Malaysia in charge of a machine-gun
unit, that's a very tricky business."[53]

The Hollowing Out of Malays from the SAF

Despite the professionalism and dedication Malay soldiers had displayed
in the military before Singapore's independence, the existentialist threat
combined with the existential crisis faced by the island-state led to great
doubt over Malay loyalty to Singapore in the event of a war against its closest neighbours.[54] This security concern of Singapore's leaders became

---

[52] Lee Hsien Loong, Singapore, *Parliamentary Debates Singapore*, no. 4, vol. 49, col. 375,
17 March 1987.
[53] Lee Kuan Yew's remarks on Malays, *The Straits Times*, 30 September 1999.
[54] "Another would be the issue of loyalty. The government may have been suspicious of the
Malays as many had relatives and families in neighbouring Malaysia and Indonesia, and
Malays also shared religious ties with the Malay-Muslim community in Malaysia and

prominent and only encouraged the subsequent hollowing out of Malays from the SAF within the first five years after independence. The country's leaders saw a need to reduce and restrict the numbers of Malays in the military. This was to ensure there was no conflict of interest for the Malays, where Malays in conscription and in the military did not have to choose between their "emotions for the nation", and their "emotions for the religion."[55] Singapore's leaders drew what Cynthia Enloe refers to as an "ethnic state security map" — to "distinguish between loyal ethnic groups, which occupy combat roles, and a range of others who either are placed at the margins of the military or are excluded from service."[56] While the rhetoric of independence called for a united and multicultural Singapore, in the case of the SAF and Singapore's immediate security concerns then, the government found it apt to limit and halt Malay presence and progress in the military.

To arrive at the restriction of Malays in the military, Singapore's leaders saw it necessary to clear the military's ranks of the high numbers of Malays, to bring in more non-Malays — especially the Chinese — and to exclude Malay youth from service.[57] Discriminate measures and strategies needed to be directly implemented towards Malays, for "local recruitment officers on aggressive campaigns [to racially balance the military still] encountered many more Malay than non-Malay volunteers."[58] The military was the traditional avenue of employment and social mobility for Malays,[59] and therefore, saw continuing eagerness from Singapore's Malay youth to join the military.

Indonesia. The government feared that Malays' religiosity would be stronger than the need to be loyal to the country. This was why the government was cautious in their policy to taking in Malay youth into the army." Wan Hussin Haji Zoohri, Accession Number 002862. Political History in Singapore 1965–1985 (10 June 2004). http://www.nas.gov.sg/archivesonline/oral_history_interviews/record-details/9b4ec773-1160-11e3-83d5-0050568939ad (accessed 12 December 2016).

[55] Peled, "Singapore: From Inclusion to Exclusion", 124.

[56] Cynthia H. Enloe, *Ethnic Soldiers: State Security in a Divided Society* (Middlesex: Penguin Books Ltd, 1980), 186.

[57] Peled, "Singapore: From Inclusion to Exclusion", 106.

[58] Ibid.

[59] Ibid., 107.

Clearing Ranks of the High Numbers of Malays

One of the first few strategies taken after independence to dampen the numbers of Malays in the military was to relieve existing Malay soldiers of their combat or field command posts.[60] Many Malay soldiers were relocated to less sensitive units to minimise potential security breaches, such as the logistics corps.[61] Malay field commanders were also redeployed to administrative duties instead of combat posts,[62] and there were also high barriers to entry for Malays to be assigned to specific military vocations such as commando and the air force. The government also introduced incentives to encourage Malay soldiers to retire earlier in their careers. Additionally, existing Malay soldiers were not placed in important posts and promotional or contract renewal prospects were curtailed.[63] At the same time alternative employment arrangements were created outside of the military, particularly in the private sector, which eventually encouraged many veteran Malay soldiers (and policemen) to become commercial security guards instead.[64]

Bringing in More Non-Malays

Singapore's leaders had to ensure there was minimal hindrance to their overall strategy of reducing and restricting Malays in the military. This was done not only by preventing existing Malay officers and commanders from rising in ranks, but also through the overall increase in the number of non-Malay soldiers. Non-Malay candidates were sent for officer training, mostly from the Singaporean Indian and Eurasian communities to make up for the shortfall of Chinese candidates at the time.[65] Malay can-

---

[60] Ibid.

[61] Ibid., 109.

[62] Ibid.

[63] Huxley, "Personnel", 102.

[64] Peled, "Singapore: From Inclusion to Exclusion", 113.

[65] The Chinese were reluctant to join the military, and had preferred to be in business or commerce. The lack of interest on the part of the Chinese in the military was made up with numbers from the Singaporean Indian and Eurasian communities instead, with Malays prevented from joining the officer courses. Peled, "Singapore: From Inclusion to Exclusion", 107.

didates and veterans within the command structure were barely considered for these courses or for military leadership, while "non-Malay civilians were transferred from their civil posts to the SAF and commissioned as officers."[66] Additionally, to facilitate recruiting more Chinese into the military and serving in senior roles, Mandarin was used as the "language of senior commanders in the military, and officers who were candidates for promotion to the rank of captain and above had to pass an oral Mandarin exam."[67]

Exclude Malay Youth from Service

Most significantly, as efforts to "racially balance" the military were not successful,[68] Singapore instituted compulsory conscription in 1967 to service the manpower needs of its defence forces by making it obligatory for Singaporean male youth to serve — and forcefully increase the numbers of Chinese in the military. The riots of 1969 stemming from racial animosity between Malays and Chinese, however, further heightened fears of Malay disloyalty to Singapore and "forced Singapore's leaders to redesign their ethnic military manpower policy."[69]

Therefore, the conscription of Malay youth into the military stalled after 1969, and "senior defence officials were instructed to carefully screen out Malays from enlistment lists."[70] The SAF dismissed Malay

---

[66] Peled, "Singapore: From Inclusion to Exclusion", 109. See also: Walsh, "The Roar of the Lion City", 271.

[67] This double standard gave the Chinese an advantage in promotions within the military. Peled, "Singapore: From Inclusion to Exclusion", 113.

[68] The strategy to "racially balance" the military was to increase the numbers of non-Malay soldiers — most particularly the Chinese. However, many Chinese were not interested in joining the military; there is a Chinese saying which goes, "good iron is never used for making nails, and good men are never made into soldiers". To which a PAP Parliament member quipped, "If good men are not turned into soldiers, then it follows that the nation will have to depend on good-for-nothing people for its defence." This may be in reference to Malays, who had largely turned to the military as a traditional form of employment. Peled, "Singapore: From Inclusion to Exclusion", 110.

[69] Ibid., 111.

[70] This is despite the fact that Malays made up between 50% to 80% of the first batch of volunteers for the new armed force after independence. Walsh, "The Roar of the Lion

youth even if they had signed official military recruitment papers. These moves diluted the number of Malays entering the SAF, and only a small number of Malay youth were allowed to trickle into the military "whenever frustration in the Malay community reached a dangerous level."[71] Malays were aware that their youth were not called up for NS, and how this "unwritten policy" of reducing the numbers of Malays in the army included informal quotas on Malays in military units.[72] Those who were conscripted found themselves becoming policemen and firemen instead, and were eventually posted into civil defence units after the mid-1970s.[73]

Ruling party parliamentarians — including Malay ones — claimed there was a need to take in only qualified Malays who had a good command of the English language and those who had at least 'A' level qualifications for conscription.[74] For example, Member of Parliament Othman Wok recognised how "the government did not call up all Malays to serve in the national service ... those who were not qualified, those who dropped out of school — they were not called up then."[75] Other incongruous explanations included how Malay males should spend more time with their families at home, and that the military did not have enough facilities and resources to train Malays.[76]

City", 274. See also: Lily Zubaidah Rahim, "The frightened Country and the Geopolitics of Insecurity", in *Singapore in the Malay World: Building and Breaching Regional Bridges*, ed. Lily Zubaidah Rahim (Oxon: Routledge, 2009), 91.

[71] Peled, "Singapore: From Inclusion to Exclusion", 112.

[72] Abdul Manaf Ahmad, Accession Number 002181. Education in Singapore (Part 3: Malay/Tamil) (20 April 2000). http://www.nas.gov.sg/archivesonline/oral_history_interviews/record-details/742e2922-115e-11e3-83d5-0050568939ad (accessed 12 December 2016).

[73] This strategic reallocation and reordering of manpower shuffled Malays into the homeland defence forces instead of the military, considering the concerns of Malay loyalty during a war between Singapore and Malaysia. Even today, Malays are arguably held to be over-represented in the police and civil defence forces, while under-represented in the military. Peled, "Singapore: From Inclusion to Exclusion", 113.

[74] Jabbar Hanief, Suhaimi Mohsen and Nuryati Duriat. "Kurang kelulusan boleh diatasi". *Berita Harian*, 28 March, 1987, 8. See also: Mohamad Maidin Packer Mohd, Accession number 003180. Political History in Singapore 1985–2005 (4 July 2007).

[75] Othman Wok, Accession Number 000774. Political History in Singapore 1965–1985 (11 May 1987). http://www.nas.gov.sg/archivesonline/oral_history_interviews/record-details/aab6a539-1161-11e3-83d5-0050568939ad (accessed 12 December 2016).

[76] Peled, "Singapore: From Inclusion to Exclusion", 121.

Further, the authorities ensured to maximise the number of Chinese conscripts in combatant roles. The Ministry of Defence (MINDEF) re-allocated about 70% of the military's logistics positions to civilians, and hired women to fill non-combatant roles.[77] Bringing more civilians and women into the military assisted in diluting the numbers of Malay youth in the SAF. The fear the leadership had of Malay disloyalty to the state was enough to relinquish the "experience and professionalism that had been built up before 1965" through Malay soldiers.[78]

NS and Pragmatism

Having traced the key and sterling role played by Malays in defending Singapore during its colonial past, the reasons for their significantly reduced role in the military after independence, and the methods employed to arrive at the goal of a reduced reliance on Malays in the military, the question remaining is how NS can be modified in order for it to better serve its two roles of defending Singapore as well as creating a nation. The answer here perhaps may be arrived at through the employment of a championed decision-making methodology, termed as pragmatism, which is informed by a precedent set in NS's past.

Pragmatism

Pragmatism is employed by the Singapore government with its politicians maintaining pragmatism as an underlying guide to decision making. Pragmatism is rooted in the idea that all endeavour has to have a clear goal and the means chosen to arrive at that goal should be decided upon by its efficiency or effectiveness at meeting that goal. For instance, if the goal is to avoid having only a President of one race, the most effective means to accomplish this goal would be for an alteration of the system used to elect Singapore's President. Alternatively, if the goal is to ensure that all Housing and Development Board (HDB) estates reflect the multiracial composition of Singapore, the most efficient and effective means to achieve this would be to have the HDB's quota system for the purchasing

---

[77] Ibid., 114.
[78] Walsh, "The Roar of the Lion City", 274.

of public housing. Arguably, based on the discussion in the second section, pragmatism was what prompted the state to come to the policy decisions with regard to NS and Malays. Singapore's existentialist threat and existential crisis taken together appeared to demand that the Malay role in the military had to be dramatically reduced if the targets were the survival of the state and the creation of the nation.

Have the goals been met? As one of the most technologically advanced and militarised states in the region, it is very doubtful Singapore still perceives the same degree of inter-state threat to its existence as it did just after independence. Hence, pragmatism has most certainly achieved one of its two goals — the survival of the state. Moreover, with the desire in recent years to stress the successful attempts to integrate Malays into all elements of the military, statements emphasising integration suggests pragmatism's second goal has also been achieved. Consider for example the then Minister of State for Defence Mohamad Maliki Osman's (who was the first Malay political office-holder in MINDEF) statement that "[o]ur Malay servicemen have made significant progress in all the services in the SAF based on their capabilities and merits, and I am confident many more will do so in the future."[79] Additionally, Defence Minister Ng Eng Hen was keen to stress that "[a] person is deployed in a sensitive unit in the Singapore Armed Forces based on his ability and beliefs to ensure that he is not a security risk, not on his race."[80] Several years earlier, the 6th Division, one of the Singapore Army's three combined-armed divisions, had in fact been commanded by a Malay brigadier general, Ishak Ismail, from 2009 to 2011.

If the integration of Malays into the military continues to make "significant progress", this suggests Singapore has largely overcome its existential crisis — a crisis that demanded them to be excluded in the first place. The integration of Malays into all elements of the military points towards a belief that the nation with a clear sense of "Us" and the "Other" has been created. After all, they could not be integrated in the past owing as Singapore was absent a nation and there were unclear lines between "Us"

---

[79] "Maliki: Malays have made significant progress in SAF", *The Straits Times*, 20 February 2015. http://news.asiaone.com/news/singapore/maliki-malays-have-made-significant-progress-saf

[80] Jermyn Chow, "Malays deployed in the SAF as sailors: Ng Eng Hen", *The Straits Times*, 16 February 2015. http://www.straitstimes.com/singapore/malays-deployed-in-the-saf-as-sailors-ng-eng-hen

and the "Other". As noted by Deputy Prime Minister and former Minister for Defence Teo Chee Hean in 2010,

> The role of Malays in the defence of our nation and in the SAF, and the associated challenges and dilemmas we face, are difficult and sensitive issues for our multi-racial, multi-religious society. They have confronted Singapore since our early days of nation-building … The SAF is a micro-cosm of Singapore society, and race relations within the SAF reflect those in our broader society. Thus as Singapore has made steady progress towards racial and religious integration, so has the SAF. Malays serve today in many more places and roles in the SAF than before …[81]

The Way Forward

If pragmatism has served Singapore so well with regard to achieving the twin goals of security and nation-building, how can NS be modified in order to serve both the state and the nation better? It is possible to argue here that for NS to do so, racial targets can be set for even greater integration within elements of the SAF serviced by conscription. The use of targets in order to turn the military into a force more reflective of the nation is not alien to the SAF. As it should be remembered, this was one of the very reasons Malays in the military had to make way for the other races in the fledgling SAF. Hence, the modified goal proposed here is for NS to be employed as an integration deepening tool where the target becomes one striving to make all three services of the SAF reflect the racial demographic of Singapore.

There is great utility to be arrived at by doing so. Firstly, regarding the defence of the state, greater integration would lead to greater diversity and the military as a whole can benefit from diversity in many ways. Research in the business field is helpful in showing how a military can benefit from greater diversity within its ranks. More diverse groups have been shown to benefit from the greater range of perspectives present and from a more inclusive environment that encourages people to contribute their individual

---

[81] Parliamentary Statement, Reply by Deputy Prime Minister and Minister for Defence to Parliamentary Question on Deployment of Malay or Muslim Servicemen in the SAF, *Singapore Ministry of Defence*, 19 July 2010. https://www.mindef.gov.sg/imindef/press_room/official_releases/ps/2010/19jul10_ps2.html

views.[82] Moreover, as revealed in a recent study, diversity is a key driver of innovation and is a critical component of being successful on a global scale.[83] Finally, as noted by entrepreneur Eric Ries, "[d]iversity is the canary in the coal mine for meritocracy" — when it is not alive and present in a meritocracy, it indicates meritocracy is not working. Moreover, one should care about diversity "not for its own sake, but because it is a source of strength for teams that have it, and a symptom of dysfunction for those that don't."[84] Secondly, regarding the SAF's second *raison d'être* which is the continued creation of commonality for generations to come, the benefits for having racial targets to strive for are psychological. Conscripts can then look around the service they are deployed to and recognise the nation they are serving within that very service — one truly representative of the phenotypic hues of the Singaporean racial demographic.

What is being proposed in this chapter is not outlandish. Singapore trusts its Malay citizens — and its other minorities as well for that matter — enough to alter its electoral system of its Elected Presidency (EP) to ensure the state avoids having presidents of only one race. It should be stressed what is put forward here is not a call for quotas or for affirmative action where the unqualified are lifted unfairly above their abilities or for military tests to be fudged. Thus, the argument for racial targets as opposed to quotas is in keeping with what Prime Minister Lee Hsien Loong has maintained about the suggestion for quotas to be introduced to correct the gender imbalance in parliament. According to the Prime Minister, Singapore has

> … no affirmative action or quota system … in any field of endeavour. We give opportunities for all and we trust that people of talent, whether men or women, will seize these opportunities and will rise up. And we try our best

---

[82] James Surowiecki, "The Difference Difference Makes: Waggle Dances, the Bay of Pigs, and the Value of Diversity", in *The Wisdom of Crowds*, ed. James Surowiecki (New York: Doubleday, 2004), 23–39.

[83] "Global diversity and inclusion: Fostering innovation through a diverse workforce," *Forbes*, 2011, 3.

[84] Eric Ries, "Why diversity matters (the meritocracy business)", *Startup Lessons Learned*, 22 February 2010. http://www.startuplessonslearned.com/2010/02/why-diversity-matter-meritocracy.html

to make sure there are no glass ceilings. So, Singaporeans know that women who occupy senior positions are there on their own merits and they can become role models for younger ones and spur them on to do their best.[85]

Instead, exactly like the proposed adaption of the EP system, individuals have to meet the high standards demanded by specific elements of the military for entry. Eschewing affirmative action of quotas through the proposed adaptation, the military instead devotes energy to help under-represented races in particular services to rise to the standards demanded to attain the target set.

Conclusion

Having commemorated the 50th anniversary of NS in Singapore, it is important to acknowledge the fact, as this chapter has shown, that Malay Singaporeans were consciously left out of NS, and as such also denied the ability to play a military role in defending their nation up to the late 1970s. However, the chapter shows that while the military was indeed hollowed out of Malays after Singapore's independence, attempts have been made in recent years to make all aspects of the SAF more inclusive. The chapter argues, though, that more can be done in order for deeper racial integration in NS be achieved — an integration of not just Malay Singaporeans but an integration to make the three services of the SAF staffed by NSmen, fully reflective of the multiracial nation it protects.

---

[85] Lee Hsien Loong, "Transcript of Prime Minister Lee Hsien Loong's speech", *National Archives of Singapore*, 14 August 2009, http://www.nas.gov.sg/archivesonline/speeches/view-html?filename=20090814008.htm

Part 4

An International Perspective

Chapter 10

Conscription in Taiwan[1]: A Problematic Evolution

Wu Shang-Su and Ho Shu Huang

Taiwan's policy of conscription is presently being re-evaluated with the aim of shifting its military to an all-volunteer force (AVF). This evolution has occurred in the context of the transformation of Taiwanese domestic politics, changing cross-Strait relations and defence reforms. The first part of this chapter explores the reasons why conscription was introduced in Taiwan and how the policy has been implemented. The second section details the criticism the policy has faced and how it has evolved because of these dissenting views. The chapter concludes that the politicisation of conscription has resulted in a problematic evolution to a specified end, but one that is still far from sight.

Why Conscription?

Conscription in Taiwan did not begin with the Republic of China (ROC) government. Even earlier, Japan, which had occupied Taiwan from 1895

---

[1] How the "Republic of China" (ROC) and "Taiwan" are used is politically contentious and therefore confusing. For clarity, this chapter will use the ROC when referring to the Kuomintang-governed state until the passing of the Taiwan Relations Act in 1979, when the United States stopped recognising it and Taiwan became more commonly used internationally. Taiwan will thereafter be used instead of the ROC. It will also be used when referencing geography. The ROC, however, will continue to be used when referring to the military and government departments as it is still part of their official names.

to 1945, had conscripted locals during World War II to help the Japanese war effort.[2] During the Chinese Civil War (1945–1949), an ad-hoc conscription policy was implemented by the Kuomintang (KMT) nationalist government.[3] It would be only years later before the ROC regime would have sufficient political capital to institute it as a national policy. The KMT's defeat by the Communists during the Civil War and its forced withdrawal to Taiwan had placed it on the back foot. The ROC regime only began to consolidate its position when it began receiving significant aid from the United States (US) in the wake of the Korean War and rising fears of the spread of Communism in Asia. Only with the stabilisation of the ROC central government could a policy of compulsory military service be implemented. Conscription began tentatively in 1953 when students were required to complete four months of military training. It was formally implemented as a national policy in 1956.[4]

To Build a Non-Communist Chinese Nation

Universal conscription was introduced for two reasons. The first was for nation-building. There was a pressing need to develop a ROC-shaped national identity in Taiwan that now included a sizeable indigenous population in addition to those who had fled the mainland. Through half a century of Japanese governance, the indigenous people of Taiwan, also known as Formosans, had broadly different cultural and historical characteristics from their Chinese counterparts. Formosans mainly spoke Japanese and dialects such as Hokkien and Hakka, and their attitudes towards the ROC regime varied. In 1945, the majority of Formosans welcomed the ROC regime's takeover of the island. The Taiwan Provincial Authority's poor governance,

---

[2] Shao Minghuang, "Taiwan in Wartime," in *China at War*, eds. Stephen R. MacKinnon, Diana Lary and Ezra F. Vogel (Stanford: Stanford University Press, 2007), 100; Hui-yu Caroline Tsai, *Taiwan in Japan's Empire-Building: An Institutional Approach to Colonial Engineering* (New York: Routledge, 2009), 180–181.

[3] Denny Roy, *Taiwan: A Political History* (Ithaca: Cornell University Press, 2003), 94–95; "一段被漠視的歷史－國共內戰台籍老兵血淚史 (The neglected history of Taiwanese Soldiers in the Chinese Civil War)," *Peopo- Citizen Journalism*, 9 June 2007, http://www.peopo.org/portal.php?op=viewPost&article (accessed 20 October 2016).

[4] Monte R. Bullard, *The Soldier and the Citizen* (New York: M. E. Sharpe, 1997), 121.

however, soon led to an island-wide uprising in 1947. The ROC's harsh military response, culminating in the February 28 Massacre, created a split between the Formosans and the government. Thereafter, the ROC regime implemented nation-building policies in the 1950s to build a common Chinese identity in Taiwan via the education system and other national programmes. These wide-ranging policies of political-social engineering focused predominantly on those born after World War II who formed a sizeable portion of the Taiwanese population. Their objective was to minimise the legacy of Taiwan under Japanese governance and enshrine the ROC regime's legitimacy in Taiwan. The military would play a significant role there. It began its involvement in education with the launch of the Youth Corps in 1952 and subsequently, military training courses introduced in 1953. Military officers were assigned to high schools and universities as course instructors.[5]

The introduction of conscription in 1956 extended the reach of this socialisation, particularly among those who had little formal education, as well as the role the military would play. During two or more years of service, conscripts learned the official language, Mandarin. The inability of locals to speak this fluently had been a significant barrier in the interactions between them and those from the mainland in the 1950s. Additionally, an extensive curriculum of political education that emphasised the Chinese identity as promulgated by the ROC regime was taught by the General Political Warfare Department. It hoped this would minimise the influence of Communism and develop loyalty to the ROC. This department, ironically a copy of the Communist Soviet commissar system, deployed political officers to all military units to ensure political education was conducted appropriately.[6] The ROC's centralised political education strengthened government command and control of its military. Previously, the ROC's forces constituted several factions whose core identities were

---

[5] Jay Taylor, *The Generalissimo's Son* (London: Harvard University Press, 2000), 194–195; Denny Roy, *Taiwan: A Political History*, 91–92; Monte R. Bullard, *The Soldier and the Citizen*, 41; Jeremiah Taylor, "Commissar", Salem Press Encyclopedia, January 2016, http://eds.a.ebscohost.com/eds/detail/detail?vid=4&sid=f0131a9b-d207-4e11-9359-3f571 fbe84dc%40sessionmgr4007&bdata=JnNpdGU9ZWRzLWxpdmUmc2NvcGU9c2l0ZQ% 3d%3d#AN=96776407&db=ers (accessed 10 July 2017).

[6] Ibid.

based on the provinces they were formed from. Factionalism within KMT forces complicated attempts to unify command and control. A divided structure which impinged combat effectiveness was one of the major reasons the KMT lost the Civil War in 1949.[7] Furthermore, an influx of conscripts who saw themselves as ROC citizens first and foremost diluted and eventually dissolved existing provincial barriers, consolidating the ROC regime's control of the military.[8]

To Transform the ROC Military: From Offence to Defence

The second reason for the introduction of conscription was to raise a sizeable ROC military capable of both offensive and defensive operations. The ROC regime had made it clear from the start that re-taking the mainland from the Communists would be part of the national agenda. To Chiang Kai-shek, the KMT leader who lost the Civil War, this was of personal importance as he had hoped to restore his reputation following its defeat. Nationally, the ROC regime had to embellish its promise to return to the mainland as that was the basis of its legitimacy as the authentic Chinese government which it once was, especially to those who fled to Taiwan. To demonstrate its seriousness and more importantly, ability to do so, the ROC military had to form a large military with offensive capabilities to retake the mainland.[9] The ROC maintained more than 20 infantry divisions, two mechanised armour divisions, one airborne brigade and two marine divisions, and a total of at least 270,000 troops throughout the Cold War.[10] To do so, conscription would provide the vast manpower needed.

In reality, this offensive force structure existed only on paper. While troop numbers were high, the quality of the military's equipment was low.

---

[7] Stephen R. MacKinnon, "Conclusion: Wartime China", in *China at War*, eds. Stephen R. MacKinnon, Diana Lary and Ezra F. Vogel (Stanford: Stanford University Press, 2007), 338.

[8] From 1956, 150,000 soldiers, about a quarter of the total armed forces, were drafted annually. Monte R. Bullard, *The Soldier and the Citizen*, 73.

[9] Jay Taylor, *The Generalissimo's Son*, 228.

[10] International Institute for Strategic Studies (IISS), *Military Balance 1965* (London: IISS, 1965), 33; *Military Balance 1970* (London: IISS, 1970), 61–62; *Military Balance 1990* (London: IISS, 1990), 177–178.

The US, the main arms supplier to the ROC, was reluctant to support the ROC's ambitious plan to arm itself.[11] It was mindful of the need to maintain the status quo in the region during the Cold War, particularly after the Korean and Vietnam wars. Furthermore, Beijing's eventual development of nuclear weapons in the mid-1960s seriously eroded any hope for the ROC to re-take the mainland militarily.[12] Compounding this, Cold War politics shifted against the ROC's favour in the 1970s. It lost its seat in the United Nations in 1971. In 1979, the US formally established diplomatic relations with the People's Republic of China (PRC). A year later, in 1980, the US ended the ROC–US Mutual Defence Treaty (MDT). These developments ended the feasibility of Chiang's offensive strategy to reunify both Chinas.[13] Despite this reality, the ROC still publicly retained a military structure geared for offensive operations until the 1990s. Conscription would therefore retain its importance as a key national policy by providing the necessary manpower for this pipe dream.[14] After all, there was no escaping the fact that Taiwan would also need a strong military to defend itself from being taken by the mainland.

The ROC was not alone in seeking reunification. The PRC, too, had similar ambitions. Conscription was touted as key to Taiwan's defence against any PRC attempt to take the island. Specifically, it could provide manpower in key areas such as the defence of Taiwan's offshore islands close to China, its navy and anti-landing operations on the Taiwanese coast.

Following its withdrawal to Taiwan, the ROC occupied the islands of Quemoy (Kinmen) and Matsu just off the mainland. Militarily, the proximity of these islands to the mainland made them difficult to defend

---

[11] Jay Taylor, *The Generalissimo's Son*, 229, 267–268; Nancy Bernkopf Tucker, *Strait Talk: United States–Taiwan Relations and the Crisis with China* (Cambridge: Harvard University Press, 2009), 94–95.

[12] Nuclear Threat Initiative, "China", http://www.nti.org/learn/countries/china/nuclear/ (accessed 21 October 2016).

[13] David W. Chen, "Taiwan's President tiptoes around politics at Cornell," *New York Times*, latest modified 10 June 1995, http://www.nytimes.com/1995/06/10/world/taiwan-s-president-tiptoes-around-politics-at-cornell.html (accessed 21 October 2016).

[14] Shen Ming-shih and Tsai Chen-Tin, "An Analysis of the Republic of China's Military Organization and Force Structure", in *Taiwan's Defense Reform*, eds. Martin Edmonds and Michael M. Tsai (London: Routledge, 2006), 104, 115.

because they were vulnerable to Chinese artillery fire. Even the ROC's US military advisors suggested abandoning them. Chiang Kai-shek, however, chose to defend them as they symbolised Taiwan's links to the mainland. They would also be key stepping stones for any eventual KMT invasion of the mainland. Consequently, Taipei deployed 100,000 and 60,000 troops, respectively in Quemoy and Matsu islands to strengthen the islands' defences.[15] In 1954 and 1958, the islands were attacked by the People's Liberation Army (PLA) though no invasion was eventually mounted. There would be repeated exchanges of artillery fire thereafter. Although this eventually ended in 1979, the deployment of forces on these islands remained significant.[16] The presence of deployment of such a large number of conscripts in these offshore islands was more of a political demonstration of resolve and intent rather than operational necessity for Taiwan's defence. Until onshore anti-ship missiles were installed, conventional artillery could do little to deny the People's Liberation Army Navy (PLAN) movement at sea in a concerted attack on the main Taiwanese island; there were no chokepoints and alternate routes could always have been taken.

Conscription was also a crucial source of manpower for the ROC Navy (ROCN) to operate its fleets. For much of the Cold War, the ROCN operated vessels provided through US military aid. Most of those vessels were of World War II vintage which required large crews. Between the late 1960s and the early 1980s, naval conscripts operated more than 30 destroyers.[17] They formed the backbone of the ROCN and performed dangerous duties. The ROCN would be at the frontline of any conflict with the PRC and it played a crucial role during the crises of 1954 and 1958. The American-supplied vessels were also not particularly well armoured. Many of the gun emplacements had open turrets. Patrolling the Taiwan

---

[15] Ralph N. Clough, *Island China* (Cambridge, Massachusetts: Harvard University Press, 1978), 106; Jay Taylor, *The Generalissimo's Son*, 233.

[16] Francoise Mengin, *Fragments of an Unfinished War: Taiwanese Entrepreneurs and the Partition of China* (London: Hurst, 2015), 104; IISS, *Military Balance 1990* (London: IISS, 1990), 178.

[17] Stockholm International Peace Research Institute, "The SIPRI Arms Transfer Database", https://www.sipri.org/databases/armstransfers (accessed 24 October 2016); H. T. Lenton, *American Fleet and Escort Destroyers 1* (London: MacDonald, 1971), 109, 131, 145.

Strait, particularly near those offshore islands and in range of PLA artillery, was particularly dangerous.[18]

Finally, despite their limitations, the mere presence of a large number of ground troops in Taiwan significantly increased the difficulty of an amphibious landing by the PLA. Large lengths of Taiwan's coastlines are unsuitable for a coastal landing. Suitable stretches were identified by the ROC Army (ROCA) and defences prepared.[19] As long as the PLA forces could be repulsed at sea, or at the very worse contained on a limited beachhead, a sizeable army would give the ROC the ability to counterattack and a good chance of repelling an invasion. Furthermore, reserve forces, themselves former conscripts, could significantly increase the manpower available to defend Taiwan's coast.

In reality, other factors protected Taiwan from invasion rather than deterrence through conscription. The PLA's main window of opportunity to quickly take Taiwan actually existed only between the KMT's withdrawal in 1949 and June 1950 before the outbreak of the Korean War, several years before the introduction of conscription. During this short period, the KMT was still reeling from its defeat in the Civil War. It was struggling to establish a functioning state on the small island of Taiwan. The evacuees were physically and psychologically fatigued from the previous years of upheaval. There were also indications that the probability of a US intervention on the ROC's side would be low.[20] Taiwan was therefore vulnerable. If the PLA could successfully cross the Taiwan Strait, it would have had a real shot at taking Taiwan.

Fortunately for the ROC, the PLA did not have the capabilities then or even during the Cold War. Its naval and air arms were too small to effectively project force across the strait immediately after the KMT's retreat to Taiwan. A land-based force then, the PLA did not have the means to stage an amphibious invasion. In the 1960s, the domestic production of Soviet-designed aircraft and vessels by the PRC defence industry raised the

---

[18] Navy Headquarters, MND, "History", last modified 24 October 2016, http://navy.mnd. gov.tw/english/Publish.aspx?cnid=836&Level=1 (accessed 24 October 2016).

[19] Shen Ming-shih and Tsai Chen-Tin, "An Analysis of the Republic of China's Military Organization and Force Structure", 102, 104.

[20] Denny Roy, *Taiwan: A Political History*, 96–97; Jay Taylor, *The Generalissimo's Son*, 196.

feasibility of an amphibious invasion. The Cultural Revolution, however, severely disrupted the development of the PLA.[21] The concurrent souring of Sino-Soviet relations during this decade culminated in a brief war between the two in 1969. This was followed by years of border confrontations. At almost every turn, Moscow managed to apply strategic pressure that hindered Beijing's ability to effectively deploy its military.[22] After the Cultural Revolution, Deng Xiaoping's cautious diplomacy and the PRC's focus on economic development reduced its likelihood of attacking Taiwan.[23] Finally, despite tensions in their relationship, Taiwan would still come under the US defence umbrella. The ROC benefited from a Mutual Defence Treaty (MDT) with the US between 1954 and 1979.[24] The Taiwan Relations Act (TRA), while more loosely worded than the MDT it replaced, was still a deterrent the PRC could not ignore.[25] These factors which mitigated the threat of a PRC invasion, however, were understated in Taiwan. The narrative that conscription was fundamental to Taiwan's defence dominated.

In 1987, Chiang Ching-kuo ended martial law. In force for 38 years, martial law granted the KMT extensive control across Taiwan, including public discourse. Its end ushered in a period of "democratisation" including greater public debate and elections. In the 1990s, Chiang's successor, Lee Teng-hui held open elections, including one for the president. The opening up of Taiwanese society would impact conscription in two divergent ways — a greater concern by the PRC that Taiwan would seek independence in a period

---

[21] Stephen P. Gibert and William M. Carpenter, *America and Island China: A Documentary History* (New York: University Press of America, 1989), 138–139; Bernard D. Cole, *The Great Wall at Sea: China's Navy Enters the Twenty-First Century* (Annapolis: Naval Institute Press, 2001), 107.

[22] Ramses Amer, "Sino–Vietnam Normalization in the Light of the Crisis of the Late 1970s", *Pacific Affairs* 67 (Autumn 1994), 358.

[23] You Ji, "China's 'New' Diplomacy, Foreign Policy, and Defense Strategy", in *China's "New" Diplomacy: Tactical or Fundamental Change?* eds. Pauline Kerr, Stuart Harris and Qin Yaqing (New York: Palgrave Macmillan, 2008), 90.

[24] Bernard Cole, *Taiwan's Security: History and Prospects* (London, New York: Routledge, 2006), 21–22; "Mutual Defense Treaty between the United States and the Republic of China; December 2, 1954", Yale Law School, http://avalon.law.yale.edu/20th_century/chin001.asp (accessed 11 July 2017).

[25] American Institute in Taiwan, "Taiwan Relations Act", https://www.ait.org.tw/en/taiwan-relations-act.html (accessed 3 May 2017).

when the PLA's capabilities were also rapidly increasing, yet a liberalisation of views on conscription domestically. While the feasibility of a cross-strait PRC invasion had steadily increased, raising the importance of conscription as a means to raise sufficient manpower to defend the island, domestic attitudes towards conscription had actually evolved from traditionally unequivocal support to a mixed range of views.

Taiwanese Independence, an Enhanced PRC's Threat and the Need for Conscription

Public opinion in Taiwan in the 1990s seemed to shift towards clear independence as a recognised sovereign state. Independence had become intertwined with Taiwanese identity and nationalism.[26] Concurrently, political and governmental reforms undertaken by the government during this period also gradually made the administration of Taiwan appear to be more like an independent state rather than a "small China" which sought unification with the mainland. This had been Taiwan's hitherto position, even if achieving it through reunification via invasion of the mainland was unrealistic. In particular, the simplification of the layers of government seemed to legitimise the independence movement. Before the reforms, Taiwan had three levels of government — central, provincial and local. These three levels, overly bureaucratic and ill-suited for governing a small island, were still adopted because they were envisaged as the structure that would be adopted after unification with the mainland. The reforms streamlined the administrative system by incorporating the provincial government into either the central or local ones, a better fit for Taiwan's circumstances. The removal of Taiwan as a province-in-waiting of a unified China was however interpreted by some as a step towards independence.[27] Additionally, the conduct of presidential elections also suggested Taiwan was behaving like a sovereign state.

---

[26] Tsai Chang-Yen, "National Identity, Ethnic Identity, and Party Identity in Taiwan", *Maryland Series in Contemporary Asia Studies* 188/1 (2007), 8.

[27] "Taiwan ends its status as a 'province' of China", *The New York Times*, 20 July 1997, http://www.nytimes.com/1997/07/20/world/taiwan-ends-its-status-as-a-province-of-china. html (accessed May 23, 2017).

Although there were no overt legislative changes, including to the constitution, these developments suggested Taiwan might indeed be moving towards declaring independence, alarming Beijing. Then and now, Taiwan's status as a renegade province is fundamentally intertwined with the PRC's nationalism narrative that it would eventually bring the island back to its fold.[28] In that narrative, the PLA is a powerful tool for the PRC to coerce Taiwan into reuniting the mainland and to give up any thoughts of independence. Consequently, the PRC began to take a firmer stance towards the island, enabled by its improved geostrategic position which now constrained it less than during the Cold War. The collapse of the Soviet Union diminished the possibility of a military confrontation along its shared borders. The PLA's modernisation had improved its Anti-Access/Area Denial (A2/AD) capability and increased the costs, time and risks for any US intervention on Taiwan's side.[29] Such intervention in the first place was not guaranteed. The TRA did not automatically oblige the US to defend Taiwan.[30]

Initial efforts by the PRC to rein Taiwan in were, however, tentative. In the 1990s, much of the pressure the PLA applied was psychological in nature. Tensions, however, seemed to reach boiling point in 1995. Prior to Taiwan's first Presidential Elections, the PLA test-fired short-range ballistic missiles, as well as conducted military exercises on its coast near Taiwan. What eventually came to be known as the "Third Taiwan Strait Crisis" ended because of US intervention and the inability of the PLA to realistically escalate the crisis by projecting force across the Strait.[31] This, however, would not remain the case for long.

A significant objective of the PLA's modernisation has been defeating Taiwan's air and sea capabilities. This has shifted the military balance

---

[28] Yu Maochun, "Political and Military Factors Determining China's Use of Force", in *If China Attacks Taiwan: Military Strategy, Politics and Economics*, ed. Steve Tseng (London: Routledge, 2006), 29.

[29] Office of the Secretary of Defense, "Annual Report to Congress: Military and Security Developments Involving the People's Republic of China 2016" (Washington D.C.: Office of the Secretary of Defense, 2016), 59–61.

[30] Ibid., 20–21; American Institute in Taiwan, "Taiwan Relations Act"; Office of the Secretary of Defense, "Military and Security Developments Involving the People's Republic of China 2016", last modified 26 April 2016, www.defense.gov/News/Article/Article/604605 (accessed 31 October 2016).

[31] Bernard Cole, *Taiwan's Security: History and Prospects*, 28–30.

across the Strait in the PRC's favour. The ROC Air Force (ROCAF) vis-à-vis its PRC counterpart is now inferior. The ROCAF has encountered difficulty procuring new fighters in the 2000s. On the other hand, the People's Liberation Army Air Force (PLAAF) and the PLAN Air Force (PLANAF) have received new locally designed and Russian-made platforms. These also include airborne radar, aerial refuelling and electronic warfare aircraft, crucial non-combat platforms required to wage a sustained air campaign. The ROCAF's small number of airbases in Taiwan are poorly defended against PLA missiles and sabotage, exacerbating its technical inferiority. Furthermore, Beijing's expanding Unmanned Aerial Vehicle (UAV) capability may enhance its ability to paralyse Taipei's air defence, possibly at lower cost.[32] Above all, a numerically superior PLA could attrite Taiwanese air defences given the limited surface-to-air missiles (SAMs) Taiwan has.[33]

The PLAN's modernisation has challenged the ROCN operational capabilities by limiting its room for manoeuvre. Targeted by the PLAN's new anti-ship missiles and submarines, the ROCN's major surface vessels could be forced to deploy away from Taiwan, limiting their operational utility in the island's defence.[34] Smaller missile boats and corvettes could be more difficult targets for the PLAN, but they have limited strike capabilities and would have to seek cover in a limited number of hideouts along Taiwan's coastline.[35] Furthermore, the ROCN has yet to modernise at an equal pace as the PLAN. Its onshore anti-ship missile launchers are limited in range. Its submarine fleet, a

---

[32] Office of the Secretary of Defense, "Military and Security Developments Involving the People's Republic of China 2016"; IISS, *Military Balance 2016* (London: IISS, 2016), 244–245; Federation of American Scientists, "Taiwan Air Bases", http://fas.org/irp/world/taiwan/af-ab.htm (accessed 1 November 2016).

[33] IISS, *Military Balance 2016*, 292; Stockholm International Peace Research Institute, "The SIPRI Arms Transfer Database".

[34] Ben Wan Beng Ho and Wu Shang-su, "Taiwan's Interest in Aegis Warships: Would They Make Operational Sense During Cross-Strait Hostilities?", The Royal United Services Institute for Defence and Security Studies, 31 October 2016, https://rusi.org/publication/rusi-defence-systems/taiwan%E2%80%99s-interest-aegis-warships-would-they-make-operational-sense (accessed 1 November 2016).

[35] Wu Shang-su, "No, stealth missile corvettes won't help Taiwan", *The Diplomat*, 9 January 2015, http://thediplomat.com/2015/01/nostealthmissilecorvetteswonthelptaiwan/ (accessed 1 November 2016).

powerful means for sea denial, is small and includes two submarines of World War II vintage. The ROCN's undersea capabilities pale in comparison to the PLAN's.[36] With the PLA's continued modernisation without a corresponding response by Taiwan, the island's air and maritime defence capabilities will invariably suffer. As it grows in strength, the PLA's ability to project itself across the Strait will become increasingly feasible. Unable to defeat a PRC invasion offshore, Taiwan's fate will therefore have to be decided on land. A sizeable ground force would be required, and conscription would be one way of raising it.

If it were to invade, the PRC would seek to swiftly overwhelm the Taiwanese defences. A speedy military victory would limit the economic impact of the war and discourage the intervention on Taiwan's behalf by a third party, particularly the US. The US' substantial economic ties with the PRC, the PLA's A2/AD capabilities and the risk of escalation to nuclear engagement, could mute Washington's response if Taiwan was already defeated militarily. A sizeable ROC ground force, however, could frustrate PRC's expectations of a swift victory. As a Russian military adage puts it, "quantity has a quality of its own." A numerically significant Taiwanese military would be a formidable deterrent. A general policy of conscription could provide for a large body of military manpower immediately, particularly with the number of Taiwanese career military personnel falling due to military reforms in the 1990s and 2000s.[37] Significantly, such a policy would ostensibly demonstrate the willingness of the Taiwanese to commit to the island's defence. Yet while the feasibility of a PRC invasion increased, attitudes towards conscription surprisingly began to shift against it. This would be the beginning of its end.

Criticising a "Sacred Cow": Negative Public Opinion on Conscription

Since the democratisation of Taiwan in the 1990s, Taiwanese have publicly criticised conscription to varying degrees. Some accept conscription in

---

[36] IISS, *Military Balance 2016*, 291.

[37] In 1991, the sizes of the active ROC Army and Marines were 370,000 and 30,000, respectively. The numbers become 130,000 and 10,000 in 2017. Bernard Cole, *Taiwan's Security: History and Prospects*, 53–66; IISS, *Military Balance 1991* (London: IISS, 1991), 180–181; IISS, *Military Balance 2017* (London: IISS, 2017), 331–332.

general but criticise specific areas of its implementation. Safety, equipping, equity in service and its actual operational usefulness to national defence have been publicly debated.

Given that conscription is mandatory, the safety of those serving naturally draws attention. In the 1990s, annual deaths and serious injuries averaged 400, a remarkably high figure during peacetime.[38] Between 2000 and 2012, these numbers fell to an average of 160. While organisational improvements contributed to this, a decrease in the number of conscripts, as well as shorter period of conscription, were also factors.[39] The larger concern was over the ill-treatment of conscripts that often resulted in their death through suicide or negligence.[40] In 2013, the death of a conscript and what was perceived to be a lackadaisical response by the authorities resulted in a significant public demonstration.[41] The equipping of conscripts with obsolete equipment, too, has been considered a form of neglect. Taiwan has traditionally invested in certain advanced and prestigious capabilities used by a few, such as fighter jets, at the expense of other aging platforms used by many more. For example, platforms such as the army's towed howitzers, air force's anti-aircraft guns and navy's landing ships were produced during the 1950s and 60s, or even as far back as World War II.[42]

A third area of critique is equity in who is conscripted. The exclusion of females from conscription has been held up as an example of unfairness. Draft dodging, and how loopholes in Taiwan's conscription policy

[38] Brian Hsu, "Relatives decry military deaths," *Taipei Times*, last modified 29 October 1999, http://www.taipeitimes.com/News/local/archives/1999/10/29/0000008577 (accessed 19 October 2016).

[39] Joseph Yeh, "Special report: Suicide in Taiwan military an issue that needs to be tackled soon", *Asian News Network*, last modified 26 June 2016, http://www.asianews.network/content/special-report-suicide-taiwan-military-issue-needs-be-tackled-soon-20905 (accessed 28 October 2016).

[40] M. Taylor Fravel, "Towards Civilian Supremacy: Civil-Military Relations in Taiwan's Democratization", *Armed Forces & Society* 29/1 (Fall 2002), 74.

[41] "Taiwan protest over Hung Chung-chiu death", *BBC News*, last modified 3 August 2013, http://www.bbc.com/news/world-asia-23561244 (accessed 28 October 2016).

[42] IISS, *Military Balance 2016*, 292; Stockholm International Peace Research Institute, "The SIPRI Arms Transfer Database"; Michael E. Haskew, *Artillery Compared and Contrasted* (Heatherton: Hinkler, 2008), 67, 94.

enable it, have drawn more attention. Living overseas has long been a way to avoid being conscripted even if one would need to be overseas till beyond the age one is liable for service.[43] Malingering by declaring medical or physical limitations to service has also been a way out of the draft. Taiwan has struggled to enforce a more rigorous medical screening process for military service.

Instead, substitute service was introduced in 1998 for those who could not serve in the military because of religious, medical or physical conditions. It was hoped alternate service would present conscription as being more inclusive and therefore fair. These servicemen have been deployed for an eclectic range of vocations in government organisations, schools, the police and fire fighting departments and even nursing homes. Additionally, conscripts with expertise in relevant fields can serve their substitute service in defence-related companies.[44] While substitute service presents conscription as being fair and equitable on paper, its implementation raises questions on how manpower is allocated in reality. Some argue screening for substitute service should be stricter given how combat roles still remain undermanned.[45] Furthermore, the ability for some businesses to seek substitute service conscripts as low-cost labour by ludicrously presenting them as being crucial to national defence has been highlighted.

[43] Lin Mei-chun, "Medics defend draft exemption", *Taipei Times,* last modified 30 April 2001, http://www.taipeitimes.com/News/local/archives/2001/04/30/0000083750/2 (accessed 28 October 2016); Chang Yung-chien, "Conscription is harming Taiwan", *Taipei Times*, last modified 26 April 2001, http://www.taipeitimes.com/News/editorials/archives/2001/04/26/0000083249 (accessed 28 October 2016).
[44] National Conscription Agency, Ministry of the Interior, "沿革 (Yen Ger, History)", last modified 27 March 2015, http://www.nca.gov.tw/web/page.php?p=P0103 (accessed 22 October 2016); Substitute Military Service Center, Department of Compulsory Military Service, Taipei City Government, last modified 2 July 2013, http://english.docms.gov.taipei/ct.asp?xItem=142994&ctNode=16148&mp=121012 (accessed 26 October 2016).
[45] 羅添斌 (Lo Tinbin), "立院預算中心：加給沒誘因 作戰部隊編現比低於50% (The Budget Centre of the Legislative Yuan: Without financial motive, combat units are manned under 50%)", *Liberty Times Net*, 13 October 2015, http://news.ltn.com.tw/news/politics/paper/923239 (accessed 22 October 2016); 洪哲政 (Hung Gercheng), "艱苦國軍部隊大缺兵 立院又打臉國防部募兵新衣 (Tough military units short in soldiers, the Legislative Yuan criticised the MND for recruitment)", 聯合報 *(United Daily News)*, 21 October 2016, http://udn.com/news/story/1/2038667 (accessed 22 October 2016).

In one instance, a dumpling manufacturer justified its request in the name of developing management talent for Taiwan.[46]

A fourth critique is the actual military utility of conscripts to national defence. The perceived low quality of equipment and harsh treatment of conscripts aside, an endemic culture of "formalism" in the military has emphasised the minutiae of regimentation at the expense of training to conduct actual military operations. Many have questioned the need to extraordinarily focus on meeting exacting standards in the barracks instead of spending more effort on military training in the field.[47] Such "formalism" suggests looking like a disciplined, regimented force is more important than actually being able to carry out operations as one. This dilution in effort and attention away from operational training also occurred when civilian requests for manpower are not rejected in order to maintain good relations. Under the guise of Operations Other Than War, conscripts have been deployed to farms to help with harvests and to cull ill livestock. The frequency of such missions has led some to worry that local Taiwanese governments may develop a dependence on the military for assistance which cannot be easily turned down. This has disrupted training for actual military missions.[48]

While these criticisms seek to improve how conscription is implemented and do not seek to abolish it outright, others have sought to end it. This is a clear break from the past where conscription was considered a cornerstone of Taiwan's national defence. The questionable operational utility of conscripts formed only part of the reason. A larger basis was a belief that war with the PRC, the oft-trumpeted justification for conscription, would only break out because of a provocative Taiwanese declaration

---

[46] Maggie Huang, "Alternative military service plan to work at dumpling franchise mocked by netizens", *Taiwan News*, 27 March 2017, http://www.taiwannews.com.tw/en/news/3126615 (accessed 10 May 2017).

[47] "「國軍：為什麼大家討厭你」列出七大點罵到骨子裡 (Military: Why do everyone dislike you? Seven points of deep criticism)", *The Apple Daily*, 12 April 2015, http://www.appledaily.com.tw/realtimenews/article/new/20150412/591004/ (accessed 6 November 2016).

[48] 林弘展 (Lin Hon-chan), "當國軍從公差變工差 (When the military becomes from civil servants to labour force)", *Fair Media*, 30 January 2016, http://www.fairmedia.com.tw/article/1260 (accessed 6 November 2016).

of independence. Going to war would therefore be Taiwan's own choice. If such sabre-rattling behaviour is avoided, cross-strait peace would be maintained, and conscription would therefore be unnecessary. Some polls suggested that 60% of surveyed youth felt they had the right to refuse to be conscripted if a war is caused by the declaration of independence.[49] Overtly seeking independence, once seen as a clear marker of Taiwanese nationalism, had diminished. While pro-independence rhetoric by individual Taiwanese politicians and non-government groups could be provocative, actual government actions remained cautious. With that central idea of Taiwanese nationalism contested, conscription was no longer a clear manifestation of it and therefore unconditionally supported. Neither Taiwan nor the PRC have crossed either's "redline" warranting a military response. Maintaining a broad narrative of peaceful coexistence in cross-strait relations became the politically sensitive position taken by both the Democratic Progressive Party (DPP) and the KMT.[50] Consequently, the need for conscription, with its attendant opportunity costs, seemed increasingly unjustifiable on grounds of national defence.

Conscription Evolves

Conscription would invariably have to evolve to match public sentiment. As part of the general military reforms of the 1990s, the military had already begun to examine the policy. With a shift from an offensive structure intended to re-take the mainland to island defence to prevent an invasion by the PRC, the army shifted its focus away from large divisions to leaner brigades. The demand for manpower decreased and how much time conscripts had to serve was reconsidered.[51] Compounded by

---

[49] Jason Pan, "Public supports compulsory military service: survey", *Taipei Times*, last modified 21 April 2015, http://www.taipeitimes.com/News/taiwan/archives/2015/04/21/2003616440 (accessed 26 October 2016); Shih Hsiuchuan, "Youth will not fight for Taiwan: poll," *Taipei Times*, last modified 13 May 2012, http://www.taipeitimes.com/News/front/print/2012/05/13/2003532684 (accessed 26 October 2016).

[50] "Majority in Taiwan support cross-strait status quo", *Taiwan Today*, 1 April 2016, http://taiwantoday.tw/ct.asp?xItem=243576&ctNode=2175 (accessed 6 November 2016).

[51] Lo Ping-Hsiung, "The Republic of China Armed Services' Human Resource Policy", in *Taiwan's Defense Reform*, eds. Martin Edmonds and Michael M. Tsai (London: Routledge,

rising public scrutiny, the evolution of Taiwan's conscription began to gain momentum.

In 2000, the military conscription was decreased from two years to 22 months. This was still largely motivated by organisational reasons.[52] The reorganisation of the army had indeed lowered manpower demands. Politics, however, would motivate subsequent changes with the election of the DPP government in 2000, breaking half a century of KMT dominance. The DPP's Chen Shui-bian administration reduced the service length of conscripts from 22 months to 14 months by 2007. The subsequent KMT's Ma Ying-jeou administration continued the reduction to just 12 months in 2008 with a plan to abolish conscription by in 2014, a promise it would eventually fail to keep (see Table 1).[53]

The KMT could not fulfil that promise because the required number of career personnel to transform the Taiwanese military into an AVF could not be recruited and retained.[54] The low fertility rates since the 1980s had resulted in a shrinking labour market with fierce competition from other

Table 1. Taiwan's shortening conscription

	2000	2004	Jan. 2007	Jul. 2007	2008	2018 (Planned)
Service (Months)	22	20	16	14	12	4

2006), 194, 198; Damon Bristow, "Taiwan's Defense Modernization — The Challenges Ahead", in *Defending Taiwan*, eds. Martin Edmonds and Michael M. Tsai (London: Routledge Curzon, 2003), 68.

[52] "Military personnel", *Global Security*, last modified on 17 December 2015, https://www.google.com.sg/#q=Taiwan,+military+service,+22+months&start=10 (accessed 2 November 2016).

[53] Andreas Speck , "Taiwan to shorten conscription term to one year", *Taiwan News*, last modified 3 December 2008, http://www.etaiwannews.com/etn/news_content.php?id= 802676&lang=eng_news (accessed 18 October 2016); John Chen, "Why Taiwan won't be able to build an effective all-volunteer force", *Georgetown Security Studies Review*, 10 April 2015, http://georgetownsecuritystudiesreview.org/2015/04/10/whytaiwanwontbe-abletobuildaneffectiveallvolunteerforce/ (accessed 26 October 2016).

[54] Jason Pan, "All-volunteer military plans postponed", *Taipei Times*, 27 August 2015, http://www.taipeitimes.com/News/front/archives/2015/08/27/2003626274 (accessed 2 November 2016).

sectors.[55] Better pay dangled as an incentive to sign up with the military was insufficient to make up for other lifestyle changes needed.[56] Furthermore, retaining volunteers is an additional challenge as they are able to seek alternative employment in a free labour market unlike conscripts.[57] Consequently, manpower targets have been reduced resulting in a smaller Taiwanese military.[58] Lowering physical standards has also been considered to boost numbers.[59] These concessions, however, could result in the capability of Taiwanese military being even lower than when conscription was fully in force, but with a significantly higher manpower cost. In 2017, only 54% and 62% of officer and non-commissioned officer positions were filled, reflecting the difficulty in recruiting and retaining an AVF.[60] An official government report has noted a manpower gap of up to 14,000 troops, a sizeable figure considering the military had planned to raise a force of 175,000.[61]

The DPP returned to power in 2016 but did not roll-back the changes to conscription. Instead, conscription for 12 months would continue as

---

[55] John Chen, "Why Taiwan won't be able to build an effective all-volunteer force".

[56] "All parties can learn from Taiwan's low salary levels", *The China Post*, 1 October 2014, http://www.chinapost.com.tw/editorial/taiwan-issues/2014/10/01/418394/All-parties.htm (accessed 6 November 2016).

[57] J. Michael Cole, "Taiwan's 'All-volunteer' military: Vision or nightmare?", *The Diplomat*, 9 July 2013, http://thediplomat.com/2013/07/taiwans-all-volunteer-military-vision-or-nightmare/ (accessed 3 November 2016).

[58] Joseph Yeh, "Military denies it will make further cuts to troop numbers", *China Post*, 6 September 2016, http://www.chinapost.com.tw/taiwan/national/national-news/2016/09/06/477671/Military-denies.htm (accessed 2 November 2016).

[59] 洪哲政 (Hung Gercheng), " 國軍研議修體測制度 「全亞洲最嚴」 體能標準不再？ (The military studies modifying physical test, no more toughest stand in Asia?)", 聯合報 *(United Daily News)*, 20 October 2016, http://udn.com/news/story/1/2036898 (accessed 2 November 2016).

[60] 王炯華 (Wang Junhua), "好慘! 國防部缺人 中尉少尉缺額近一半恐影響戰力 (Terrible! The MND's manpower shortage: Close to half positions of lieutenants are empty and it would affect defence)", *The Apple Daily*, 10 May 2017, http://www.appledaily.com.tw/realtimenews/article/new/20170510/1115572/ (accessed 10 May 2017) .

[61] Aaron Tu and Jonathan Chin, "Report questions all-volunteer military", *Taipei Times*, 29 January 2018, http://www.taipeitimes.com/News/taiwan/archives/2018/01/29/2003686629 (accessed 3 April 2018).

long as AVF recruitment did not meet 90% of its target.[62] Be that as it may, conscripts would no longer serve in regular units and their service would be reduced to just four months of mandatory military training by 2018.[63] While this satisfied administrative and political goals imposed by the political commitment to shift to an AVF, conscripts would be structurally marginalised. Bereft of conscripts, regular units, the sharp end of Taiwan's military, would also be undermanned. This arrangement would have knock-on effects. First, excluding conscripts from regular units would invariably result in an effectively smaller military if recruitment and retention targets are not met, which they have not.[64] Second, four months of basic training for conscripts would not equip them to participate in large-scale operations, limiting their operational use. Third, the capabilities of Taiwan's reserve force which conscripts eventually form will diminish increasingly as conscripts with minimal training start filling its ranks.[65]

Political considerations, not military ones, would ultimately shape Taiwan's conscription policy. Both the KMT and DPP presently believe ending conscription is politically expedient.

It is unusual to see both the KMT and DPP share a common stance on conscription. Both have historically had diverse political ideologies based on differing conceptions of Taiwanese national identities. The KMT has promoted a common Chinese identity but has sought peaceful bilateral relations with the PRC. Abolishing conscription would plausibly

---

[62] "Ministry says army conscription to be maintained in 2017", *Taipei Times*, 17 August 2016, http://www.taipeitimes.com/News/taiwan/archives/2016/08/17/2003653293 (accessed 2 November 2016).

[63] Chen Wei-han, "MND works 'toward' 2018 end to draft", *Taipei Times*, 14 December 2016, http://www.taipeitimes.com/News/taiwan/archives/2016/12/14/2003661192 (accessed 11 May 2016).

[64] Joseph Yeh, "Military getting flexible", *The China Post*, 21 December 2016, http://www.chinapost.com.tw/taiwan/national/national-news/2016/12/21/487283/military-getting.htm (accessed 12 July 2017); Office of the Secretary of Defense, "Annual Report to Congress: Military and Security Developments Involving People's Republic of China 2017" (Washington D.C.: Office of the Secretary of Defense, 2017), 82.

[65] Ian Easton, Mark Stokes, Cortez A. Cooper and Arthur Chan, *Transformation of Taiwan's Reserve Force* (Santa Monica: RAND, 2017), 6–8, 27–28; Jean-Pierre Cabestan, "Recent Changes in Taiwan's Defense Policy and Taiwan–USA Relations", *East Asia* 31/4 (2014), 349–350.

jeopardise its ability to defend itself against the PRC but seeking peaceful co-existence with it reduces the importance of that concern.

In contrast, the DPP has adopted a more hardline stance on defence and Taiwanese independence. The party promotes a stronger Taiwanese identity unique to the island. Conscription would be a means to defend this. Reducing the length of conscription seemingly goes against this.[66] Its early initiatives to reduce the length of service were puzzling, and some found it surprising that it did not use its landslide victory in 2016 to reverse previous reductions in service.[67] One reason why the DPP has continued with the reduction of conscription is its short-term desire to not upset voters with radical shifts in policy. Completely reforming conscription would take more time than the four-year electoral cycle and would be a great political risk to undertake.[68] Additionally, as long as peace remains, the need for well-trained conscripts would always be questioned. Therefore, despite intensive political struggles and debates between the KMT and the DPP, the current DPP administration has continued its KMT predecessor's policy to transform the Taiwanese military into an AVF and reduce conscription even further.

Conclusion: When Will the Evolution End?

Conscription was implemented as a means to defend Taiwan against a perceived clear-and-present threat of the PRC. While the threat may have been overstated during the Cold War as the PLA did not actually possess the means to invade Taiwan, occasional skirmishes were a reminder of its possibility. With the US establishing diplomatic relations with the PRC in 1979 and the international isolation that followed thereafter, the belief that

---

[66] Victoria Jen, "Rise of Taiwan identity helped DPP trounce KMT: Analysts", *Channel News Asia*, 19 January 2016, http://www.channelnewsasia.com/news/asiapacific/rise-of-taiwan-identity/2438726.html (accessed 2 November 2016).

[67] J. Michael Cole, "Taiwan's all-volunteer force pains: There's a way out", *The Diplomat*, 24 April 2015, http://thediplomat.com/2015/04/taiwans-all-volunteer-force-pains-theres-a-way-out/ (accessed 2 November 2016).

[68] "Additional Articles of the Constitution of the Republic of China", *Laws and Regulations Database of the Republic of China*, last modified 10 June 2005, http://law.moj.gov.tw/Eng/LawClass/LawAll.aspx?PCode=A0000002 (accessed 2 November 2016).

Taiwan could rely mainly on itself for its defence strengthened support for conscription. The PLA's rising capability, Beijing's open threats and the Third Taiwan Strait Crisis of 1996 reinforced the need for conscription. Yet the end of martial law and the democratisation of Taiwan revealed diverse interpretations of national identity, often a contest between pro-unification (with mainland China) and pro-independence movements. Consequently, the hardline justification that conscription was needed to defend Taiwanese sovereignty began to fracture. Conscription became politicised and different administrations embarked on a policy to shift the Taiwanese military to an AVF and abolish conscription.

The net result of the politicisation of conscription has been a problematic evolution following a series of hasty decisions across administrations to abolish conscription and shift to an AVF. Short-term political gains justified abandoning one of Taiwan's foundational public policies. Working towards a politically viable AVF by abolishing conscription was thought to be easier than reforming it and addressing the numerous challenges it faced. This goal has proven to be elusive and Taiwan is now saddled with a problematic hybrid AVF-conscript system with long-term concerns over its operational usefulness. Driven by politics, the policy of conscription will continue to evolve. While its stated objective — to be eventually phased out for an AVF — is clear, when this end is ultimately achieved remains uncertain.

Index

www.ingramcontent.com/pod-product-compliance
Lightning Source LLC
Chambersburg PA
CBHW051956270326
41929CB00015B/2676